My Sweet Wild Dance

Mikaya Heart

First published by Dog Ear Publishing
4010 W. 86th Street, Ste H
Indianapolis, IN 46268
www.dogearpublishing.net

ISBN: 978-160844-070-2

This book is printed on acid-free paper.

Printed in the United States of America

Acknowledgments

This book was many years in the writing, and I don't even remember everyone who was involved. Thanks to all of you who were willing to help, most especially: Shay, Kay, Barbara, Sage, Tine, Jesse, and Dayana.

And I must also acknowledge all my teachers throughout my life. Since that includes everyone I have ever met, I'll just mention a few people: my mother, my father, May Burns, Jesse, Maggie, Cindy, Caryn, and Dayana.

I extend inexpressible levels of gratitude to all the non-human beings who take such good care of me, providing invaluable assistance, and enabling me to triumph over all manner of challenges.

Thank you!

Preface

This is a true story. However, in this world, truth (with a small t) is very personal. Therefore some individuals may believe my truth to be lies. That's OK.

A great deal of this book is about feelings. Since feelings don't relate to past, present and future, I have used the present tense. The first half, which occurs in the U.K., is written in British English. Since the second half occurs primarily in the U.S.A., I have used more American English.

In general, I have changed names. I could say that is to protect the innocent, but really, those concepts—*guilty* and *innocent*—are meaningless in this context.

Some characters appear only very briefly, and what matters is how they affect the protagonist, Chris, at that time period. To assist in the flow of words, I have sometimes given these transient characters the name, *John*. You will find a number of *Johns* in this book.

This is a story of how one woman forged a path through life's jungle. It is not intended to make statements or judgments. It has no moral. My hope is that some of you will find it as fascinating as I did, and perhaps the trail that she made will help you on your way.

Prologue

It is a gorgeous summer in Montana, and I spend my time doing what I enjoy. I ride a horse who belongs to some friends, sail a small catamaran on the lake, and paint the four houses at the retreat center where I am staying. This last occupation pleases the retreat center coordinator, but it makes her very nervous to watch me balance at the top of a long ladder. Since I enjoy being up the ladder, and I'm confident that I will be fine, I don't appreciate her anxiety. "Don't watch me," I tell her sternly.

"What if the ladder slips?" She asks in a concerned tone.

"Well, then, you'll find me standing there beside you," I say. "Just envision me healthy and happy. That's the most helpful thing you can do."

When the wind is up, I run down to the lake and rig my little catamaran. When I've had some experience sailing, maybe I'll be able to buy a boat big enough to live on, and small enough to sail single-handed on the ocean. I love the sensation of the water carrying me, and I love to watch the light on the water's surface, in its endlessly varied manifestations, depending on the amount of wind and sun. I'm looking forward to the time when I can get out on the ocean, far from land.

Riding horses is not so different from sailing. You're sitting on top of something that is much stronger than you, and predictable only within limits. Considerable skill and coordination are necessary so that you remain in constant communication with what is beneath you. Sonny is a thoroughbred who won a lot of races before he had an injury that permanently removed him from the race course. He still loves to run. Sometimes he's nervous, to the point of making me feel like I'm sitting on a bomb, but if I let him run as fast as he wants, he calms down. He covers the ground so quickly that it's hard to find safe places where I can really let him go. The most amazing thing about him is that if I fall off, he stops, and waits, quite still, until I get back on. What a wonderful trait!

John, his owner, is pleased that I'm exercising him, though he gets anxious about my falling off. One day when I come home, I tell him about the dog that scared Sonny. "He shied so fast that I came right off and he went running away without me, but as soon as I called him, he came back to me." I'm *very* delighted with Sonny about this.

John's focus is elsewhere. He says, "You've got to stop falling off."

"It's fine," I reply, "I landed on my feet."

"Yes, but you won't always land on your feet."

"How do you know?"

"Well, it just stands to reason, you can't always land on your feet!"

"Hmmm…you'd be amazed how often I can land on my feet." I take off Sonny's saddle, and remove the blanket, soaked with his sweat. His gorgeous black body is a perfect tapestry of muscle. I run my cheek down his neck, filling my nostrils with the scent of horse. I think, *the next time I fall off, I won't tell John.* True, he's only concerned for my wellbeing—but that kind of worried concern only invites tragedy. And I'm not into tragedy, I'm into joy.

Chapter One

I'm sitting with my mother on the bench outside the front door. The cat, a tortoiseshell quite like the one I grew up with, is curled between us and I'm idly rubbing her head. The sun is shining, though not, of course, as strongly as I'm used to after ten years in California; still, strongly enough for Scotland in April. My mother is sipping her lunch-time drink—gin and tonic. To my right is a hydrangea, just like the one that sat there thirty-three years ago, when I first saw this house, at the age of six. In front of us lies the gravel driveway, and then the curving edge of the lawn, that I once cut with our noisy old lawnmower, long gone to a well-deserved grave. Past the lawn is the holly tree, and then the handsome beech tree that I used to climb. Even now, from an adult viewpoint, it seems like a big tree. The rope that once dangled from its first fork, ten or so feet above the ground, is gone, and so is one of its huge branches, cut to make light for ornamental shrubs that grow beneath.

Beyond the beech tree is the stone wall that marks the division between our garden and the field that I once trudged over on my way up the hill to go fishing. This year the field's green surface is dotted with white sheep, heads down, busily munching. Other years I remember it brownish red with newly ploughed earth, or golden in the late summer with yard-long stalks of ripe wheat, rustling and rippling in the breeze.

The cat purrs and stretches. "It's so nice to have you here, Christine," says my mother, with a warm smile. "I wish you could visit more often." I know she means it, and that knowing touches me deeply. It wasn't so very long ago that I believed she wished I didn't exist. I'm well aware that if I visited much more often than I do, I would get heartily sick of both my parents, but in this moment, I too want more time with my mother.

"Yes, I wish I didn't live quite so far away. I hope you're going to be able to come over to California."

"Well, it looks like Kay is really serious about taking me. I must say, I do really want to see where you live. It's so hard to imagine a place when you've never seen it."

Kay is my mother's sister. She and her husband have plenty of money and they've offered to pay my mother's fare to the U.S. My parents have lived in high class poverty since before I was born. My father always refused to take any job that involved working for anyone else, and the living he makes from badly written books and training gundogs is still meager.

I notice how gray my mother's hair is, and how lined her striking face has become. She leans forward a little awkwardly, elbow resting on knee, drink clutched in her right hand, while her other hand absently strokes her cheek. She seems more ill at ease in her body than she used to be…she has lost her poise.

I take a deep breath. "Mother, do you mind if I ask you about how your brother John died?"

She looks startled, but quickly regains her composure, saying, "Well, no, of course not. That was all such a long time ago now. What is it you want to know?"

"Well, how exactly did it happen? How old was he?"

"Didn't you ever hear the story?" She sounds surprised.

"Only that he was accidentally shot." I refrain from saying that no one ever told me anything when I was growing up. Oblique references were the norm, and questions were discouraged, to put it mildly.

She sighs. "He was twelve. He'd been out shooting for the day with a friend of his, Peter, one of the Kerrs from Easthame. As a matter of fact, Peter still lives at Easthame with his wife. I just heard the other day that he's been sick." As she talks, I watch her profile, noticing that she has the same mobile lips as I do, and they reflect her tension in just the same way. "Anyway, they had two guns, a shotgun and a rifle. When they came back in for the day, Peter sat down and read a book while John cleaned the rifle. After he'd done the rifle, he picked up the shotgun to clean it, and Peter got up, and started to take it from him, saying it was his job to clean it. The gun was loaded and it went off into John's throat. He was killed instantly."

"Where were you that day?"

"Well, actually, I was the first to see the body." She laughs a little, flicking her left hand, a nervous gesture that's become a habit. "I was nineteen, already engaged to your father. I was cooking in the kitchen. Mother—your grandmother—was upstairs at a Women's Institute meeting in the drawing room. Peter came into the kitchen, white as a sheet, and said, 'I think I've killed John.' Of course I didn't believe him…" she laughs again, "so I said, 'You're joking!' and he said, 'No, I'm absolutely serious, come and look.' So I followed him down the hall to the gunroom, and there was John, lying in a pool of blood." She swirls her drink in its long stemmed glass, flicks her free hand, and looks at me, smiling.

I'm frowning. "Jesus. What did you do?"

She gives another nervous laugh. "Well, I did just what I shouldn't have, really...I ran up to the drawing room, threw open the door, and said, 'Mother, come quick, John's been shot!'"

I don't ask why she shouldn't have done that. Of course his death would have been made public, but the family *should* have been in charge of when and how. That's supposed to be one of the prerogatives of the upper classes, to be able to doctor and control public access to the truth.

I can imagine all the ladies from the Women's Institute crowding to the door of the gunroom behind my grandmother to see the gory sight. No doubt it was the crowning glory of their boring lives.

My mother continues. "The worst thing was all the hoo-ha afterwards. Father was away at the time, of course, and he blamed Mother because, he said, she shouldn't have let the boys use guns without supervision." I roll my eyes. My grandfather was not a man who took his share of the blame for anything if he could avoid it. He would never have made sure the boys had supervision. He never had time for his children, and anyhow it's been a tradition in this family forever, that the sons are allowed to use guns from a young age.

"And then the worst thing of all was the hate letters!" Now she sounds quite outraged, and her face twists as she looks directly at me.

I'm surprised. "Hate letters? From whom?"

"Well, as soon as it was in the papers, they came pouring in, from all kinds of people! 'Serves you right for letting your son use guns!' 'What do you expect if you teach your children to hunt?' You know, all that kind of garbage. Can't you imagine how awful it was, to have to deal with all that nonsense on top of John's death? Poor Mother. Honestly, it must have been so hard for her."

I nod somberly, thinking it must have been very hard for *my* mother too.

"Where was Arthur at the time?" Arthur is my father. It's one of those arbitrary rules of the upper classes, that you don't call your father *Dad*, or your mother *Mum*. The alternative is *Daddy*, which I can't stand, precisely because it is a word loaded with class.

My mother shrugs and smiles again, this time with a rueful edge. "He was in London. We were engaged to be married. I phoned him up right away, of course, and he said he'd get the next train up, but he didn't manage to get here till four days later, after the funeral."

"Why not?" I can't imagine what could have delayed him for four days.

"He kept getting drunk and missing the trains."

I'm walking on the beach with my father. He strides along, shotgun over his arm, the cold sea breeze whipping his kilt around his bare knees. You only notice him limping when he runs. The dogs are ahead of us. I hope they don't flush any duck; I don't want to deal with dead birds. The waves roll gently up the sand a hundred yards to our left, and ahead of us the river widens as it meets the sea. My father's been mouthing off about the latest book he's writing, forecasting its fantastic success. He always has something to say, and most of it is bullshit. But I have learned to guide the conversation into interesting arenas, and these days he respects me enough to allow me to do that. I seize my opportunity.

"I wanted to hear the story of how you got shot," I say.

"Oh come on, you must have heard that story a dozen times," he says, raising his expressive eyebrows in my direction.

"No, I've never heard the full version." Why do my parents think I know about these things?

"Really? Well, all right then, if you insist. You know I was in command of a tank. It was one of those old Saracens, piece of junk, I can assure you. Somehow or other we managed to keep it going. Anyhow, after we chased the Huns out of North Africa, they shipped us over to Italy. That was '44, and the Italians were already pretty beat, but there was a lot of cleaning up to do. After we reached shore we were advancing inland, and it was incredibly slow going. Boring as hell, sitting inside one of those tin cans for hours on end, let me tell you. There was a long line of tanks, one behind another, for miles, and we'd just move a few yards at a time and then sit for hours. Eventually, I decided to get out and have a look, see what was going on. So I climbed out and looked around, 'course there was nothing to see, so I was about to climb back in when someone let loose with a machine gun. I dropped to the ground and all but the last two bullets missed—" he pauses to look at me, adjusting his cap "—you know, the last couple of bullets in the belt usually go high because the gun kicks up at the end. The gunner was aiming too low to start with."

I nod as though I know what he's talking about. We're getting close to the river and soon we'll have to turn back.

"Anyway, they got me in the thigh. So there I am, lying on the ground, bleeding like a stuck pig, and I can't pull myself up to get back in the tank. I had a helluva time persuading my sergeant to get out and help me back in! He was terrified, damn fellow." He snorts with disgust. "But he finally did, I'm glad to say."

How typical of my father to risk getting killed because he was bored. And the truth is I would probably do the same thing. I'm too like him to be able to lead a regular kind of life.

"And then once he got me back inside, he tried to tell me, with a smirk on his face, that he was in charge now! 'No, you're damn well not,' I told him, 'as long as I'm in this tank, I'm the one who's in charge!'"

"What happened next?"

"Well, once we got to Naples, they put me on a ship back home." He starts into one of his favorite subjects, how the doctors made a mess of fixing his wounded leg, and he really should sue them. Reaching the river, we turn to walk along the bank towards the sea. I'm trying to imagine how it must have been for him to go through such a nightmare. My father was one amongst millions of men who went through World War II. A whole generation of kids...he was nineteen when he joined up. Of course you'd have to learn not to feel your emotions. The daily horror of the war…inexpressible.

I interrupt his monologue on how the doctors messed him around, to ask, "How long was it before you could walk?"

"I was on crutches for months. Then I went to the stables in Devon where I met your mother, and the minute I started riding, I was able to walk again." He laughs. "Of course, to begin with, I had trouble getting on the horse. But it didn't take me long. Damn fool doctors, they said I'd never walk again. Hah!" This time it's a triumphant snort. "I was fine until I went to work in London. Then I started falling down. It was very embarrassing, I'd be walking along in my business suit, wearing a bowler hat and carrying my brief case, and all of a sudden my damn leg would give way and I'd be sitting on the sidewalk. People thought I was drunk. Truth is, the only time I didn't fall down was when I was drunk!"

He starts into a rant about the beneficial effects of alcohol. I know better than to mention the times I have known him to fall down when he was drunk. Considering how many times I've seen him drunk, there weren't so very many when he fell down.

At the edge of the shore itself, we turn back towards the parking area, with the waves licking the sand to our right. It's too sheltered in this bay for the sea to get fierce. We stride along together. He's nearly seventy, and he has half the muscles in one leg that everyone else does, but he still moves along as fast as ever. I remember the times I ran to keep up with him as a child. I feel a fondness for him now, a grudging admiration for his willpower. I can't remember a previous time in my life when I didn't hate him.

There are so many things I want to throw in your face. I want to destroy you with words about the past, just as you destroyed me with words in the past. Needing to play those horrible games where I was always the loser, you treated me like a plaything. I was an easy tar-

get. You never tried to deal with the resentment and anger and pain and fear and grief that fueled your cruelty, you just emptied it out little by little on me and my sister, and later, when we were gone, on my mother.

It amused you to watch me struggling to understand and comply. When I asked a question, you purposefully distorted your answer (if you bothered to answer at all) and I relied on other adults to set me straight, if I was fortunate enough to find out that you had lied. You framed a horribly twisted view of the world, and of who I could be in it.

You honed laughter into the cruelest weapon. You knew how to use laughter to pull the rug out from under someone's feet. You used it to put people down, to take the power out of their arguments. You laughed at me when I was serious, whenever something was important to me. You laughed at me when I was right, so that I felt like I must be wrong. You laughed at me when I was unhappy, to show that my unhappiness was unimportant. You laughed to make a lie out of what was true. You laughed when you felt unsafe. You laughed to cover your feelings, as a ruse to distract everyone from the awful truth of your humanness. You laughed out loud, long and loud and harsh, discordant and drunken. You laughed at pain: your pain, my pain, the pain of the world, all of our pain. You laughed at everything so that nothing could be important enough to cause you pain. You laughed with hatred, and you laughed fondly, belittling your fondness. Your laughter had no humor. It was a disguise, an ambush, a barrier.

It's taken all your energy all these years to prevent your own healing. And you have never understood what enormous strength lies in vulnerability. Your world view has kept you stunted, and you'll die stunted, a puny bitter caricature of the man you could have been.

I know that insistent need to find someone to blame. You taught me well. I know exactly how to belittle and undermine, to say one thing and yet to convey quite another with a tone of voice that cuts to the bone, that slices out someone's self-esteem with quick quiet sweeps of the razor's edge. I was more subtle than you, of course. I learned to be subtle because I had promised myself I wouldn't be like you. So then when my desire to destroy got out of hand, I had to pretend that I wasn't doing what I was doing. Besides, I had no children to bear the brunt of my sadistic need, I had to find my victims else-where, and they often refused to put up with my inhumane treatment. They weren't tied to me the way I was tied to you.

I'm staying with my sister, Elizabeth, for a few days before I go back to the U.S. She and her husband own a farm here in Perthshire. It's beautiful, but freezing cold. I'm glad I live in California, where there is hot sun and much more open space.

I've been out of touch with my sister and brother for the last twenty years. It's interesting to meet them again now. My sister's husband, Simon, treats me respectfully, which I don't normally expect from Scottish men. My sister smokes cigarettes and talks constantly. In the evening, I sit at the kitchen table with her, trying to comprehend her view of the world. It's not easy, since, like my father, she is an artist at making drama out of the simplest story.

"How do you get along with David and Diane?" I ask. My brother is recently married.

"Oh, they're all right. Diane's a bit...you know..." she wrinkles her nose a little and flicks the ash off her cigarette. "Did you like that casserole we ate for dinner? I could heat that up for lunch tomorrow if you want. I have to take the boys to Perth in the morning, but I won't be long."

I couldn't care less about tomorrow's lunch. I try to steer her back to the subject of interest. "Wait a minute, Diane's a bit what?"

"Oh, you know..."

"No, I don't."

"Well, they're both so smartly dressed all the time. They come out here wearing white jackets and then they get all upset because the dog jumps up on them with muddy paws. Honestly, what do they expect? Why do they wear white jackets? They're such city people." She leans forward conspiratorially, lowering her voice. "And they're mean with their money. They've got plenty of it, for Christ's sake. Their lifestyle is so posh, they're downright snotty. They're yuppies!"

Sitting back with an air of triumph, she takes a drag on her cigarette. Not wanting to argue, I say, "Well, yes, I see what you mean, they are kind of yuppie-ish."

Now Elizabeth's on a roll. She nods vigorously. "Yes, that's what they are, they're yuppies. And you know, they've really alienated Mummy and Daddy. Did you know what David said to Daddy the other day?" She tightens her lips and folds her arms, so that I know I am about to hear something really shocking. "He told him he drinks too much! Can you believe the cheek of that?"

Suppressing the desire to laugh, I say, "Well, he does."

"Well, maybe, but who the hell does David think he is telling him that? He's got no business telling Daddy how to run his life!"

Later, we are talking about my mother's health, and out of the blue, Elizabeth puts down her cigarette, saying, "Did you know that Mummy was considering leaving Daddy when I was pregnant with William? Oh, that reminds me, I must get William's clothes ready for tomorrow, he's got rugby. What are you planning to do tomorrow?"

"Wait a minute, *when* was she considering leaving him? And why didn't she?"

"Well, she asked me how I would feel if she left him, and I burst into tears. I was eight months pregnant, and I was just feeling really...well, you know..." She rattles on for a minute or two while I remain silent, not trusting myself to speak. I am furious. She could have encouraged my mother to free herself from the impossible man she had married. Why hadn't my mother asked *me* what I would feel about it? I would have helped her!

I know why she didn't ask me. I wasn't around. Once I got out from under my parents' thumbs, I was gone.

I catch another snippet of my sister's conversation. "Of course you know she had an affair with John. I don't blame her for that, I wouldn't mind having an affair, Simon's such a bore sometimes, I really need some other company. Not that there's anyone worth having an affair with, all the men I meet are so boring. Do you need another drink? A wee drop of whiskey?"

"Wait a minute, you said she had an affair with John? When was that? How long did it last? How do you know about it?"

"It was obvious! Everyone knew about it except Daddy! Oh, I must remember to send off those forms tomorrow. Honestly, that bloody secretary, she's absolutely—"

"Wait!" I'm almost yelling at her now. "When did she have this affair with John?" John was an old friend of my father's.

"It happened when John and Mary were living at Elmdale, and they spent a lot of time together, the four of them. Daddy was going through a period of getting really drunk. He'd pass out every night and Mary always used to go off to bed early, so that left John and Mummy alone together. Even Grandpa knew about it! He was the one who told Daddy in the end."

"He told Daddy?"

"Yes, they were having one of their usual arguments about who knows more than the other one, and Grandpa finally said, 'Well, I know something you don't!' and Daddy said, 'And what might that be?' in that scornful way he has, and Grandpa said, 'Your wife's having an affair with John.' So of course Daddy said, 'Oh, don't talk such rubbish,' but the beans were spilled by then. Grandpa gave him a good talking to about neglecting his wife, and they both snarled at each other, and Daddy went and talked to Mummy. Once it was all out in the open, John and Mary moved away. I'm going to pour myself another whisky, are you sure you don't want one?"

My brother David is much saner than my sister, although a little less hospitable. His wife cooks dinner in their impeccably furnished Edinburgh flat, and we sit around the table afterwards, drinking wine. The subject soon turns to our parents.

"So, I gather you're not getting along with Arthur and Margaret?" I ask.

"No." He looks down at his plate. Pushing his chair back, he gets up from the table, walking over to lean his elbow against the mantelpiece, just the way our father used to do. His handsomely chiseled face is set and serious. "Arthur's impossible to get along with, he's so bloody arrogant and competitive."

"Yes, well, he's always been that way."

"I didn't experience him like that when I was a child." He twists the stem of his wine glass in his fingers, watching the red liquid swirl.

I'm surprised. How could anyone have experienced him any other way? "You didn't?" I question.

He looks directly at me for a moment, then back to his wine glass. "No. He always seemed to me like the model father. Whenever I was home on holiday from school, he was always taking me out shooting or fishing, and all my friends loved him. He enjoyed young people, he always had a good story to tell and he loved to entertain us. Then I was living abroad for twenty years, so I hardly saw him. It wasn't until recently that I ever saw this side of him." Diane comes in, and he puts his arm around her. The gesture jolts me, and I realize how rarely that kind of easy affection is demonstrated in our family.

Meanwhile, I am considering my brother's words with amazement. A model father? That brute?

I hypothesize. "I suppose you were favored, being the only son, and you were away at boarding school from the age of seven, so you didn't see that much of him. I lived with his presence every day for eighteen years. And we always rubbed each other wrong anyway. We're too alike, he and I. I hated him from a young age. I planned to kill him. I was going to push him off the top of the Law."

My brother's eyes widen, and he laughs: a short, humorless bark. The Law is 400 feet high with a sheer cliff on one side. "Hm. Well, he always did have a sarcastic tongue. He never turned on me the way he did on you, though, he just seemed like a fun guy, always making jokes. Until now." He rubs his leg in a nervous gesture that is familiar to me from his teenage years; strange how he still seems uncomfortable in his gangly but powerful body. He has never been able to assume my father's façade of ease. I like him better for that.

"Yes, it's ironic that I can get along with him now," I say. "I feel like he respects me now in a way he never did when I was younger. And it's the other way around with you."

David twirls the stem of his wine glass again and his eyebrows furrow, as he stares into the distance. "Yes. I think he feels like a failure now that he's old, and I've made a success of my life, and he can't stand having that mirrored back to him."

"What about Margaret? Do you get along with her?"

"Yes, well enough," he shrugs. "But ultimately she'll always support him, and it's impossible to see them separately for long, because he always turns up and wants to dominate the conversation."

"You just have to tell him to shut up," I advise. I discovered this the last time I visited. I found that if I told him to shut up enough times, he would eventually wander off, grumbling, to his study.

He sighs hopelessly. "I've tried that. He just gets more obnoxious than ever. I really don't want to have anything to do with him any more, he's *so* unpleasant."

I shake my head sympathetically. "Well, he certainly can be unbelievably rude."

My brother laughs, relieved that I seem to understand. "Yes, *unbelievably* is the right word! No one would ever believe it unless they saw it!" He shakes his head too, and sips from his wine glass, then chortles as he turns back to me, his eyes wide. "Did you hear what he did when some friends of ours asked him what he wears under his kilt?"

"Oh, no!" I wince. "He didn't show them, did he?"

Chapter Two

One morning, my older sister and brother and I are called in from the garden where the three of us are playing, and ordered to clean up. We are going to lunch at my grandmother's house. My grandmother regularly entertains different members of our large extended family in the beautiful red stone building overlooking the stream where I later learn to fish. My grandfather, the local laird, officially lives there too, but he is so often away on "business" trips that I have never really thought of him as a resident. The house is huge, with three separate wings, and acres of garden, which are all wonderful playgrounds. As our car pulls into the driveway, my father addresses us in the stern baritone that is so familiar: "Now you listen to me, you three brats, I don't want any nonsense out of you! Your Great Aunt Vera is visiting from the South, and you'd better be on your best behavior."

As the youngest, I am sitting in the least favorite place, in the middle of the back seat of the car. So I am last out, and I run across the crunchy gravel to catch up. John is holding open the perfectly paneled front door with its gold knob. Today he is the butler. Other days he is the yacht hand, the handy man, or the chauffeur.

"Guid morrnin', m'lady," he says to my mother, smiling, and she replies, also with a smile, "Good morning, John, how are you today?"

"Ah'm verra weel, thank you, and yerrsel'?"

"I'm very well. The good weather always helps, don't you think?"

"Aye, indeed, that it does!"

I scoot in, squeezing my little body between the adults, as John grins down at me. Leaving him there, we turn towards the sitting room where everyone will be waiting for lunch. As we enter, a tall person, with short gray hair cut like a man's, comes striding across the room to kiss my mother on the cheek.

"Margaret, darling, how *wonderful* to see you! Arthur, you're looking so well!" it booms in a strikingly deep voice. The usual series of postulations follow: how are we, and how is she, and how is Jessica (the woman she's come with), how long are they staying, how wonderful it is to get such nice weather for their visit, what particular brand of alcohol are they drinking right now, and so on and on. I observe with interest from my three foot high vantage point. My brother and sister and I are briefly introduced, and Vera expresses amazement at how much we have grown. It is standard conversation, but Vera is far from standard. I have more great aunts than I am yet able to count, and not one of them is anything like Vera.

She wears not a scrap of makeup and makes no pretense of a hairdo. Her clothes are plain, and her divided skirts are more reminiscent of trousers than skirts. Her shoes are plain, flat-bottomed and sensible. She moves decisively, without any awkwardness or hesitation, as though she is used to working with her body. Her voice is not only deep, it is commanding and loud. Strangest of all, the men treat her with a deference and respect that I have never seen them accord to a woman.

Lunch is declared, and we make our way down the hall to the dining room. Like the sitting room, it is furnished in impeccable taste, with side-tables and paintings that are probably worth tens of thousands. Nothing garish or modern mars the proper and slightly somber setting. I am too young to be aware of the importance of the furnishings and the care that has been taken with them. To me it is just a dining room, and I don't think about it. A number of years pass before I realize that only a privileged few can afford to decorate their homes like this.

The middle of the room is dominated by the huge polished oak dining table. A dozen or more of my relatives are present, along with a couple of family friends, and we are soon seated according to my grandmother's wishes. Four or five conversations, fueled by alcohol, are occurring at once. It is deafening and boring to a four-year-old, so I concentrate on the delicious food that is delivered to us on beautiful china by silent servants. From fragments of conversation, I gather Vera is a photographer, and I want to ask about this. It isn't until the end of the last course that I manage to make my small voice heard over the cacophony. Then there is one of those sudden unforeseeable silences when, by some miracle, everyone in unison ceases their gabbling. I seize my opportunity.

"Uncle Vera, "I say, as loud as I can in case someone interrupts, "Are you going to take photos of us?"

In a split second, the atmosphere becomes intensely and tangibly electric. I look around in surprise, wondering what happened. Then everyone starts gabbling louder and faster than before. From across the table, Vera smiles broadly at me, saying, "Yes, I want to take some photos of you."

Later, we children are dismissed to play in the garden. My father intercepts me in the hallway as I am running to keep up with my older sister and brother. He leans down over me and takes a hold of my arm, speaking quietly so that no one else can hear. "Poppet, that's your *Aunt* Vera, not your Uncle Vera."

There is a hint of amusement in his tone, so I dare to disagree. "No, it's an uncle!"

This time his tone allows no opposition. "If I say she's your aunt, then she's your aunt, do you understand?" His fingers are painfully tight around my arm. I nod my agreement and he lets me go. I run out in the garden to find my siblings.

My mother takes me to stay with a friend, Caroline, for the night. She lives about ten miles away—a fairly long drive on the narrow, winding country roads in our beat-up old Ford. I met Caroline at the tiny school that I've been attending for a few months now, and her mother is acquainted with mine, so that makes it OK for us to exchange visits. She has already been to stay with me, and I'm quite enthralled with her.

She lives in a big rambling stone house a little like ours. Indeed, all my parents' friends seem to live in big rambling stone houses. When we get there, I shyly greet her mother—who looks a little like my mother, with not too obviously styled hair, a sprinkling of make-up, a loose skirt of some nondescript color that comes to just below her knees, and a harassed expression carefully hidden beneath a welcoming smile. I run off with Caroline, and we are soon playing on the swing that hangs from a big oak in the garden. I work at making it go fast and high, leaning forward on one sweep, and far back with my legs in front of me on the other sweep. I am exhilarated by the sensation of my stomach being left behind. Then, at the top of the swing, I let go and fly off, rolling in the sandpit below.

"I bet you can't go so high! Can you jump off like that?" I dare my friend, as I scramble to my feet.

She looks slightly hesitant. "I don't know...I've never tried..."

"You should try it! It's fun! Try it!"

She gets on the swing and I stand behind, pushing with all my five-year-old strength, to make the swing go at its maximum speed and height. To and fro it goes, higher and higher, her little arms fully stretched and then fully bent, her little hands gripping the ropes tightly. I exhort her to jump off, but she doesn't, and finally I have another idea.

"Here, let me get on behind you, I'll stand." I grab one rope of the swing to slow it down, and climb on behind her. Off we go again, laughing and screaming, with my feet either side of her hips, my hands gripping the rope above hers, and my body flexing with the movement of the swing.

I notice the slide. We don't have a slide at home. I run over to climb up the steps. She follows, and pretty soon we have used it in every possible permutation: sitting down individually, sitting down together, headfirst, feet-first, on our bellies, on our backs. After our twentieth slide, she grabs me by the hand, and says: "Come with me, I'll show you my secret house!"

We follow a path through some bushes till we get to a clearing where a cardboard structure sits. We crawl in through the makeshift door, finding a blanket and a small mattress in a room with two windows cut into the cardboard walls. It's a perfect size for the two of us. We wrap ourselves up in the blanket, giggling and tickling each other. I love being so close to her. I love her little girl body, just like mine, only slightly smaller. We lie side by side, facing each other, telling nonsensical stories and laughing at nothing, until we are called in for tea.

Later, when it's bedtime, she leads me up to her room. There are two small beds, with brightly colored bedspreads. We play in the bathroom, throwing water at each other, until her mother comes in to say it's time we settled down. So we say goodnight to her and she kisses Caroline, patting me on the head. I get into my own bed, but the minute we are alone, I hop across the room into bed with my friend.

"Let's play nurses and doctors!" I've loved this game when we've played it before.

"OK, you take your jammies off, and I'll be the doctor!"

I eagerly oblige, and she stands by the bed in the mild light of the small lamp that has been left on for us, while I lie face up, giggling, and she pokes and prods me. Pretty soon she instructs me: "Now you have to open your legs, I have to look at your pee-pee. There's something wrong with it!" She manages to keep her voice stern until the last word and then we both break out into peals of giggles. We entertain each other, becoming bolder and bolder in our investigations of each other's bodies. In a while, it's my turn to be doctor and I'm kneeling over Caroline with my hand between her legs, *fiddling* gently, while she wriggles and squirms and oohs and aahs. So entranced are we, that neither of us notice her mother has opened the door of the room until we hear her shocked voice: "What *are* you doing? Christine, get in your own bed!"

I leap up in a paroxysm of guilt. Quickly pulling on my pajamas, I climb into my own bed. Caroline's mother watches, thin-lipped. Her voice is cold: "If you can't behave, I'll put you in separate rooms!"

I'm not invited to Caroline's house again, nor she to mine.

Sometimes, when she wants to get rid of us, my mother sends my sister and me up the road to see Tom McFarlane, who was once my grandparents' chauffeur, now retired. Tom is always delighted to see us.

Today I am sitting on Tom's knee, when suddenly the door opens, and there is John, one of the gardeners, his big body framed in the doorway. There is a brief respite as he takes in the scene in the gloomy cottage, lit only by the light from one small window. Then he throws his head back, laughing uproariously. In one quick moment, he steps back and departs, closing the door.

What has just happened? It is as though a powerful wind blew through the room and then suddenly ceased, leaving the air hot and stuffy, thick and still. Astonished, I glance at my older sister, dwarfed in the armchair on the other side of the fireplace. She has an unmistakably angry frown on her sweet eight-year-old face. The frown seems to be directed at me, although I cannot imagine why. Tom, quickly pulling his hand out from my pants, is shaking. Looking at his face for clues, I see that he is blushing red to the roots of his gray cropped hair. Setting me down, he stands up, pulling his old ungainly body out of the armchair with much more speed than usual.

I have never seen an adult act with such anxiety. I am confused and concerned, because it is clear the other three all understand something I don't. Since their reactions are extreme, it must be something important. Yet I'm not aware of anything unusual.

Elizabeth climbs out of her armchair, and takes my hand, saying, "It's time for us to go now."

Usually Tom is reluctant to let us go, even when all the sweeties are gone, but now he just mutters, "All right, all right...you come back soon!" He doesn't even demand a kiss.

As soon as the door has closed behind us, I ask my sister, "Why did John laugh like that?"

Her brow once again furrows in a disapproving frown, and she says, "You shouldn't let Tom do that to you!"

I'm astonished. No one has ever said that kind of thing is wrong. Is my sister really suggesting that I have the power to stop Tom from doing it? That's ridiculous. It isn't that I like Tom putting his hand down my pants, but I've learned just to concentrate on the candy he feeds me. I do prefer him fiddling around down there, uncomfortable as it is, to having him clutch me so tightly that I am afraid of suffocating.

Besides, I can clearly remember Tom doing similar things to Elizabeth; not recently, it's true, but surely that's only because I have taken her place. *That*, as Elizabeth calls it, is something many of the men we meet want to do to both of us. Although most of them don't actually put their hands down our pants, they certainly hold us tightly in the same way, they touch our bottoms, and insist on kissing us with their wet lips and bristly chins. They leer at us with that look in their eyes, give us chocolate if we sit on their knees, and go on about how pretty we are. I know I am meant to let them do these things because my parents get angry with me if I don't hide the fact that I don't like it. My father says I am rude and I need to learn some manners. I don't want to be thought rude, I know it will get me in trouble.

There are all kinds of rules about being polite. Sometimes I have to wear really uncomfortable clothes and I have to be really careful what I do so that I won't get them dirty. I have to smile at the right people at the right time, even if I want to cry. I have to be very sure to thank my friends' mothers when I leave after visiting them, even if I haven't enjoyed myself. I have to eat things I don't want to eat, pretending I like them. What's different about allowing men like Tom to feel my body?

The strange thing on this occasion was John's entrance, and his laughter. Why had his arrival had such an effect on Tom? Why had he left so abruptly instead of coming in to say hello? Perhaps I have done something wrong. I feel foolish. I desperately want some kind of explanation.

So when we get home, I muster enough courage to ask my mother about it. To my relief, she isn't angry. She says that Elizabeth and I won't go to visit Tom any more, though she doesn't explain why not. She tells me not to worry about it, without explaining what *it* is. I don't feel much better.

Growing up is fraught with strange contradictions. The feelings that emanate from people are very real to me. Yet, what adults *say* frequently seems to conflict directly with what those feelings are telling me. Apparently, I should pretend some things are not happening even when they are so obvious that I'm sure everyone knows they are happening. I decide this thing with Tom is another one of these weird grownup games. Like you aren't meant to mention needing to do a number two when there are people around. I've got into trouble with my mother for that, and now I know that you should only whisper about it or not mention it at all. That's part of being polite.

I am beginning to grasp the concept of embarrassment, and I understand that it is to be avoided at any cost. I continue to let men do *that* to me, since trying to prevent them is a losing proposition. I pretend they are just being loving, like my mother or my grandmother. As long as everyone plays along, there will be none of the shame associated with allowing such secrets to come to light. As I grow older, I understand that it is part of my role as a girl to keep everyone happy. I am a good girl. I never make a fuss.

We've been out for the day and it's six o'clock by the time we get home. My mother, who has been short-tempered and uptight for the last half-hour, heads straight to the drinks cabinet. "Phew! Time for a whiskey," she says, smiling, and she is soon sitting down at the table with a glass of Scotch. She opens her handbag to pull out a pack of cigarettes.

"Damn, I forgot to buy more cigarettes," she mutters with a frown, as she applies the flame of her lighter to the end of the slender white tube sticking out of her mouth, and inhales deeply. My sister, who is playing with one of the dogs, pipes up, "Daddy says he won't buy cigarettes for you any more, he says it's a disgusting habit."

"He's quite right," responds my mother, "it *is* a disgusting habit, and it's really time I gave it up. Make sure you don't smoke when you're older! Waste of money and bad for your health!" She makes this pronouncement in a tone of certainty, as she blows a cloud of blue smoke in our direction.

I have observed that most adults are even more concerned about having access to alcohol than to cigarettes. They don't seem able to get more than a few hours through the day without having a drink. So I offer my opinion: "No, I won't smoke, and I won't drink either!"

To my surprise, my mother's expression of indulgent amusement turns to a look of horror. "Oh no, don't deny yourself the pleasure of drinking! Life would be no fun without drink!"

I'm walking along the road with my mother. She is on the inside next to the grass, and I'm wheeling my bicycle between us. Stopping, she says, "Wheel your bicycle on the outside."

I change my position, asking, as I so often do, "Why?"

She smiles down at me. "Because if a car comes by too close, I'd rather it hit your bicycle than hit you. We can get a new bicycle but we can't get a new Christine!"

I look up at her with a slightly awed sense of pleasure. That must mean she likes having me around. Previously, I'd assumed it would be a relief for her if I didn't exist.

When I'm playing with some friends, one of them makes a remark I don't understand. The others, who are all older than me, snigger a little. Somehow my ignorance shows and they make fun of me. One of them laughs scornfully, "You're seven, and you don't even know the facts of life!"

Brazenly, I reply, "Of course I do!" but I feel like a fool.

I ask my mother to explain what the facts of life are. She tells me that in order for a woman to have a baby, a man has to put his penis into her vagina. I am perplexed. I've seen boys' willies, and they're puny little soft things, a bit like short fat worms. It seems very awkward to try fitting them into women's vaginas. My mother explains that when a man is excited, his penis gets bigger. She says this is something that men and women only do when they love each other. I try to imagine it. I ask her if they do it standing up. She says no, they usually do it in bed. Sensing her growing irritation, I drop the subject, although I still have many half-formed questions. What is this kind of love that magically makes a man's penis grow? How and when and why does it happen? How long does it last? Do you get to choose who it happens with, or is it quite random? Do you always have a baby when you do this?

I decide I'd better just pretend to understand.

Chapter Three

In the summer I spend a great deal of time down at the burn, as we call the stream that runs through the valley. I sit for hours at the edge of the water, discovering the myriad different animals who make it their home: insects with long legs that run across the surface where it is still; things like living pieces of wire, wrapping themselves around the plants that grow along the banks; tadpoles, thousands of happy little black splodges with tails, wiggling to and fro in pools; sticklebacks, only an inch long, the fierce red and blue males with three spines on their backs; trout, from shoals of transparent tiny ones in the shallows, to bigger ones, maybe six inches long or more, that wait in the deep pools for food to come down in the gurgling water.

My eyes become accustomed to differentiating the shapes under the surface from the illusory pictures created by the light shining onto the surface. I recognize the shapes that are merely surface reflections, versus those that are multidimensional. The outside world, the dry world, the world of air, *my* world, is turned into a liquid dream painted on top of what is real. Everything underneath is brown and smooth and constantly moving, from the weed that covers the stones that are rounded by centuries of water flowing over them, to the fish themselves. I learn to watch the brown movement under the flow of water, and tell what is light on a stone, or a weed waving like a transparent fish fin, or a fish waiting. I learn to see the slightly darker shapes that are the trout with fluid fins that hold them stationary (but flowing, always flowing) against the water, facing upstream.

I learn what will feel solid when I touch it, and what (such as the weeds or the illusory water itself) will disappear between my fingers like air. I learn to move through the water so slowly, so naturally, with such smooth concentration and careful grace, that the fish don't notice my approach. I can get close enough to see the red of their gills moving in and out, to see the markings on their backs, to see the white of their bellies and the hint of rainbows on their sides, to see the lines of their fins waving lazily. One day, moving like this, I find myself standing beside a fish as it rests just above the layer of stones that pave the bottom of the burn. Slowly, soothingly, delicately, I reach my hand down through the water until I am almost touching the fish, and then I abruptly close my fingers before it realizes its life is being threatened. I know how to hold it, with my fingers in its gills, so that the thrashing of its little muscular body is to no avail. I wade out of the water triumphantly with my prey.

Ever since I can remember, the ten-foot-high stone walls that surround our garden have challenged me. Some have loose, pointed stones on top and these are obviously more dangerous (and therefore more fun) than the ones with flat stones on top, which I have quickly mastered. I can walk along the flat stones at normal speed. The ones with loose stones I have to negotiate more carefully, using my hands.

The farm next door is an exciting place, providing fertile training grounds for my climbing skills. There are several huge barns, with walls built out of stone, and horizontal beams from the top of one wall to the other. I spend a lot of time in those barns. Using cracks in the old stone walls, I can hoist myself high enough to get a grip on the first beam. Once I have my hands around the beam, I can scramble up until I am sitting on it. Then I can traverse the full length of the barn, from beam to beam, on all fours. Soon I discover the pleasures of swinging by my arms from the beams, and flying through the air to land in the thick piles of straw that cover the floor of the barn. From there I progress to swinging hand-over-hand from one beam to the next, using the weight and momentum of my body to propel myself. It leaves me shaking with exhaustion. I set myself tests, seeing how far I can go before my arms give out. Within a very few days I've progressed to five...six...seven...and in no time, I'm setting my sights on going the whole length of the barn, a total of fourteen beams. It takes me two weeks of practicing every day. My arms are nearly pulled out of their sockets. I make it to the second-last beam, and panting desperately, barely able to muster the last swing, I grab the fourteenth one. I hang there triumphantly for a second before I drop to the ground, aching, exhausted, and very pleased.

I swagger over to tell my friend and neighbor, Robert, the shepherd's son, about my latest achievement. I find him walking along the dirt road that runs between our homes, idly waving a stick.

"Hey, Robert!" I call to him exultantly. "I can go the whole length of the barn swingin' from the rafters by my hands!"

He glares at me, hitting the ground with his stick. "I dinna believe youse!"

I am insulted. I feel my face darken. Robert and I are both nearly ten years old, but I am bigger than him. We often fight with each other, sometimes for the joy of fighting, sometimes to establish who is boss (me), and sometimes because we're pissed off with each other. At this particular moment, we are about to have a fight because we are pissed off with each other, since Robert has just issued a challenge I cannot ignore.

"Well, come and watch then!" I say. Right now I would rather show off my new skill than fight. But Robert is in a bad mood.

"Why should Ah? Ah dinna wan' tae! Ye're lyin'!" he sneers. I take a threatening step towards him and he raises the stick to ward me off. This incenses me further.

"Ah'm gonna ge' you!" I say, and I rush in. I don't even notice the stick hitting my side. Swinging wildly with my fists, I catch Robert on the cheek. He swings back, hitting my shoulder. Employing my favorite tactic, I hurl myself on top of him. We're both scrambling about on the ground, pushing, pulling, grabbing, hitting. I'm tired from the energy I expended swinging my way across the barn, and Robert starts to get the better of me. He manages to roll over on top of me, pinning me down. There's a brief lull in our struggle.

Breath rasping in his throat, he says, "Ah've go' you now, d'y' give in?"

The words are like a red rag to a bull. I plant my feet, and with a surge of strength I raise my hips so that he is lifted in the air, then I roll over on top of him. We struggle for a few minutes more until I have him pinned, straddling his belly, my hands firmly around his wrists, which are outstretched on the ground above his head. Twist and turn as he might, he cannot get away from me; I know exactly how to distribute my weight so that I am very heavy. He tries again and again to free himself, without success. Finally he lies still.

"Well, d'y' give in?" I demand, gleeful, even though I am panting so hard that I can hardly talk.

His face is a mask of fury. He sputters something that might be assent. I decide to be magnanimous (and anyway, I am exhausted), so instead of forcing him to acknowledge defeat more politely, I get up, freeing him to leave. Rolling over wearily, he stands up, rubbing his red wrists. He glares at me under his eyebrows as he limps off. Over his shoulder, he shouts, "Ah hate youse!"

I go home, a little saddened that he's not as pleased as I am that I have once again defeated him. Poor Robert. There used to be a time when he would occasionally beat me. But in recent months, I have always been the winner. Every time he gets anywhere close to beating me, I summon up supergirl strength, and I turn the tables. In that state, I don't feel the pain of his blows.

It doesn't occur to me that it may be galling to him to be so consistently beaten by a girl. It doesn't occur to me because I do not think of myself as a girl. It's not that I think of myself as a boy, either. I know I'm not a boy. But somehow I believe that I am not a girl in the sense that most girls are girls. I am a not-girl. I will not be a girl. That is, I will not grow up to be a woman. I decide this deep in my small child mind when I am still very young, that I am not going to be like my mother and my grandmother and my aunt, and all the other women I know who stay at home, and cook and clean for their men, and complain behind their husbands' backs. I won't wear makeup or dresses. I will be like my father and my brother. I will go out and have exciting adventures in the big wide world. I'll go walking on the moors with my dogs, carrying a gun, and afterwards I'll stride around boasting loudly about my prowess. People will listen to me. I will be one of the men. I will be powerful.

However, forces are gathering against me. When I get home, I wander into the kitchen, hungry from my exertions. My mother is stirring a pot on the stove, one hand on her hip. My sister is there too, chopping something on the counter. She's being helpful. Suddenly I am aware that my shirt is ripped, my clothes and my face are covered in mud, and I have a graze on my cheek. My mother looks at me disapprovingly. In a tone that does not bode well, she asks, "What have you been doing, Christine?"

"Fighting with Robert," I say, torn between backing out the door and peering in the pot to see what's for dinner.

"It's time you stopped fighting with Robert, you're too old for that nonsense." Her voice is cold and biting.

I cannot believe my ears. I look at her in amazement, saying, "No' fight with Robert? Why no'?" I'm so appalled at what she has said that I accidentally slip into the forbidden Scottish accent. In front of my parents I must speak the Queen's English, as all upper class people do. At this moment, however, my mother is preoccupied with other transgressions and she ignores my lapse.

"Because you're growing up!"

"But why can't I fight with Robert?"

"Because I say so!"

I know better than to push for further explanation. I drop the subject, feeling surly and misunderstood. I glare at my sister, meekly chopping vegetables. My mother says something to her, using quite a different tone from the one she used with me. *You're such a goody-goody*, I think resentfully.

I cannot comprehend why my getting older means I shouldn't fight with Robert any more. It's one of my greatest pleasures. She might as well have said, don't climb trees. Of course I'll continue to fight with Robert.

And I do. But my mother's complaints about my torn, dirty clothes and body get more frequent. More and more often, she wants me to dress up in girls' clothing. She tries to make me look smart and clean, and gets very angry when I don't manage to stay that way for more than two minutes. I have already been thrown out of the local

Scottish country dance classes, for standing on the other children's toes. Now I am expected to wear a skirt and go to church on Sunday with my grandmother. On Sunday, one of the days I have to myself, when all I want to do is roam in the woods! And I have to go with my mother and my sister to visit people, sitting quietly in a chair for hours, listening to boring conversations, drinking tea out of ridiculous china. I am supposed to learn to cook and sew. I loathe poring over a piece of stupid cloth, I always manage to get the thread thoroughly knotted and tangled after the first stitch. It's not my idea of fun!

I resist and I resist. I continue to play in the barns on the farm. I stop climbing on the garden walls because that's too conspicuous. Instead I climb trees where I can't be seen, or I go down to the river. I stalk rabbits, catch them by hand, and then let them go because I don't want to kill them. I spend hours watching the fish in the river, learning to catch small trout in my hands. When I take these home to eat, my parents actually seem pleased with me. My father gives me a brief, impatient lesson in using a fishing rod.

But mostly he ignores me, especially when my brother is home from boarding school.

The barns on the farm are home to dozens of pigeons, who raise their young in makeshift nests. I take a couple of the babies home when they are still too young to fly. They are covered with stiff sheaths of feathers, and over that, still a smattering of yellow fluff. At this stage they don't coo, they whistle a single repetitive note. There is a small aviary in our garden, left over from the previous owner, where I keep the birds. I give them some grain that I find on the farm. When I put it on the shelf where I normally feed them, one happily eats the ears of wheat, while the other gets very upset. He picks up the grains and drops them off the edge of the shelf. I watch in surprise.

Later the one that ate the grain dies in convulsions. It must have been poisoned feed, left out for the rats.

The remaining bird, whom I call Pablo, becomes a very close friend. He sits on my shoulder, whistling happily and nuzzling my ear. He is always delighted to see me, and his trust in me is deeply touching. He quickly grows up, filling in his feathers and losing his yellow fluff. Soon he can fly very adequately. Keeping him in the aviary is too confining, and we are both happier when I let him fly free, although I am nervous that he will fly away.

I love him.

Then I am at school all day, and in my absence, he makes friends with the wild pigeons at the farm. Every day, when I come home, I stand by the aviary calling him, and he comes flying from the farm, spiraling down to sit on my shoulder and kiss me. Gradually it takes longer and longer for him to come when I call, although he is always very loving when he does arrive. Finally one day he doesn't come. I watch the pigeons flying in swirling flocks around the farm, wondering if he is with them. I know it's right for him to be free, and I miss his generous loving.

I reach puberty early, without any awareness of what is about to happen to my body. Horror accompanies the gradual realization that I am developing breasts. And then, even worse, a dark shadow begins to appear and spread just above the place between my legs which I never, ever, touch. I burrow under the blankets of my bed at night trying to distract myself from reality with fantasies of being a war spy (male, of course), captured by the enemy, giving nothing away in spite of horrible tortures, then valiantly escaping to become a greatly admired hero. The fantasies become progressively more vivid, occupying a great deal of my mind when I am not distracted by daily work and play.

But the shadow under my underpants grows. Individual curly black hairs begin to take shape. I am only nine-and-a-half, and this all seems very unfair. None of the other girls I know have bodies that are anything but white, flat and hairless. I have never seen a naked adult. I cannot imagine having an adult body. I cannot imagine being an adult.

Even my sister, nearly two years older than me, is barely filling out the way I am.

After my sister has already been sent to a school in Edinburgh, I still go to the village school down the road, which has only twenty-six pupils. One day we have a health check. The doctor arrives with a bustling nurse in a white uniform. All the girls have to line up in the dining room, from youngest to oldest. One by one, we are called forward and ordered to undress, in front of all the others. The first girl is my friend Moira, who's much smaller than me, has no breasts and no hint of hair on her smooth white body. I am second. I wait in terror for my turn, painfully aware that I look quite different from Moira. The jolly nurse calls me forward. I start to take off my clothes, hoping some miracle will occur and save me. Nothing happens except that I stand naked in front of them all, deeply humiliated. The doctor pokes me, weighs me, looks in my ears and eyes and pronounces me as healthy as a horse. I am allowed to put my clothes on again.

Chapter Four

Since my young mind is constantly trying to make sense of the world, I listen carefully to the adults around me. I frequently hear my mother complaining about not having enough money. This is most apparent when the mail arrives. She picks up the pile of white envelopes and flips through them, frowning anxiously, and muttering to herself, "More bloody bills!"

Then she walks into the dining room where my father is drinking his coffee while he peruses the paper. She tosses one or two of the envelopes on the table in front of him, saying something like, "I don't know *how* we are going to pay this!"

One day when I am laying the table for tea, I get some butter out of the refrigerator. As I am taking it out of its wrapper to put it on the butter-dish, she says, in a self-righteous tone, "Soon we won't be able to afford to buy butter!"

I'm a little surprised at this, but I assume it's true. Why would she say it if it wasn't true? Later, when we are all sitting down to eat, spreading butter on the bread that she makes, she repeats it, with the same air of certainty. "It won't be long before we can't afford to buy butter any more!"

I've known for a long time that we don't have enough money. The few occasions when my mother is forced to buy new clothes for me, instead of fitting me out in other people's cast-offs, are always agonizing. I hate it when she is so worried. The next day, when we sit down to eat our tea, I put jam on my bread without any butter. I really like butter, but I figure giving it up is the least I can do to help with a difficult situation, and I really don't want to feel that I am using up what is obviously a much more important resource than I had previously realized.

Noticing what I am doing, my mother leans forward with a puzzled expression. "Christine, why aren't you having butter on your bread?"

Everyone looks at me and I feel my face flushing. I can tell that she thinks I'm doing something silly. I stare down at my plate. "Umm...because you said we won't be able to afford it soon."

They all laugh. With a conciliatory smile, my mother says, "Well, if I were you I wouldn't worry about it. Just appreciate it while we have it!"

From then on, I have butter on my bread. Years later, I understand the significance of butter: the fear my mother was expressing was not that we would have nothing to put on our bread, but that we would be reduced to eating margarine, which is a working class food. We were never in danger of starving, only of being unable to maintain the illusion of class.

My father is astoundingly unmoved by my mother's constant state of desperation. He refuses to get a job, and my parents spend years staggering from overdraft to overdraft, occasionally reduced when he gets paid for the books he writes on hunting and fishing.

How do they manage to pay for my brother to go to an expensive boarding school in England? They don't. My grandparents pay for that, since it wouldn't do for their grandson to get anything less than the best education. It is the educational system, after all, that maintains the power of class privilege.

They don't pay for my sister and me to be educated, since we are girls. Our parents manage to scrape enough money together to send us to schools in Edinburgh. Even though we are merely girls, it's out of the question for any member of the laird's family to continue attending the local school past the age of ten.

And so I begin the daily bus treks to school in Edinburgh. A thousand girls crowd the forbidding stone staircases and hallways of the huge Victorian building. In such unfamiliar territory, I am lost, lonely and frightened, although I don't identify these emotions.

When people ask me I if enjoy school, I mumble yes. What difference would it make, if I said I didn't like school? I don't want to be asked to explain myself. I have no idea what it means to *enjoy* something, or not.

The playground is a small rooftop where there is no room to run. We stand around in groups trying to act like the young ladies we are supposed to be. One day a girl brings a short handwritten story that her brother has given her, about a girl who has sex with her uncle after he reads her a bedtime story. It is quite graphic and detailed. I have never read anything like it before. It makes me feel acutely uncomfortable, deeply disturbed in a way that I cannot find any words for. I know that sex is taboo. Yet, the girl in the story apparently enjoys what went on between her and her uncle. Does this mean that sex...that awful dirty word that makes us all blush and giggle...is really something nice? I know the teachers at school disapprove of it, but then they also disapprove of fighting and climbing trees.

I love to accompany my father on his daily shooting expeditions. It is the one time when we have a truce, when I am not required to act in some foreign adult fashion. He strides along in front of me, shotgun in the crook of his arm, dogs running ahead searching for game. I have to move at a half-run, so as not to be left behind. When a rabbit bursts out of the brush to our left, flushed by one of the dogs, my father stops abruptly, raising the gun to his shoulder. There is a long pause. I am holding my breath. This is always a moment of intense confusion for me. On the one hand, I want the small furry animal not to be hurt. On the other hand, I want my father to be a successful hunter. I think of my ambivalence as weakness. It's irrelevant anyway. My father pulls the trigger, a bang resounds in the hills, and the rabbit tumbles over and over. It screams as it falls, sounds that tear at my insides. As one of the dogs streaks after it, my father calls, "Good girl, bring it here!"

When the other dog starts to move off, he snaps, "Not you, you bloody animal, sit down!"

It continues to run, and he roars, "I said *sit down*, damn you!"

It cowers, tail between its legs, as the other dog returns with the rabbit hanging from its jaws. Praising the dog, he takes the trophy, kills it with one quick chop to its neck, and hands it to me. I haven't yet recovered from the horrible sound of the screams. Seeing the stricken expression on my face, he pats my shoulder, saying, "It's all right, poppet, it's only a rabbit."

I place the warm dead body in the game bag that's hanging over my shoulder. That's my job, to carry the birds and animals that he has killed. And when we get home, I will pluck or skin and clean them.

Sometimes, on successful hunting trips, I get very tired carrying the heavy bag of game. I'm still short, and the bag hangs down almost to my knees. We stride over the hills, often up steep inclines that leave me breathless even when I'm not weighted down with a full bag of game. Once or twice I am reduced to tears of pain and exhaustion, as I fall in ditches and trip over roots. I try very hard not to let my father see when I get into this state. I will overcome the failing of my female-ness. I will learn to be tough, show no weakness, and tolerate all hardship. I will prove myself, and eventually, when I am old enough, I will be allowed to carry a gun. I will be an excellent shot, and the dogs will obey me instantly. I will return home with bags full of game.

Occasionally we are graced with visits from our English cousins, John and Peter. John is about Elizabeth's age, and Peter a little younger than I. The three older children are a formidable gang, regarding Peter and me as legitimate prey. Their favorite pastime is to tie one of us to a tree, threatening all kinds of torture. I usually feel uncomfortable when they choose Peter as a victim, since I know only too well that it could be my turn next. On the other hand, it seems sensible to side with the strongest when I am offered the opportunity.

One day, after tying Peter to a tree, they're busy collecting wood to make a fire around him. Peter is snarling, calling us every name he can think of. I decide to play my part as one of the oppressors, so I tell him to shut up and put my hand over his mouth, whereupon he bites me very hard. The other three all laugh. The shock of intense pain jolts me. Later, when the others have gone wandering off, I go back to untie him. His simple, unsmiling *thank you* gives me far more pleasure than I'd ever got from tying him up.

The next day, when David and John decide to tie me up, I resist with every ounce of strength in my little body. Thankfully, Elizabeth doesn't help them, so although the struggle that ensues is vicious, and lasts a good half hour, it ends with me free. I'm covered in stinging rope burns. Since we have a very strong taboo against telling on each other, I don't dare go to my mother. However, as I am making my way to my room, sobbing with pain, I pass my grandfather. Seeing the red welts all over my arms and legs, he asks in horror what has happened. That allows me to speak, which I do with great but disguised pleasure. The telling-off my brother gets as a result does nothing to improve my relationship with him. Many years pass before he speaks to me in anything other than a tone of ridicule.

One winter evening, my father offers to teach me how to play draughts. I'm intrigued by the complexities of the game, by the far-reaching consequences of moving each little round red or black piece. The next evening we play again, and the next and the next...it becomes a ritual. I sit in a hard-backed chair poring over the checkered board, deliberating over each move for several minutes. He sits in the blue armchair, reading a book while he plays, paying little or no attention to the game, yet never falling into any of my carefully laid traps. Night after night, I lose. But I'm getting better. After a while he has to give the game more of his attention, because I'm no longer so easy to beat. Soon I'll be able to play as well as him.

Sure enough, one evening I win. I'm exultant. He responds to my grinning face with an indulgent smile, says "Well done!" and returns to his book. The next evening, as usual, I pull out the board. To my amazement, he shakes his head. "Not tonight, poppet."

The next night and the next night, he says the same thing. It dawns on me that he'll never play with me again.

Christmas arrives. In the sitting room, my sister and brother and I are opening our presents, ripping off the paper in unrestrained excitement. My brother has a package that is a very interesting shape, long and cylindrical, so I have half an eye on him even as I am busy tearing at my own presents. Hearing him say in a voice of awe, "It's a gun!" I immediately run over to look. There it lies, brand new gleaming metal barrel and shiny wooden stock, oozing power. I'm suddenly flushed with desire. I glance up at my father, standing with his hands clasped behind him, rocking on his heels, and looking very proud. Proud of his son.

"Now you'd better make sure you take care of it, do you hear me? I'll take you out later today and we'll see if you can bag a duck or two on the foreshore. Now listen, when you clean it..." As he bends forward to pick it up, I interrupt.

"Will I have to wait till I'm fourteen to get one?"

He stands up straight, holding the gun, and fixes me with a look, his eyebrows drawn together, his mouth thin. His expression of pride has been displaced by annoyance.

"*You!*" I shrink from the disdain in his voice. "*You* are *never* going to get a gun! Women in this family don't use guns!" He turns back to my brother. I slink over to my disappointing presents, holding back the tears.

Chapter Five

It's New Year's Day. My sister and brother and I are playing in the haystack on the farm. I love making tunnels in the stacks of bales. But as the afternoon wears on I become increasingly aware of a growing pain in my belly. It's a heavy ache that seems to pull at my insides. Eventually, unable to ignore it, I reluctantly return to the house. Going to the bathroom, I pull down my jeans and pants, sitting down to pee...then I'm shocked to see that there is blood in my underpants. Am I bleeding from between my legs? I look to see what I can see. No sign of any cuts or grazes. I'm frightened. I quickly decide I won't tell anyone.

Wiping away the blood with toilet paper, I pull up my pants and trousers and go into the bedroom I share with my sister. I must look worried, because she immediately asks what's wrong. Hesitantly, I tell her there's blood in my pants. She tells me it's OK, it happens to all girls and I must go and tell Mummy. I resolutely refuse to do so. Before I can stop her, she runs downstairs. A few minutes later I hear my mother's footsteps on the stairs. I wait in dread, but to my relief, she's quite understanding. She finds me a clean pair of underpants and gives me pads to put between my legs to catch the blood, which she says will carry on for a few days. She calls the pads STs, short for sanitary towels. She tells me the bleeding is normal, it happens to all girls, and it will happen every month from now on. I'm only slightly reassured. My mother calls it *the curse*. Am I now cursed for life?

How come it's happened to me and not to any of the other girls I know? How come nobody talks about this if it's as common an experience as my mother says?

Fishing in the burn one day, I slice my finger open. The wound gapes wide, as blood mixed with water streams over my wrist. I regard it anxiously. It smarts. Usually I ignore the many cuts and grazes inflicted upon me due to my lack of regard for my body, but I decide this one needs a bandage. It's about half a mile home, mostly downhill, and I fly on my sturdy green bike. When I get home the cut is still seeping blood and my hand aches. My mother is in her bedroom, putting clothes away. I am always a little nervous of interrupting her. I decide the cut is bad enough to warrant her attention, so I knock on the half-open door, saying, "Mummy, I've cut my hand."

Without turning towards me, she snaps, "Well, go and put something on it then!"

I leave at once, since I know from the familiar tone of her voice she doesn't want to be disturbed. (I have the strange idea that she may have been crying, though I have never seen her cry before). I look through the medicine cabinet in the bathroom and find a band-aid. The cut is in an awkward place between my fingers, but I do my best to patch myself up.

Later, my mother sees the wound. "Dearie me," she says, "that *is* a bad one."

I can tell she feels guilty for fobbing me off earlier in the day and I'm gratified that she thinks the cut is bad. Maybe, after all, it was OK for me to ask for help. On the other hand, I feel uncomfortable with her guilt. I want to make her feel better.

She tries to put a band-aid on but nothing will hold those raw gaping edges of flesh together. With time, the skin heals itself. There will always be a scar.

I'm walking up the lane when I see a movement in the grass at the side of the road. It turns out to be a rabbit with myxomatosis, a disease that's been spread on purpose amongst the rabbits to try and reduce their numbers, since they are a great pest. Myxomatosis makes their heads swell until they can't see, hear or smell. At home, I tell my father I've seen this sick rabbit. He orders me to go back and kill it, saying it's wrong to leave an animal to suffer.

I go back down the road. The animal is too far gone to be able to run away. Steeling myself to do what needs to be done, I hit the rabbit repeatedly on the head with a rock. Now it lies on its side with blood oozing from its mouth, but its feet still move and I am afraid it's still alive. In desperation, I take it by its hind legs, swinging the body as hard as I can on the bar of a gate. Now I think I've broken its neck and it's really dead. I go home, feeling sick.

It's lunchtime. My father is in one of his frequent moods, and he is leaning towards me with that look on his face. I don't even hear his words, just his tone. I sit very still, slightly hunched forward, staring at the grain of the polished oak dining table in front of me, and the circle of my plate against it. I think, *I must listen to what he's saying, then maybe I can make the right reply and he'll leave me alone.* It doesn't work, of course. He's leaning closer. I glance frantically towards my mother. Perhaps she will intervene. I know she can stop him. But she's busily reading a book. My father takes my arm, digging his cruel fingers into my flesh.

"Ow, that hurts," I whine, thinking perhaps now my mother will intervene; I know she doesn't like it when he hurts me physically. He lets go of my arm, his face twisting contemptuously. His tone drips scorn: "Baby!" he says with a snort of disgust. He launches into a list of my shortcomings. I keep my gaze on my plate, feeling the softness of the cat as she rubs against my leg under the table. I desperately want to reach down and stroke her. The tears are starting to sting behind my eyes. I am torn between allowing them to show, which is likely to end the torture sooner, and keeping them under control, which will prove I am not a baby...won't it?

I no longer have any choice. As he leans over me again, I flinch away, glancing up in anticipatory fear, and a sob bursts from my tightened throat. More sobs follow, I've lost control. I feel deeply ashamed. My father sits back away from me.

"Oh for God's sake, child! Can't you ever take a joke? You're never going to get along in this world!"

Silently, furiously, I stare at the table through my tears, hating him, and promising myself that in spite of all he says, I *will* get along in this world. I wonder if it is safe for me to get up and run out of the room. Will he grab me before I get to the door?

Now my mother has noticed. "Leave her alone, Arthur," she says testily. It's enough to make him transfer his attention elsewhere. I manage to finish my meal.

My father seldom has anything good to say about anyone, and he often launches into loud diatribes about how stupid people are. His favorite target is my mother's father, who is the laird, and many of the other members of my mother's large illustrious family, although he is superficially polite to them when he meets them in person.

My father's father, who lives with us and always sits opposite me at the dining table, adores me. He and my father nurse a mutual hatred, or so it seems to my child mind. It may have been distorted love. In any case, they are always at each other's throats. Weeks go by when they do nothing but shout at each other. My father, being younger, better of hearing, louder of voice, cleverer with words and more underhand, usually gets the better of their arguments, and my grandfather often stomps out of the room cursing. Though there are occasions when he diverts my father from tormenting me, his support of me often spurs my father on to greater extremes, in order to prove that he isn't going to be swayed by Grandpa.

Sometimes, when I run out of the room in tears, my father follows me upstairs where I lie sobbing on the bed. Speaking in a kind tone, he tells me how he is only treating me like this because he loves me. "You need to learn to laugh at yourself. When you grow up, you'll appreciate what I'm doing for you."

I don't find this reassuring. On some level, for no good reason, I am sure life doesn't have to be like this.

I work out a plan to murder him. I am going to push him off a very steep, high cliff. I will lure him to the edge by pretending one of the dogs is in trouble. He often goes shooting near the cliff I have in mind, so it is a feasible plan. I reckon we'd all be much happier without him.

I never get as far as trying to carry out my plan.

My grandfather is always smacking me and my sister on our bottoms, telling us to give him a kiss. When I was younger, I enjoyed running away from him, but now I hate his game. I've always hated having to kiss him. His mustache is all bristly. My parents have told me many times that I must humor him, as well as all the other relatives who want me to sit in their laps or kiss them.

One day my father notices him slapping my bottom as I walk by. He's seen Grandpa do this many times before without remarking on it. Now he says to my grandfather, "Don't do that, they're getting too old for that sort of thing now."

From then on, my grandfather no longer slaps our bottoms or asks for kisses. I'm grateful, though confused. It used to be something I had to let him do, now it's something he's not supposed to do. What's suddenly changed?

We've just been into town to see a film, which is a rare treat. As we exit the well-lit but dingy cinema into the parking lot, my father removes his cap with one hand, brushes back his hair with the other hand, and then replaces his cap. This is a familiar gesture, and I know it prefaces an Announcement. I wait anxiously. He says, "Well, that was a boring load of Hollywood rubbish!" I breathe a sigh of relief. The movie was a fairly complex love story with subtleties beyond the comprehension of my limited world view. Although I don't personally have any judgment of it being good or bad, I might be asked what I think of it and I want to make sure that I respond correctly. Now I have my cue.

We pile into the car, a battered old Rover, and set off home. As always, I'm sitting in the middle in the back, with my sister on one side, my brother on the other. My father drives so fast on the narrow winding road that we're all flung from side to side.

"For God's sake, Arthur, can't you slow down?" demands my mother.

Laughing with a slightly maniacal edge, my father reduces his speed a little. "No, I'm being chased by a blonde bitch in a red sports-car!"

He's referring to a character in the film we've just seen. My mother says, "God, she was such a pain in the neck!" and my brother chimes in, "She was so stupid!"

Something takes me over, obscuring my common sense like a fog blotting out the light. Or is it a light shining through the fog? Before I can stop myself, I am telling the truth. "I thought she was nice!"

Raucous laughter follows my statement.

"For God's sake, child, have you no discrimination?" roars my father from the front.

Sneering, my brother turns towards me, saying with utter scorn, "*You* are such an idiot!"

I've learned to knit, with much sighing and groaning, and I manage to knit myself a sweater for school. It takes a great deal of frowning concentration and several long winter evenings by the fire in the sitting room, where the wind howls up through the floorboards, lifting the carpet like some beast trying to force its way in. The long worn velvet curtains muffle the sound of the rain lashing against the windows as I struggle with tangled wool and needles that won't obey me. Finally it's done. I sew the sleeves up, sew them onto the body and put it on. I'm very proud of myself, yet, though I wear the sweater for years, I really don't like it. It is the inevitable school blue. It is chunky and shapeless. Other girls wear smart store-bought sweaters that look good on them.

My mother is pleased that I have learned to knit, partly because it saves her money if I make my own clothes, and partly because it proves I am capable of some feminine activities.

Chapter Six

We children are always supposed to help in the kitchen. One day when I am tearfully trying to get away without doing my chores, I mutter under my breath that my family sees me as nothing more than a bloody slave. Hearing me, my brother immediately tells my parents, who think it is hilarious. They bring it up again the next day, and the day after that, and the day after that, and the day after that. It becomes a family joke. I have to listen to my parents telling other relatives what I said, amidst guffaws of laughter. Soon, all it takes for them to break into hilarity is for someone to say "Poor little BS." It goes on for years. When I am eighteen, they are still saying it.

I'm out on my bicycle, and I stop at a berry patch by the side of the road. I'm busy popping the juicy black berries into my bag to take home to my mother, when a smart white car zips past me, then pulls up, reversing back towards me. The driver, a youngish woman with a stylish hairdo, rolls down the window. She's clearly not a local, since I've never seen her before. She must be lost. These small back roads are poorly signposted.

"Can you tell me where the Countess of Chesterhame lives?"

Of course I know where my grandmother lives, and I'm eager to be helpful. When I have explained in detail how to get there, she thanks me, and drives off.

Once the bag is filled with berries, I get back on my bike and ride home. My mother is pleased, and makes stewed blackberries and apples for dinner. I chop the apples. Later, at dinner, I casually mention my interaction. "When I was picking blackberries, a woman driving a car asked me the way to Granny's."

My father turns on me in an instant, his eyebrows drawn fiercely together. His tone fills me with dread. "You didn't *tell* her, did you?"

I am immediately certain the answer is meant to be no, but the fact is I did tell her, and it's too late now to hide the truth. I stutter a little. He puts down his fork and glares at me more fiercely than ever. "You *did* tell her, didn't you? You stupid little brat!"

I make one shot at defending myself. "I thought…I didn't know I shouldn't! I was just trying to be helpful!"

"Oh for God's sake, you don't understand anything, do you? Trying to be helpful, my God!" He rolls his eyes and groans, then turns back to me. I look at my plate. "She was a reporter, you idiot! You just sent a reporter to harass your grandmother! You never give directions to strangers, do you understand? For God's sake, use your common sense for once! Do you understand? *Do* you?" There's a long pause while I pretend not to exist. But he isn't going to let it go.

"Well, *do* you or not? Answer me!"

I mutter into my plate. It's true that I understand something: my grandfather has scandalized the county by trying to divorce my grandmother, and no one in my family wants to talk to the newspapers about it. I *don't* understand how I am supposed to know when not to be helpful.

When my friend Moira from down the road joins the Girl Guides, I follow suit. I like it well enough: it gets me out of the house, I meet other children my age, and I occasionally go camping. My father adopts a superior attitude, with flippant overtones. After I've been to a meeting and we're in the dining room, eating supper, he asks, smiling indulgently, "So, daughter number two, how was the Girl Guides today?"

I never know quite how to reply to this kind of question. "Fine," I say, hoping he will leave me alone. I concentrate on my meal, watching out of the corner of my eye.

He regards me with that slightly bored expression, languid and tolerantly amused, one eyebrow raised. "You *do* know that they are a bunch of fascist reactionaries, don't you?"

I hesitate. It's often a mistake to admit I don't know something, but I may well make a fool of myself if I pretend to understand his remark. "What's a fascist reactionary?"

He snorts, twirling his narrow stemmed glass, filled with red liquid, between his fingers. "You don't know what a fascist reactionary is?"

I say nothing, looking down at my plate.

"Well, I'm sure your Captain knows what a fascist reactionary is, why don't you ask her?"

The captain of my Girl Guide troop is a middle-aged local woman whom my father rarely meets, although of course everyone knows everyone around here. For some reason, he seems to regard her as a comical figure.

I frown anxiously, uncertain what I might be letting myself in for. He repeats, "Why don't you tell her the Girl Guides are fascist reactionaries, and ask her to explain to you what that means?"

There's something in his expression that warns me this might not be a good idea. But I'm much less afraid of Captain than I am of my father. And can I really get into trouble for asking a question that I have been instructed to ask?

"But don't tell her I told you to ask her!" he says. "Don't tell her that I was the person who said that, all right? Do you understand?"

I nod. Now I'm a seriously intrigued.

At my next Girl Guide meeting, I say to Captain, "Someone told me that the Girl Guides are fascist reactionaries."

She turns to face me with a horrified expression. Her tone is self-righteously indignant. "*Who* said that?"

"I promised I wouldn't say. What is a fascist reactionary?"

"*Who* would say something like that?" She is almost fuming. I'm slightly alarmed at the level of her outrage, although it makes me want an answer to my question more than ever.

"I can't tell you. What *are* fascist reactionaries?"

"I don't believe anyone would say that! What nonsense!"

I let her fume for a few moments longer, and then I query again. "What *are* fascist reactionaries?"

She purses her lips. "Hitler was a fascist. His followers would be called fascist reactionaries."

"Oh!" Now I understand what a loaded remark it was.

She harasses me a little more to find out who said it, but I manage to avoid telling her.

When my mother's father, the Earl of Chesterhame, insists on a divorce, my grandmother goes to live in a small house, near the sea. I like to go with my mother to visit her there, since I get to play with all the little creatures that live in the waters of the estuary, but when my father accompanies us, our visits are short and awkward. My kindhearted grandmother doesn't tolerate his tendency to act the bully, and isn't deceived by the veneer of humor that covers his short temper. He makes fun of her behind her back. Her genuine sincerity gives him plenty of fuel.

The house is a far cry from the mansion where she used to live, and there is barely room for all of us to sit. Her cooking is sometimes strange. Although she has never lacked for money, living through two drawn-out wars has left her with a strong sense of frugality, so she won't always throw food away when it's time to do so.

One day, my sister, brother, mother, father and I are all squashed into the tiny kitchen for lunch. First she serves us a very peppery mash. Examining his plate, my father inquires, "What *is* this you're feeding us?"

My grandmother replies, "It's leftover sausage from the other day, mixed with brussel sprouts and potatoes. And leeks from the garden." While she's over at the stove with her back turned, my mother glares at him, muttering, "Just eat it, for God's sake!"

We all eat what we can. When we are done with that course, she serves us a kind of sponge cake with jam and cream on top. As my grandmother sits down, we pick up our spoons to dig in. She says, "I hope this tastes all right, you wouldn't believe how much mold I took off the top of the jam. But it tastes fine to me. And that cream had been in the fridge for about six weeks. Really, I do think that refrigerators are wonderful inventions." Her voice indicates her very real appreciation.

My father snorts and then coughs. Each of us takes a mouthful or two. It does taste a little strange.

My mother's father manages the family estate. In order for him to support his mistress, he is forced to sell part of the estate. So when I am eleven, a boys' boarding school buys the big house where my mother was born.

I spend my summer days fishing in the river, or just combing the woods for new and exciting things to see, animals to watch, trees to climb, bushes to hide in. Now these pastimes are interrupted by obtrusive teenage boys from the school. At first they just shout abuse, and I ignore them as best I can. One day a red-haired boy is friendly to me. He is there the next day and the next, as I work up and down the river with my fishing rod. Although I can't figure out what he wants, it's nice to have a friend. He takes to walking half way home with me. One day he awkwardly takes my hand. I realize that I have a boyfriend.

John is excruciatingly boring. I never know quite what to do with him, although I bask in the joy of having someone attentive to me. Nothing happens between us for a long time except we walk places together holding hands. One day he clumsily kisses me. It's all wet and sloppy. The other kids on the bus to school have already made fun of me for having a boyfriend who never does anything beyond holding my hand, so I know that cool people like to kiss. In spite of disliking John slobbering all over my face, I very much want to be cool and have a boyfriend. I put up with being kissed.

One day another boy speaks to me when I am fishing, asking if he can walk me home. I assume he's just being nice. When we get to the top of the hill, he stops under a tree, puts his arms round me and kisses me. I'm not particularly pleased that someone else as well as John wants to do this, but I resign myself. We kiss, while I am sandwiched between boy and tree trunk, then he slides his hand up my shirt to touch my nipple. Without warning, an electric shock rips through my body. It's an extraordinary sensation, that takes my breath away. Such an intense, uncontrolled physical response has no place in my reality. I don't have time to mull over what has occurred, or why, before the boy removes his hand from my breast to thrust it down my pants. The sensation of him fiddling between my legs is simply unpleasant, but he's holding me so tightly that there isn't anything I can do. When I struggle, he tightens his hold on me, kissing me all the time, so I can't talk. He seems quite carried away. After a short while he releases me and steps back, panting, looking quite pleased. I don't know what to think, although the fact that he looks happy is reassuring.

From then on, my sex education continues apace. The second boy is soon replaced by a third. I'm not sure how any of them lays claim to me. I have an uneasy feeling that I am being treated as something that can be owned and taken or given away. The boys all have one thing in common: they want to slobber over my face and stick their hands down my pants. This activity is acutely distasteful and chronically boring to me. Since it is clearly very compelling to them, I don't know how to avoid it without creating an unpleasant scene. I soon have the dubious pleasure of feeling an erect penis. Even through clothes, I am impressed and a little appalled. When I first see one hanging out in full view, I can hardly believe my eyes. It is undoubtedly the ugliest thing I have ever seen. I decide I will avoid looking at them whenever possible.

This must be what my mother meant when she told me about men and women making babies. I gather from various passing remarks that it is a big deal to *go all the way* or *not go all the way*. I certainly don't relish the idea of a boy sticking his penis inside my vagina. I really don't want to have anything to do with my vagina. I never touch myself *down there*, and I feel very uncomfortable at the idea of doing so. I want to pretend that *down there* doesn't exist.

Fortunately, the boys I initially have sex with don't seem too intent on going all the way, or I am able to dissuade them by one means or other. They don't seem much concerned about me at all, just as long as they have what I learn to recognize as an orgasm. If I really object, they get angry. In general they get it over with more quickly if I don't protest too much. I perfect the art of distracting my mind while they make use of my body.

The forces that dictate my womanhood are inexorable. My schoolmates make it abundantly clear that I will never fit in if I continue to climb trees, play cowboys and indians, go fishing, and fight with the boy next door. They giggle and look at me pityingly when I talk about things like that. I am already the odd one out at home—the one who's no good at being sweet, the one who asks too many questions, the one that can't seem to grasp important unspoken rules—and my father makes sure I know what a disappointment I am. I very much want to fit in somewhere. Gradually, I give in to pressure. The boy next door, my fighting companion, has moved away. I have to wear a skirt to school. I am being forced to conform, at least on a surface level, to the irrevocable fact of my female-ness.

I have one very good friend at school though, and our friendship makes my life bearable. Sadly, Janet's into boys. I follow her lead. I learn to put on make-up and dresses. Instead of going fishing, we go out and pick up boys. I begin to worry what I look like. I spend less and less time in the woods that sustained me through my pre-teen years.

I quite often spend weekends at Janet's house, since we live miles apart. We sleep in a double bed together, and sometimes we play doctors and nurses, which involves touching each other's bodies in various ways and places. I like it a lot. It never occurs to me that there is a connection between what I do with her and what boys do to me. I know there isn't any connection.

One day, when I want to play this game, she refuses, saying we're too old for that kind of thing. I'm disappointed and confused. What *is* that kind of thing? And why are we too old for it? I don't dare admit my ignorance to her. Soon afterwards, we stop sharing a bed when I stay at her house. I miss the warmth and comfort of her body. I'm vaguely aware of feeling lonely. I never allow myself to feel this for long enough to name it.

The boys I meet through her want to do exactly the same sort of thing as the boys from the boarding school. I get used to being groped in bus shelters and phone boxes. Janet seems to like it, and there's nothing else for me to do while I'm waiting for her. I know the fact that I don't like it means there is something wrong with me.

Nobody seems to want to talk about this activity called sex in any real way. They disapprove of it outright, only refer to it obliquely, or they leer and make incomprehensible jokes. Gradually, I begin to perceive that my woman-ness is an indispensable part of this pastime that the male species finds so desirable. I begin to learn that most men are easily manipulated and very replaceable. If I have to be a woman, at least I can use this apparently universal male weakness to my advantage. Perhaps I am not completely without power.

Chapter Seven

At the age of sixteen, old enough to earn my own money, I answer an ad in the paper for a temporary typing job. After talking to my potential employer on the phone, I'm on my way to his apartment. I go up two flights of stairs—those bare stone stairs with a wooden banister that are everywhere in Edinburgh—to ring the doorbell of number three. A middle-aged man with balding gray hair and saggy cheeks opens the door, standing aside for me to enter. His manner is very friendly, perhaps a little too familiar. I don't immediately warm to him, but then why should I? It doesn't seem of any consequence whether I like him or not, I'm only there to earn money.

I follow him into a room with a desk, a sofa, and many books around the walls. It's quite dark, with half-drawn curtains, which seems strange for an office. I wonder what he needs typed.

Waving at the sofa, he invites me to sit down. Walking to a drinks cabinet across the room, he pours himself a glass of whiskey, asking me if I'd like one.

"No, thanks." I'm starting to feel uneasy. I just want to get on with the work, get paid and go home.

He stands smiling at me, the drink in his hand, while I try not to fidget. He says "So you're Chris, are you?"

I agree. I don't like the way he's looking at me.

He sits down beside me, asking where I live, how old I am, where I go to school. He's obviously not in any hurry to get on with the work and just wants to chat for a while. I relax a little. Then he asks me if I have a boyfriend, which makes me uneasy again. When men ask me this, it's usually a prelude to sexual advances. I say no, and what kind of typing does he need done? He gets up, gesturing at the typewriter on the desk. Just some casual work, he says, let's see what you can do. I sit down at the typewriter, relieved that now we're going to get on with it. He stands close behind me dictating a sentence, then leans over me to see what I've typed, putting his hand on my shoulder.

I feel acutely uncomfortable at the proximity of his body and even more so at his touch, but what can I do? It would be unthinkably rude to ask him to remove his hand. My only option is to ignore it. He dictates some more. Now he is standing directly behind me with a hand on each of my shoulders, and he's starting to knead them as he talks. Now I am more than uncomfortable—I am frightened. I remember that he locked the door behind me when I entered. I continue to type, pretending nothing is happening. He asks if I enjoy massage and I make some un-identifiable response through my tight throat. He laughs. I am vaguely aware that I hate the sound of his laugh. To my horror, his hands start to slide down inside my blouse. He leans over me, saying that I have lovely breasts. I feel his breath on the side of my face. I am terrified, my fingers frozen in place over the keys of the typewriter. My mind races, desperately searching for some way to extricate myself before something absolutely unthinkable happens.

Just as his hand encircles my breast, I blurt out the words, "I really have to go soon or I'll miss the bus home."

He laughs again, saying, "Oh, surely there's no hurry." His hands are caressing my nipples. I think of leaping up and running to the door, but I'd never have time to pick up my bag and then I'd have no money to get home with. Besides, the door is locked.

I am caught in the nightmare. I make more excuses about having to catch the bus. His hands continue to play with my breasts, and he laughs, asking me questions like, why am I in such a hurry? Am I feeling uncomfortable? Why don't I just relax for a while? I tell him I have to go, I'll miss the bus, my parents are waiting for me.

It seems like centuries before he removes his hands slowly from inside my blouse and steps backwards with a sigh. He smiles as I leap up, grab my bag and coat, and back towards the door. He comes forward to let me out. "Same time tomorrow then?"

"Of course," I reply with some semblance of a smile. Does he really think I would willingly come here again? To my immense relief, he opens the door. I rush out, gulping in the cold fresh air. At full speed I flee down the stairs.

His laughter follows me: "I hope you catch the bus!"

Out on the street, I turn the corner, running all the way to the bus station. I'm still trembling when I get there, though trying to compose myself. I don't want to attract attention. I will not tell anyone about what has just happened to me, of course. That would be much too embarrassing.

Why am I so shaken by this behavior with an older man, when I am unmoved by what teenage boys do to me?

My existence, like that of my parents, is a shallow sham, a pretense. I do whatever I have to do, to survive the lies that everyone is so desperately perpetuating. Some day I will find the key to another world. I have no idea what this other world will be like, but I know that this is not all there is to life. I am very sure of that. Meanwhile, I am searching, although there is really nowhere to look; or perhaps the problem is that I always have to go home and deal with my family. And I am bored. I am always bored as a teenager. From my upper-class family and the nerds my mother tries to foist on me, to the middle class girls and teachers at school, to the working class lads I go out with when I visit my friend Janet, I find no one with anything worthwhile to say. Everyone avoids anything that smacks of reality. No one tells the truth about what they really feel or think.

Being bored makes me vulnerable to feelings, which are dangerous. Alcohol leaves me with a hangover, but it is a distraction.

New Year's Eve in Scotland is traditionally a time for great celebration. Everyone gets very drunk and gathers at the nearest Town Hall, waiting for the clock to chime midnight. When it does, there's a massive uproar, and the men kiss as many women as they can lay their lips on.

Now that we are both seventeen, Janet and I are allowed to go to the pub, but licensing hours dictate that the pubs close at 10:30

p.m. We leave the pub where we sat drinking half pints of lager and lime, and go to the off-license on the corner to pick up something to take to the town square. The store is crowded with men talking and joking loudly, jostling each other for space. I stand at the shelves covered in bottles full of differently colored liquids, all with fancy labels. I'm not looking at the labels—I'm looking at the prices pasted underneath the bottles, while I finger my purse anxiously. Dare I splash out on some hard liquor? I hate the taste of alcohol, but I want to be drunk tonight. How else will I stand dozens of men slobbering all over me? I glance at the clock on the wall. It's only 10:45. One and a quarter hours to wait. That's a long time to be hanging around. Nothing exciting will happen before midnight. Decisively I pick up a bottle of vodka. It's the most innocuous tasting of all the spirits.

Outside we dawdle. A friend of Janet's comes up and chats for a while. I'm bored. Watching the boys, I pick out the attractive ones, aware all the time of the cold biting at my thighs below my miniskirt. I huddle into the coat that covers only the upper half of my body, thrusting my hands deep into my pockets. The bottle sits there warmly, a promise of more warmth to come. When Janet's acquaintance departs, I pull out the bottle, unscrew the cap and take a long swig before I pass it on to my friend. For a while we're conservative with it, but as I get colder I start to chug it seriously. I take a look at what's left: about half, and it's 11:30. I put the bottle to my lips and drink it all down in ten or twelve burning mouthfuls. I stop with a gasp and smack my lips, taking in breaths of air to cool my burning throat. I leave the empty bottle sitting on a wall. Janet looks at me slightly disapprovingly.

"You're going to be awfi drunk," she says. I laugh with bravado. Somewhere inside me I am aware of an aching. I'm not able to put a name to it: I don't know that I am suffering from unrequited love for my very heterosexual best friend. I don't know how to recognize love.

We wander down to the square, which is rapidly filling with people, most of them already very drunk and all of them in the process of consuming some kind of booze. We hang out on the edge of a group of boys who soon share their whiskey with us. All this alcohol is going to my head. I'm laughing a lot and talking very loudly. The crowd begins to stir; it's five minutes to midnight. The hands of the huge clock are only a blur to me now and I have to lean on a lamppost. The tension mounts; only two minutes to go. Janet gets hold of me, leading me away from the group of men we've been standing near. She doesn't like them. I'm beyond any discrimination. I feel fine and I'm having a good time. I don't much care who we are standing near. The chimes of midnight begin, and the square explodes into an uproar. A dozen arms grab hold of me, and I'm swept up in the melee, laughing all the while that I'm being kissed and hugged. Janet manages to stay nearby. Some time passes and I'm not aware of much, but finally the crowd is beginning to thin and I gather that I have been chosen by one of the many boys who've been sampling my kisses. Janet's been chosen by another. We seem to be going somewhere. I can't focus on anything and can barely stand. I realize that I've repeatedly been asking Janet in a very loud voice if the boy I'm with is good-looking. She's been trying to shut me up.

He calls a taxi, since I obviously can't walk very far. By the time we are delivered to his house, I'm feeling very sick. He has a room separate from his parents' place (must be middle class—none of the working class lads I know would have such a luxury). Since I'm feeling really ill, I immediately lie down on the bed. He gets on the bed beside me, taking my clothes off. I desperately want to be left alone to sleep, but my arms and legs feel like very heavy water, so I have no ability to resist. He gets on top of me, pushing my legs apart. We're both naked now under the sheets. His dick is hard and it's pushing at my vagina. Other boys have tried this before. Somehow I've always managed to preserve my virginity, perhaps simply by bracing against their attempts to force me open. Now I'm in no state to keep out his rigid and determined penis. I'm not thinking about what he's doing except insofar as his urgent movements contribute to the churning of my stomach. I'm trying hard not to throw up. He's oblivious to my discomfort. He brought me here because he wanted to fuck and now he's going to fuck.

Brought back to the reality of the moment by a sharp pain between my thighs, I make a futile attempt to push him away. It's hopeless, I'm too weak, and he's well on his way to coming, as his penis thrusts in and out of me as fast as he can wield it. Nausea overwhelms me again, and the pain passes. His breathing quickens, he heaves against me harder than before, then pushes in one last long time with a moaning sigh. I'm intensely relieved when he rolls off me. I lie on my side groaning quietly.

We sleep for a blessed interval, not touching. I wake with him shaking me, saying I have to get dressed and leave before his parents wake. I climb into my clothes with considerable difficulty. I still feel awful. Realizing I can't contain myself any more, I rush to the door to throw up beside of the concrete path. Such a relief to get rid of the reeking alcoholic puke, even as the retching racks my body. Afterwards I stand up straight and look around me, bleary eyed. It's dawn. The boy is glowering at me from the doorway. "Did y' have to throw up right there? Ma parents'll see it!"

"Well, that's too bad!"

"Anyway you have to go now, my mum'll be up soon."

"Well, where am I going? Where the hell are we? You have to tell me which way to go, at least! Aren't you going to walk me home?"

He growls something non-committal, making it clear he doesn't want to walk me home. I'm pissed off. "You can't just bring me here and then throw me out when you want to get rid of me! You brought me here, now take me home!"

He glares at me. "Well, you weren't much good in bed! I thought from the way you were acting back there at the square that you were going to be some fun. Now there's blood on the sheets and you've thrown up on my doorstep!"

"Blood on the sheets?" I'm surprised. I definitely shouldn't be bleeding, and I feel guilty for messing up his sheets. Then indignation takes over, who the hell does he think he is? I never promised him I'd even go to bed with him, much less give him a good time! "Well, hard luck, you didn't get what you want, and I feel lousy. You think I enjoy throwing up? You think I planned it? The least you can do is pay for a taxi!"

He relents finally, agreeing to walk me part way home. By the time we've walked a couple of miles, and the fresh air and beauty of the dawn has improved my health and my mood, we're getting on OK, as far as I ever get on with the boys I'm sexual with. About a half mile from Janet's house he leaves me, and I walk on alone. I meet Janet saying good-bye to her pick-up at the corner just before her house. We sneak quietly in the back door of her house so as not to wake her parents. She asks me if I'm going to be seeing that boy again. I say no, I didn't even think he was good looking, and he was pretty rude besides. She liked hers, and she's going to see him again tomorrow. Neither of us talk about the details of what we did with our boys, although I do describe throwing up on his doorstep.

Later, I put two and two together and realize this was the occasion when my hymen broke. It doesn't alter my experience of sexual activity. There's not that much difference between penetration and almost-penetration. I'm not into it anyway.

Chapter Eight

J anet's family is much more loving than mine. My parents are distant and disapproving, and have no idea how to relate to teenage girls (or perhaps no desire to relate to them). Janet's mother is supportive and sweet, and hugs me more in one weekend than my mother has hugged me in years. She makes sandwiches specially for us and genuinely seems concerned that we should enjoy ourselves when we go out. Her father, too, is friendly and warm. I love going to visit them.

But it turns out her family is a little too loving—if that's what it can be called. Janet has an older brother, John. He's much more polite to her than my big brother is to me. I say to her, "John is really sweet with you."

"Yes, well, sometimes," she replies shortly, and there's something in her tone that makes me look at her sharply.

"What do you mean? What's the matter?"

She looks away and I can see she's embarrassed. I wait. After a moment she says, "He comes into my room at night."

"Oh!" I'm shocked. She must mean that he has sex with her. Brothers aren't supposed to have sex with their sisters. "Don't your parents hear him?" Her room is right next to her parents.

"He's very quiet. He goes into Alice's room too." Alice is her older sister.

I furrow my brow. This is very confusing.

Later, when I am a little older and have become an accomplished flirt, John creeps into my room to share my bed. I don't object. It's quite exciting. He's engaged to be married, so there will be no pretense of his owning me in public.

As he lies on top of me, humping to and fro, he pants, "I love you!" and then stops for a moment to explain apologetically, "Well, actually I love Marie, you know." I don't find this surprising: I know by now that the use of the phrase *I love you* is never to be taken seriously. Marie is his fiancée. He's supposed to love her more than me.

I do find it rather strange when he jumps up just as he's about to come, and jerks off out of the window. He explains that this is so that his mother won't see stains on the sheets. I wonder, has she remarked on stains before?

John takes after his father. One Christmas I'm at a small party at their house. I'm wearing my short, red, corduroy dress with a zip up the front. Men can't stand that zip: it makes them want to take the dress off right away. After a number of drinks, I'm having a great time, with Janet's father, brother and her sister's fiance all vying for my attention. I'm a little sobered when I realize that Janet, her sister and her mother are all sitting on the other side of the room glaring at me and the men. I can tell they're not pleased. But surely I'm just doing what women are meant to do?

A friend at school tells me that Janet's father came on to her. She is genuinely shocked. She talks about how disgusting it is for a man of his age to be chasing his daughter's friends. I say nothing. I think she is stunningly naïve. It may be disgusting—and it happens all the time.

When I'm eighteen, I fall in love with one of my boyfriends. That is, I fall into a state of wanting to be with him all the time, and with all of me. It happens very suddenly, so I have no time to adjust to this extraordinary turn of events. I have never wanted to be fully present with any of my boyfriends before. In fact, I have rarely wanted to be present with my self. I have certainly never wanted to *give* myself to someone before.

However, I don't know who I am, or, in fact, where *I* am. The real me is buried under layers of not-me, safe from the ravages of various adults. The real me is not present. How then can I give myself to anyone? The false me is not a gift worth giving. It doesn't even exist.

We are in my bed. My parents are away, and I have taken the liberty of bringing John home. My grandfather is somewhere around, but he never comes to this wing of the wandering old house with its long passageways and staircases, so I feel somewhat secure. Of course there's always the general fear of being found out, but I'm used to that.

We are naked, the sheets pulled up to our chests. I'm lying on my side staring at John, trying to see the person that I knew before this extraordinary transformation. Now I can't make him into anyone except some kind of Greek god. He's touching my nipple, and vital sensations of electricity are demanding that I pay attention to strange, disturbing feelings that I've always previously managed to avoid. He sits up, pushing the sheets away, and pulls me up to sit in front of him. He takes my hand and puts it on his penis, hard and throbbing between his hairy legs. I'm amazed, not at the sight of his erection (I'm fairly used to those), but at the surge of—of what? What is this thing pulsing through my body?—something wonderful, yet terrifying.

I look at my hand on his dick, feel the slight silkiness of it against my palm. Everything around me is very still. I am coated with the silence inside my head. He says, "Don't just hold it, move your hand up and down."

I look at his face, wanting very much to please him. But I cannot move. I am paralyzed with the strangeness of what I will one day recognize as sexual desire. I am caught in a whirling empty space inside my head. I am trapped in the deathly stillness that is the eye of a storm I dare not bring to consciousness.

Even the astounding intensity of my turn-on when I am around John is not enough to break me out of my paralysis. Feeling sexual is not part of my reality. I am completely at odds with myself. I cannot turn away from John, as I have always done with other boys, yet I cannot move towards him either.

I fall into a strange kind of dreamlike state. Since John isn't a particularly patient person, he gives up after a few days. It is a relief not to have to deal with the complexity of the situation any more, although my deep loneliness is now stirred up. For a few days my chest aches with an oddly unfamiliar (and yet very familiar) need. Another boyfriend is easy to come by, and I soon fall back into my old patterns.

But something changes. I feel stirrings of a sexual desire that is quite different from making conquests.

In the meantime, I start going steady with another boy. It's my first serious relationship...at least, *he* takes it seriously. I like the sense of being loved and taken care of, and he is certainly one of the sweetest men I know. Sometimes I even enjoy sex with him. And he keeps me safe from all the other potential predators. But no matter how hard I try, I cannot imagine being his wife. I'm only eighteen—the world is finally opening up to me. I'm just starting to break away from my parents, and there is so much to see and experience. To be willingly tied down again? That's ridiculous.

I'm appalled and a little frightened, when it dawns on me that marriage really is the main focus of life for all my girlfriends—including Janet. She's not just playing a game, like I am. She is really looking for a husband! Of course that's what we all have been told we will be doing, but up till now I had thought it was a myth, rather like my mother telling me sex was something you did with a man you loved.

My father becomes more and more infuriated that I choose to hang out with people who don't meet his standards of class. I just don't seem to get along with the kind of people he wants me to be friends with. I don't feel at ease when I am trying to be posh. I don't do well with the kind of pretence that upper class people seem to require. In contrast, the people I meet through Janet are not trying to live up to some unspoken standard. They have no clue about social circles where it's vitally important what school you went to or how your father earns his money. They are down to earth and straightfor-ward. They all have Scottish accents, and they're proud of being Scottish. The only time I feel awkward with them is when they ques-tion me about why I don't speak with a Scottish accent.

When my current boyfriend phones me, my father answers, hearing him ask, "Can Ah talk tae Chris?"

I am doing homework in my room. My father stands at the bottom of the stairs with the phone in his hand, calling tersely up to me, "Christine, there's some son of a plumber on the phone for you!"

I leap down the stairs to snatch the phone out of his hand. Has my boyfriend heard what was said? Does he even comprehend that I come from a world where calling someone's father a plumber is an insult? How can I protect my friends from my father's acid tongue?

I get a job in a restaurant, washing dishes, over Christmas. My father curses me upside down and sideways, telling me I am good for nothing, and threatening to disown me. I manage to stand firm against his onslaught.

Chapter Nine

I earn enough money for a short trip to Germany with a friend from school. We stay with a family that she already knows, and hang out with a gang of hippie teenagers who smoke hashish and take LSD, colloquially known as acid. Since I've found life so shallow, and I'm desperate for anything that might give it more depth, I'm very interested in trying these drugs. My girlfriend is not, which turns out to be a very good thing since I get stoned out of my head, so that I am really incapable of taking care of myself. When we leave, one of the long-haired boys we've been hanging out with gives me a tab of acid, a small white pill wrapped in a piece of tinfoil. "This is Californian Sunshine," he tells me. "It's a really good acid trip, but make sure you take the whole tab, don't split it." He looks at me sternly to make sure I've got the message, repeating, "Take the whole thing, don't split it."

On our way back home, we begin our journey in a very slow German train. As I sit in the carriage staring at the boring scenery—buildings and roads dirty white from recent half-melted snow—I think to myself, maybe I should just take that tab of acid right now. I turn to my friend. "Is it OK with you if I get stoned?" She shrugs, knowing even less than I do.

So I swallow the pill. In a little while, I find myself completely unable to stop laughing. An uncontrollable grin wants to split my face in half. Some part of myself that thinks it ought to be in control is painfully aware that it's not, creating a background of anxiety. Things begin to appear strangely un-solid. Looking at the faces of the people in the train carriage, I realize they are all melting. They are not attractive, although I can't stop smiling at them.

When we get off the train, we have to make our way to the ferry terminal. I ask my friend to hold my hand, to stop me floating away. Crossing the road seems impossible since the cars that appear to be far in the distance on one glance are very close at hand on the next glance. Space, time, sound, edges and color are all alternately elongated and then, without warning, shortened. Somehow we manage to board the boat, which is an overnight ferry. Since negotiating the physical world is tricky, my friend leaves me sitting in a booth on a lower deck. I occupy myself by alternately admiring the huge chunks of ice that heave to and fro laboriously in the harbor water, like the body of some vast monster, and watching the people walk down the aisle towards me. I stare fixedly at them with my inane grin. The colors and shapes of their faces and bodies are fascinating. To my alarm, a man sits in the adjacent seat, trying to engage me in conversation. It is a useless project, because the sounds he's making are too bizarre to comprehend. In any case, I can't make my own mouth work to produce any response. He vibes like a predator, which makes me want him to leave, and soon he obliges me, presumably fed up with my strange behavior.

Then a particularly extraordinary apparition walks down the aisle. It is a Christmas tree: the top a huge flaming red halo, in the center two bright blue crystals, and all suffused with green from below. I stare, fascinated, as it approaches. It stops beside me, and I realize it is a young man with bushy orange hair, blue eyes and a green scarf. He addresses me, and to my pleasure I understand his words: "Hallo! May I sit down?"

I nod, not trusting my tongue. I still can't take my eyes off him. I'm trying hard not to giggle with delight. He sits down, arranges his possessions, and then turns towards me, asking me a question. This time the sounds are all stretched out again, so that I can't understand him, but since I like his vibe, I want him to stay, so I try to say something coherent. I manage to articulate a couple of words, until my lips and tongue get tangled up, and I lapse into silence, hoping I am not drooling.

He speaks again, looking directly at me with a very sweet smile. "Are you tripping?"

I'm immensely reassured by these words, and I feel the grin getting even bigger, although the muscles in my face are already aching. I nod. Looking satisfied, he says something I can't make sense of, but now I know that he understands what I am going through. He will not expect a coherent reply.

Time passes, he hangs out, my girlfriend comes back bringing food, which I attempt to eat—another profound experience, which amuses the Christmas tree. I'm concerned that I may never again be able to function, and I want to ask him about this, figuring that he can be trusted to know. I finally manage to articulate the words, "Will I be normal again?"

He smiles, saying, "Oh yes, trips don't usually last longer than twelve hours."

I'm relieved.

And he's right. By the time the boat docks, I am feeling fairly normal again, though I never will be quite the same. The acid trip has changed me. Now I understand that the standard human perception of reality is just one of many, and a limited one at that. I take acid again on a few future occasions, and I'm always amazed at how it facilitates an awareness of the world as an indescribable place of fluidity and wholeness. But I never feel easy about being so out of control of my body.

My parents send me to Austria to stay with some relatives, hoping my undesirable tendencies will be miraculously transformed. The relatives in Vienna are not interested in me, and there's no one to tell me what I can and cannot do. I get a job in a hotel to earn enough money to act as a jumping board. Then I'm off, hitchhiking the length and breadth of Europe on my own, experiencing a freedom that is exhilarating beyond anything I have ever known. Of course it is terrifying, too. I keep my terror well wrapped up.

Without the constant influence of people who know me, I begin to get in touch with who I am: with the core of me, that I have so carefully hidden under layers of apparent acquiescence. Inevitably, that means I begin to get in touch with my anger.

I often sleep under bridges, in parks, on beaches, or in woods by the highway, but I don't like to sleep outside when I am in a city. Too many other lost souls are wandering around. One evening, I am walking through the streets of a German town at dusk, making my way to the youth hostel. I eat up the pavement with my usual fast stride. The street is empty but for three figures approaching— teenage boys talking in animated German. They look me up and down as they pass, and I look straight ahead, aware of the impor- tance of not catching an eye. I don't look behind after I have passed them, but I can tell they have noticed me and they stop, then turn and run to catch up with me. Two on one side and one on the other, they begin to harass me, firing questions in rapid German, laughing and grabbing at my arm. One of them gets in front of me so that I have to sidestep around him. I walk on impassively, staring straight ahead. Inside my rage is beginning to boil. I am so very very tired of being seen as prey. The boy gets in front of me again and I look directly at him for the first time. Skinny, blonde, a little taller than me, but probably no heavier. My punch is a simple reflex, just the desire to strike that has finally escaped control. I hit him square on the nose, catching the expression of utter astonishment in his eyes as he claps his hands over his face and crumples to the ground.

I walk on past him, lengthening my stride just a little. I'm wor- ried—three against one. They will certainly be able to exact revenge if they choose. I risk one quick glance behind. They are conferring in a group. Then I hear one set of footsteps approaching at a run and I turn just before the steps reach me, ready to protect myself. But the boy isn't preparing to attack. He walks along beside me, talking in German too fast for me to follow, and gesturing with his hands, but now keep- ing a respectful distance between us. As I note the look of chagrin on his face, it dawns on me that he is apologizing. They hadn't intended any harm, he says, they only meant to help. I continue to stride along, watching him out of the corner of my eye. The straps of my rucksack are digging painfully into my shoulders. The boy skips along beside me, almost begging for a response. Suddenly I burst out laughing. "OK, OK," I say, "it's OK, just leave me alone, OK?"

Relief floods his face, and he stops, leaving me to go on alone. I round a corner and they are gone. I slow a little, catching my breath and shaking my head in wonder. Is that all it takes to stand up for myself? Would other men be as intimidated at demonstrations of outrage?

Sadly, I have to learn this lesson again and again, before I finally believe that it is OK to say no.

I become a barefoot hippie, care-free and wild. I hitchhike north and south, down to Morocco, and up to Stockholm. I sleep with men when it's convenient and drop them with little thought when they become inconvenient. I make many friends and leave them all behind. I watch the world go by from the cars that pick me up. I make my own decisions from day to day about where to go. When I want to be safe, I sleep in youth hostels.

And so, one morning, I find myself in the large sterile waiting room of a youth hostel in Copenhagen with four other women. They are travelling in two separate units, and have evidently never met before. One couple is American; the taller is friendly, but the smaller is expressionless and stoney, giving the impression she doesn't like people much. Nevertheless, she is very popular because she can apparently read palms. As I watch her read one of the British women, I'm impressed with their *oohs* and *aahs*, although I am only an incidental onlooker who doesn't know any of them. She sits holding her client's hand, poring over the unseen messages that it offers her, making laconic remarks about the woman's boyfriend and the town where she lives. The other half of the couple, standing by, says in a tone of amazement, "How did you know that?"

The reader looks up a little impatiently, saying, "I can see it." She puts the woman's hand down. "That's about all. I hope it was useful."

"It certainly was!" says the British woman.

I make a quick decision. This is too interesting to pass up. From the other end of the table, I say, "I'd like you to read my palm, too."

The small woman looks at me as though she is bored, and says, "I need you to pay me first." Sitting down beside her, I give her the money she asks, and she takes my palm in her hands, while the other three women watch, the British couple obviously greatly intrigued.

There is a long silence while she sits with my hand in hers, her head down. As the silence lengthens and thickens, we four spectators become uneasy. The atmosphere in the room stretches tight with tension. Still she says nothing. I begin to question her, asking, "What's going on? What do you see?" At first she doesn't answer. I notice the tears dripping from her face onto the table at about the same time as I find hot tears filling my own eyes. The feeling of grief in the room is frighteningly strong, like a weight pressing down. No one seems to be able to separate from it: the British women are sobbing in each other's arms, and the other American is wiping her face with her handkerchief, pushing aside her glasses. With my free hand, I mop the tears on my cheeks. A dozen thoughts run through my mind: is she going to tell me I am about to die? That I am terminally ill? Why isn't she talking to me? I speak urgently, almost angrily. "Please, tell me what's going on!"

She remains silent until I almost scream at her through my tears. "Please, tell me what you see!"

Finally she finds her voice, low and hesitating. "You must go home to your parents at once. You're making them very unhappy, especially your mother. She needs you to go home. Both your parents are suffering, and it's your fault."

I take a deep breath and release it. This is no news to me, although I am not pleased to find out that others see it, and I certainly don't like this woman telling it to me. I really don't want to think about it. My father has been saying for years that I am making my mother unhappy, and I have long ago ceased to believe him, if only from a sense of self-preservation, knowing that I cannot sacrifice myself to someone else's demands.

The woman glances up at me, her expression tense and grim. Her friend is offering her a handkerchief and she puts my hand on the table while she wipes her eyes. She takes up my hand again, saying once more in a firmer voice, "You really must go home at once. Your mother is very unhappy and it is your fault. She will feel much better when you go home."

I sigh. I have paid for this? "Is that all you see? You don't see anything else?" I want to know how many kids I will have, and who I am going to marry, and what I will do for a career. I don't want to know that my parents' needs are following me around the world.

Wiping my palm with her thumb, she says, "I see that you will have two children. You'll put them to sleep on the sofa, you won't bother with cribs and things like that. But you'll be a good mother, you'll treat them well." She puts my hand down, turning to her friend. I sigh again, glancing at my watch. I'll have to go if I want to catch the next ferry to Sweden.

Not quite as immune to her words as I would wish, I decide to return to Scotland a few weeks later. I'm out of money anyway.

Bob is wild-looking, his long hair in dreads, a bright Indian lungi draped around his long lean body. Such obvious rejection of convention fascinates me immediately, from the first moment I see him sitting on the steps of the American Express Office in Amsterdam. He turns out to be as interesting as he looks and also, to my surprise, interested in me. He is smart and knowledgeable, yet above all he is kind, a rare quality. He shows interest in getting to know me as a real person. Unlike other men, he asks me questions about how I feel and what I think. He seduces me in a very different way, with his heart and his mind instead of his dick. It is a much more effective way of reaching me. The respect and caring I feel from him are in stark contrast to the aggressive, inconsiderate sexual demands that I have come to expect in my dealings with men.

We set off for England in the evening. John drives, while Bob and I lie in the back of the van talking, cuddling, snoozing, and admiring the beauty of the sunset. We arrive at Calais at 10.30 p.m., in time for the last ferry to Dover. I am excited to be going home after traveling on the continent for six months, and excited to be with Bob. We make the usual preparations for going through customs, cleaning out the van and removing all traces of anything illegal.

The Channel is calm, and it's an easy crossing. We drive off the ferry in Dover quite unprepared for our reception. John, sitting up front, has short hair and we might have gone through immigration without any hassle if they hadn't looked in the back and seen Bob, so clearly an undesirable. Since it's late at night, the border officials have plenty of time to harass us.

They order us all out of the van. They are cold, distant and unsmiling. Two of them search our bags while the other two examine our passports minutely, questioning the Americans thoroughly about how much money they have, how long they are planning to stay, where they are going and why. They take their passports away. We wait and wait. Finally one of them returns, saying to Bob, "This way, please."

I start to follow, but the immigration officer stops me. "You can wait here." The door is closed and Bob is gone.

Again we wait and wait, trying in vain to find something to amuse ourselves in the big sterile room with rows of sterile seats, a sterile counter at one end, sterile white paint on the walls. At three in the morning, no one is around. I am impatient and nervous, desperate for distraction. Eventually one of the uniformed men returns with John's passport. "You may go," he says formally to the two of us, "your friend is being detained."

I am outraged. "Wha'd'you mean, he's being detained?" I shriek, beside myself with righteous indignation. "He hasn't done anything wrong! What are you going to do with him? You can't just hold him without any reason!"

They can. They won't answer any of our questions and are completely unswayed when I insist that my parents will vouch for Bob. But when we make it clear that we won't leave without seeing him, they agree that we can camp in the parking lot overnight and see him in the morning.

I don't sleep much. My sense of helplessness enrages me. What right do these men in uniforms have, to take someone away so absolutely, without any explanation or excuse? I am up at dawn, and in the office, demanding to see him. Again I wait and wait. Again they simply ignore my questions. Customs officers are trained to remain remote and impassive in the face of the most impassioned plea, and the British tend to be naturals at that anyway. I may as well have been one inch tall for all the attention they pay me.

Eventually I am shown into a small room. Bars separate me from Bob, who looks haggard and worried. He tells me they are sending him back to Holland on the next boat. He has no idea why. He assures me they won't be able to keep him out of the country. He will come in at some other port of entry and meet me in Scotland. His obvious determination makes me feel better. He doesn't seem to think it's hopeless. So we say good-bye, sure we'll meet again soon.

We never do. He is refused entry at Newcastle two days later and then again at Edinburgh airport. Finally the Dutch authorities send him back to Brazil, the country where his family lives, and they put him in prison for using LSD. I hear from him once, a sad letter, telling me that in order to get his father's help in dealing with the charges against him, he has to agree to marry a suitable woman, and he's forbidden to contact me again.

I am beginning to understand that becoming an adult is not going to mean the freedom I have hoped for.

Chapter Ten

My parents are not the only people appalled at the hippie identity I adopt after my travels. Now I am alienated from my friends as well. They are not flouting convention the way I am. They are still becoming ladies.

Fortunately, I'm off to university in a new city where no one knows me. It's easy to assume a new persona, and there are lots of new and exciting people to meet. Attaching myself to a gang of long-haired hippies, I go around wearing the patched jeans and jackets that make me a far cry from the seductive young woman in miniskirts that has been my modus operandi in the past.

It so happens that within the first week of my arrival at university, a man I know from my college days in Edinburgh is passing through. I've always found him interesting and I don't want to pass up the opportunity to be with him. This presents a dilemma—he may have great difficulty relating to me in my hippie clothes. I put on my short red dress, the infamous one with the zipper down the front. He takes me out, and later we have sex. It's OK, he's a nice guy. But in the morning, when I wear my torn stained jeans, I feel right, I feel at home. The dress is just that—dressing up. It was a prop for a role I played before I knew there were other options.

Since I'm studying biology at university, I take a course in ecology. I learn that if progress continues at its present rate, we will soon destroy the world. We are poisoning it with our excretions, just like bacteria who find an environment in which they thrive, and reproduce as fast as possible until their own waste products build up, poisoning them so that they begin to die off.

It is only 1972, and the ordinary person on the street has never heard the phrase *environmental concerns*.

I say to my professor, "What you are teaching us is that we are doing irreversible ecological damage to the planet. Isn't that so?"

He shrugs, purses his lips and looks over my shoulder. "Perhaps. I expect we will find ways of dealing with the problems."

"We should be addressing these concerns now. It's unforgivable to continue to produce these amounts of pollution, knowing what damage they are doing."

"Well, perhaps. But you can't stop progress."

"You can refuse to be a part of it."

He laughs cynically. "Sure, if you want to live in a cave for the rest of your life!"

I seriously consider the prospect of living in a cave, or at least being independent of the system. After weeks of righteous and frustrated outrage, I decide to form a group that will take action on environmental issues. I apply to the student body for a grant. This means I have to explain to them why I think it is worth being concerned about the environment.

As I wait in a room with two or three dozen others who are asking for grants, my anxiety level soars. By the time it is my turn to stand up in front of the six haughty, impatient and bored men who comprise the student council, I'm close to passing out. I stutter a few incoherent words. It is not enough. They refuse us a grant.

I need to feel like I am doing *something*. Fortunately, most of my friends are both supportive and brave. We get some labels made up that say *this product is over-packaged*, and paste them all over the relevant products in a local supermarket. The manager is angry, to say the least, but we manage to avoid getting arrested.

Soon after this, I drop out of university. I cannot stomach being part of a system that is destroying the planet, and I will never be satisfied with academic work that removes me from the natural world. Inevitably, I become involved in radical politics, which at least offers me a sympathetic space in which to express my feelings.

My radical politics involve, amongst other things, demonstrating against the British government's policies in Northern Ireland. When the government decides to increase its military presence in Belfast, we—my radical friends and I—are outraged. Pro-Irish, anti-English demonstrations occur in various cities around England. After one of them, a group of us decide to occupy an army recruiting office. Eleven of us lie down in the doorway of the office, effectively blocking the entrance. Most of the staff in the office are tolerantly amused. Only one man expresses any anger. He makes a point of walking on our prone bodies. His obvious pleasure at stomping on us is alarming, though he does remarkably little damage.

The cops soon turn up, which means the worst is over. I have seen the police beat people with batons, but only during demonstrations where the energy is running very high. Although I'm aware that my faith is not shared by my friends, I think the police are unlikely to harm us here—we are all thoroughly trained in nonviolent resistance and in spite of the apparent drama, we are stationary bodies posing no real threat. They have no reason to get riled up. They are not particularly rough as they drag us away, throwing us into the van that takes us to jail, where we sit in cells in threes and fours, singing protest songs loudly. Dourly, they search us, take all the details they need to book us on charges of disturbing the peace, and let us out on bail. They barely acknowledge that we are human, but there are eleven of us, and in our noisy defiance, we aren't affected by their unspoken scorn.

We all turn up in court the next morning, defended by a radical lawyer who is working without pay. The courtroom is crowded with our supporters. The case seems to hinge upon the issue of whether the police gave us adequate warning that we were going to be arrested. Since we had all decided before we took the action that we were willing to be arrested, it seems to be a moot point, but obviously in this strange justice system, we are supposed to pretend it's relevant. We stand up in the witness box one by one, to be cross-examined. It's very reminiscent of being cross-examined by my father when I was a child, except that there are some rules preventing the lawyer from being too underhand. Since I'm practiced at this kind of verbal play, I quite enjoy it. When it is my turn to put my hand in the air (not on the Bible—none of us are willing to go there), repeating the words, "I swear to tell the truth, the whole truth, and nothing but the truth," I wonder for a moment: *am I really going to tell the truth?* My concern passes quickly—what a ridiculous idea, that truth even exists within such an utterly loaded situation. I know what I think is right, and that's why I'm here.

In the end, we are acquitted. Since the whole thing is a farcical game anyway, it's a wise move on the part of our opponents (otherwise known as the establishment) to let us go free. It would only cost them money to take it any further in court, and the publicity would look bad for them. Nevertheless we declare it a triumph.

The unspoken aspects of it leave me uneasy. Although my comrades-in-resistance and I are temporarily treated as heroes by other activists, which is fun, I don't feel I achieved anything worthwhile for the amount of energy that was expended. I've had an interesting experience, and that's about it.

I occasionally sleep with John. He's a nice guy, always friendly and sweet, quite undemanding for a man. Although I don't really want him as a regular boyfriend—he's too much of a pushover—it's nice to have company when my sense of loneliness overwhelms me. He's also quite fast and efficient at fucking, doesn't linger over it too long, doesn't slobber over my face for hours.

One night when we get into bed, I do the preliminary cuddling up to him, and a little bit of kissing, then I feel his growing erection brush against my thigh, his body becoming assertive and pushy. The usual surge of revulsion, more active than ever, begins to choke me. I turn abruptly away from him, curling up on my side, facing the wall. My body will not carry through with the usual pretense.

Like many men, John isn't so sweet when it comes to sex. He raises up on one elbow, saying sharply, "Hey, what's your problem? What did you start something for if you're not going to go through with it?" It's the first time in the six months I have known him that I've heard him sound angry. I roll over and let him get on with it.

I don't know why I have so much conflict around sex. I think there's something wrong with me.

One of my friends very much wants to go to bed with me. I don't want to go to bed with him. He grabs me one evening when we are walking together on campus, trying to kiss me. When I push him away, he won't let go, trying to hold me still. A struggle ensues, until I succeed in freeing myself. Although I'm angry, I only mention it in passing to a couple of friends. None of us think it's a big deal.

I have no boyfriends for about a year, which is a great blow to my self esteem. I have not yet acknowledged the very unacceptable fact that I don't much like being physical with the male species, and a great deal of my self image is still tied up with being attractive to them. It makes me feel powerful to be able to seduce anyone I choose, and I am still searching for sources of power. I've rarely had trouble getting a boy into bed before, even though I am often bored and disgusted when we get there.

Finally, I meet Dan. We begin to spend more and more time together. I'm quite interested in him, and after a few weeks I'm sure it's reciprocal.

We've just spent the evening tripping on acid and now we're sitting on my bed smoking joint after joint, and laughing hilariously at nothing at all. Sex is in the air, and tonight will be the night we sleep together. I'm really wishing he would get on with it. At last he leans forward to kiss me. It's a sloppy and skill-less kiss but I put up with it. I need a boyfriend, after all.

Without too many words, pretending that we don't feel embarrassed and scared, we eventually get naked in bed. I'm expecting at last that we will have sex, but after he's been slobbering inexpertly all over my face for a while, I reach down between his legs, and discover he's completely soft, still just a useless worm. Nothing I can do (though it's true I haven't had a whole lot of experience at dealing with this eventuality) makes any difference.

After the second night we sleep together, when he still isn't showing any signs of an erection, I ask him if he's a virgin, and he reluctantly admits that is the case. I make the extremely radical suggestion that there are other things we can do, something in between intercourse and kissing. His only response is to turn away as if he's going to sleep. On the third night, he manages to get an erection, and we actually have intercourse, which is quite a relief after the interminable slobbering, although he comes very quickly, and it's all quite unsatisfying. The truth is, Dan will always be a lousy lover. Just as I had come to hope for something a little better.

I go with Dan to India. A far-away land where it's always warm and the people laugh a lot; where it's strangely impossible to tell truth from fantasy, fact from illusion. A mysterious place, like something out of a dream. A culture so different from mine that it cannot be described, only experienced. India. Dirt, dust, heat, flies crawling everywhere: over food, over people's eyes, noses, mouths, and open, running sores. Mice running over food stacked on a slab of stone that serves as a shop counter, while the store owner sits crosslegged behind the slab, happily uncaring. Cattle lumbering around narrow streets that have never heard of lighting or street signs. Houses built of mud, like part of the landscape. India. Never-ending noise and hustle. A million pairs of brown eyes incessantly staring at the white woman. A million men, wide smiles splitting their faces, blinded by two things: money and sex. India. Bright cloth, every shade of yellow, orange, red, purple, blue and green, worn on skinny bodies or laid out by the side of the river to dry. Tiny winding bumpy roads, and trucks that sport strings of prayer flags, and every possible garish decoration imaginable, roaring along with little apparent concern for life and death. India, where women rush out like dung beetles to pick up steaming fresh cow manure with their bare hands. It is their only source of fuel. India, the country of holy men and ashrams, where magic and miracles and yogis and snake charmers are all real. The country of starving people, thin as rakes, walking along the road with a piece of material flung over their heads, meager protection from the unforgiving sun that beats down on their naked boney shoulders. A gaunt hand, all knuckle, cupped in supplication, as its owner stares up, eyes pleading, thin lips forming the word "rupees," that word that is like a continuous hum in the background, a never-ending mantra. India, where you can buy special *lassi* in the restaurants—yogurt laced with marijuana. Where, if you choose the right spot, you can live naked for months on stretches of clean, unspoilt beach, with thick green buzzing jungle just behind. Or make your home in a temple carved out of solid rock, abandoned because the waves of the ocean have begun to wear it away. Or go up into the Himalayas, amongst the pine trees and the snow, where you can rent a room for next to nothing and experience a peace that you won't find anywhere else in India; where you can listen to the red-robed Buddhist monks playing their eerie horns and chanting in the dawn. India, where westerners who are not rich enough to create a haven of western-ness to keep themselves sane, are required to reach into the core of their being to hold onto who they are. If they lose that vital sense of self (and the India-ness of India erodes it without mercy), then they dissolve into madness.

Dan dissolves. He becomes a weeping anguished ghost overflowing with volatile emotions, very unpleasant to be around. When I try to leave him, he flings himself on the ground in a fit of hysteria, screaming incoherent abuse. I know he will probably die if I go. A misguided sense of responsibility makes me stay with him, though a great deal of my energy is taken up with trying to get away from him at the same time.

My desire to leave him is tempered by the fact that he provides a little relief from the Indian men, whose insolently roving hands enrage me over and over again.

I think he will never return to the Dan I have known, and wonder how I will explain what happened. To my surprise he pulls himself together as soon as we reach English soil, regaling everyone with stories, almost completely fabricated, to illustrate what a wonderful time he has had during our months away.

Our relationship deteriorated into hatred early on in our journey, and we haven't been physical in seven months. When we arrive in England, he forces himself on me. It is an act of power-over, subjugation, and we both know it. I could hold him off—my body is honed into a lean mass of muscle from carrying all our luggage when he was barely strong enough to walk—but I have not yet fully convinced myself that I have the right to make a fuss. Besides, we are staying in my sister's London flat. It would be embarrassing to cause a commotion that might wake her up. He is supposed to be my boyfriend after all.

Our travels shake up all my concepts of reality except one, and that one is reinforced: most men regard me as a sexual object, and nothing else. My body is considered their legitimate prey. During my teens, with a dull ache of resignation, I had accepted the oppression of being born female. Now, the disrespect I experience from friends and strangers alike whets that resignation into active rage. The thin skin of social pressure that contains my rage is stretched to its limit.

Chapter Eleven

Jilli is different from other women I have met: she seems more alive, more vibrant, more willing to speak of what is going on. Perhaps it's partly because she is Australian and hasn't been subject to that subtle but powerful pressure that affects so many British women, keeping them subdued in a way that is very pervasive, though not obvious to casual visitors.

Jilli has also recently been traveling in India, so we have that in common. We travel to Switzerland to visit some of her friends. We talk openly with each other about many things, including sex, which is new for me. She quickly becomes an integral part of my life. When she is not around, I feel a lack. I have a kind of reverence for her that I have never felt for another woman.

Gradually I realize that what I find so attractive about Jilli is a kind of erotic energy that she exudes. The excitement I feel when I am with her reaches deep inside me—it is physical and emotional as well as mental. I'm careful not to think about this too graphically because it makes me feel agitated.

Although she obviously enjoys my company, and is physically affectionate with me, she is clearly attracted to men. I am very uncertain that she feels the same desire for me that I do for her. I am afraid that if I tell her I want our intimacy to deepen, she will withdraw from me.

However, my desire does not lessen. Although it feels like it would be a natural progression of our pleasure in each other, potent unseen barriers prevent me from reaching out to stroke her skin in that very special way. She sleeps with various men, and I begin to feel jealous of the access they have to her body, even though I know it means little to her.

Eventually I find myself feeling awkward with her. I avoid discussions about sex. I hold my body stiffly to limit the expression of my longing. I decide I must talk to her about it, rehearsing what I will say. But no matter how determined I am, the moment I am faced with the reality of her presence, I am tongue-tied.

Needing an outlet for what has now become torment, I write a letter to a friend about my feelings. It offers me a little relief. A few weeks later, Jilli and I are visiting this friend. By coincidence, the letter is lying open on my friend's desk, and Jilli sees it.

In her usual forward manner, she says, "Oh, is this a letter from Chris? May I read it?"

My friend is embarrassed. "Uh...I'm not sure..." She glances at me for some direction.

Realizing that this may be the most painless way of telling Jilli how I feel, I nod. "Yeah, go ahead."

Unable to watch her read it, I go into the kitchen. When I return, with a cup of tea for both of them, they are talking about what to eat for dinner. Later that evening, when we are alone and I am ensconced in an armchair with a sleek black cat on my knee, Jilli says to me, "I appreciate you letting me read that letter."

"Mmmm," I reply, racking my brains without success for some more intelligent comment. I stroke the cat's ear between my thumb and forefinger, taking comfort in her softness as she stretches out and purrs.

"I'd like to talk more with you about it sometime," says Jilli.

"OK," I respond. We go on to discuss what time we have to leave tomorrow.

That's the last time it's mentioned. Over time, Jilli and I see less and less of each other.

Jilli has opened up one avenue for me: I feel able to talk about sex—not so much with the men I sleep with, who mostly have no desire to talk about it, but with my women friends. Now I know that women are meant to have orgasms (previously I've believed this was some kind of male myth). Well...I have experienced lots of sexual sensations. I am sometimes even aware of a very intense wanting that seems to be sexual desire. Such a physical ache, a body-taking-over sensation, out of my control, and uncomfortable in its intensity! Is this what is meant by an orgasm? The theory goes that an orgasm is unmistakable, but I'm not so sure about that.

After listening to descriptions of what Jilli and a couple of other women experience, I realize I haven't had anything that merits the label orgasm. Of course, lots of women don't have orgasms. But I don't know that, because other women who are experiencing conflict about sex are as reluctant to admit it as I am.

I'm living in a small farming community, learning about organic growing. I'm also learning a great deal about living and working with people. I sleep around with a few of the men, although no one really interests me.

John and Sonya are one of the couples that live here. People stay out of Sonya's way. She is an impatient person who doesn't mince her words. Fortunately, she doesn't work on the farm much, but she rules John with an iron hand. He has to be home for dinner by six, he has to take her into town when she says, he's often forbidden to go out to the pub on Saturday evening with the rest of us. Nevertheless, he is apparently devoted to her.

When an old school friend of Sonya's moves close by, she starts spending a lot of time with him. It's all the gossip: everyone is speculating whether she will leave John or not.

One night I wake to hear someone enter my room, and a voice, that I recognize as John's, whispering, "Are you awake, Chris?"

"Kind of." I wonder sleepily what he wants.

There is no light in my little trailer. Feeling his way to the bed, he kneels beside it. "Can I get into bed with you?"

John and I have never even flirted before. I can tell by his voice that he is upset, and anyway, I know he wouldn't be here if things were fine between him and Sonya. So I say, "Sure," and pull back the covers. Stripping off his shirt and jeans, he gets in beside me. He's shivering, so I put my arms around him to warm him up, then I realize he isn't cold. He is shaking with emotion.

"What's going on with you and Sonya? Does she know you're here?"

"No. She's with Dave." Dave is the guy she's been interested in.

"Oh, I'm sorry. That must be hard for you."

"Yeah..."

I can't tell if he is crying or not. I wonder if he wants to be sexual, thinking probably not, since he is clearly very upset. Although I could do it if he really wants to, I hope he doesn't. He lies next to me for a while, and then his hand strays across my chest, grazing my nipples. It's not an accident. I sigh inwardly. It would be too unkind to say no right now.

"Chris...I came here because..." There is a long pause. His hand rests beside my breast. I listen to his breathing, irregular in the darkness. His body next to me is rigid with tension.

"Yes?" I try to sound encouraging. I assume he came here because he needed to be with someone.

"I...I've never been with anyone but Sonya."

"Hmmm." Mulling over this piece of information, I turn my head towards him. I am half wanting to be able to see his face so I can read him better, and half relieved that we both have the darkness to hide in. "Do you want the experience of being sexual with another woman?"

"Yes...is that OK?"

"Sure." I'm relieved that he isn't pretending he's in love with me, or something stupid like that. Worse, he could be genuinely in love with me. That would really be a mess. He's still shaking uncontrollably and I can't quite imagine that he will be able to have a good time, or even get it up. But if he wants to try just for the sake of the experience, I'll go along with it.

We kiss, and he puts his mouth on my nipples, stroking my thigh with his hand. The shakes don't leave and I know this isn't going anywhere. He stops, turning on his back, and now I can tell he is crying for real. Feeling helpless, I put my hand over his on his chest and wait.

"I'm sorry...I just can't do it..." he manages finally.

"Oh, that's OK, you have nothing to apologize for," I assure him. "I'm sorry things are so difficult."

He sits up, swinging his legs over the edge of the bed. "I have to go now."

"OK. Take care of yourself."

Pulling on his clothes, he disappears into the night. I go back to sleep, barely remembering his visit in the morning. I'm pulling on my boots in the barn, getting ready to bring the sheep in, when Sonya appears.

"Chris, I want to talk to you."

"Oh, OK. Shall I come over to your place when I'm finished with the sheep?"

She agrees, and departs. One of the other workers, who has observed our brief interchange, grins at me. "Got a summons, have you?"

I laugh. "I guess so!" I don't take it seriously. I didn't invite John into my room, he came of his own accord.

Later, I arrive at Sonya's place. She does look a little grim and I wonder if I should be worried. We sit down at the heavy wooden table in the center of her kitchen. The room is gloomy, lit only by the light of one small window set into the thick stone walls. In the days when this farmhouse was built, stone was very cheap and glass was very expensive, so light wasn't a priority.

"John told me he went to your trailer last night." Sonya's voice is edged with righteousness.

I think, *what do you expect him to do while you are with Dave?* I say, "Yes, he was pretty upset."

There's a long pause. Finally Sonya says, "Don't you have anything to say to me about that?"

I look at her blankly, while she looks back at me almost impatiently. *What is it she wants?* I rack my brains. Suddenly it dawns on me.

"Oh! You want an apology. Well, I assure you I have no desire to hurt you, and I have absolutely no intention of damaging your relationship with John. That's the last thing in the world I would want to do."

She looks slightly mollified, but I think I'd better lay it on a little thicker, just to make sure. "I really wouldn't want to hurt you at all. I'm really sorry if you feel hurt."

Now she looks almost satisfied. She talks for a little while about her relationship with John, and how important he is to her. Wondering how long I will have to sit here, I try to look as though I'm listening attentively. Then she says, "So are you intending to sleep with him again?"

Thinking that I never intended to sleep with him in the first place, I say, "No, I don't think we'll be sleeping together again." Then I amend it: "I'm *sure* we won't be sleeping together again."

Magnanimously, she responds, "Well then, I think I can forgive you, as long as it never happens again."

Chapter Twelve

I **never heard the word lesbian** while I was growing up, but by my mid-twenties, I've certainly thought about the option of lesbianism, especially after my wannabe affair with Jilli. While I don't hold out much hope that it will be radically different from sex with men, that doesn't seem like a reason not to try it.

I have a casual relationship with John, who is married to Kerry. Everyone I know is resoundingly heterosexual, except for Kerry, and I don't take her very seriously. She laughs at inappropriate times, her voice is high and a little squeaky, she holds her body tight and stiff. Her face is attractive, but hidden behind bookish glasses. She looks shy, and indeed she has never learned the niceties of social chitchat. In some ways that appeals to me, since my upbringing has left me with an aversion to people who hide under a social facade.

One day when we are alone together in the dairy, straining the milk, she leans towards me, brushing the hair off my face with the back of her hand. "You're very beautiful, you know," she says with a smile that is awkward, but genuine. I stare at her blankly, uncertain how to take this. I only remember being told I'm beautiful once before, by a man.

John knows that Kerry is interested in me. He thinks it's sweet. One day when I am visiting, he magnanimously goes off to bed on his own, leaving me and Kerry to share the only other bed, since it is too late for me to go home. I've slept with girlfriends before, but I know that this will be different.

Undressing, we get under the covers. It's cold, the sheets are damp and chilly, so there can be no hanging out on the other edge of the bed. She reaches for me without any hesitation. I might be bolder out in the big wide world, but she is bolder by far in bed. She makes love to me sweetly and gently, slowly and eagerly, stroking my body, my skin, my breasts, my belly and my sex with a reverence that I have never experienced. It is all too strange, to be so intimate with a body that is such an immediate reflection of my own, a body that I really don't know what to do with, just as I don't know what to do with my own.

I'm carefully not feeling anything, especially not the fear that might explode if I pay it too much attention, especially not the desire to let go of my well-patrolled barriers. I am watching from a guarded intellectual distance, observing clinically so that I can examine what the experience of sleeping with someone of my own sex is like. Is it something I want to repeat?

My carefully groomed consciousness has never been in charge as much as I have wanted, as much as I have pretended. The day after sleeping with Kerry, I find myself in an uncontrollable fury, apparently about my living and working situation. My fury culminates by the end of the day in a decision to go traveling in Africa. I don't allow my lack of money or traveling companion to deter me. I went to India with a nerd who was useless, surely I can go to Africa on my own. Four days later I am gone. No chance to sleep with Kerry again.

I get as far as Switzerland where I stop to stay with Jilli, who is married now, and living here with her husband. Ostensibly, the reason I come here is to earn some money. But I am deeply churned up. I talk with Jilli about this strange dis-ease that is roiling around inside me. I tell her I am thinking perhaps I might be a lesbian. Of course she doesn't like that. She sets me up with a man. This time the experience is more than boring, it's disgusting, and I know I don't want to repeat it any time soon. Does this mean I am doomed to a life of loneliness? Or is there really a possibility that women might turn out to be a viable alternative?

Jilli thinks part of my problem is that I don't have orgasms, and she thinks I will have one if I masturbate. The idea of masturbating isn't appealing. Jilli talks me into persevering beyond my discomfort. So I lie in bed at night, forcing my hand to go through the motions of stimulating my clitoris, which I've previously been barely aware of. My mind clamors with anxiety and excuses. At first I always abandon the experiment at the point where I get painfully tense. Jilli advises me to push past that, to let my body focus on what it wants.

One night, the energy builds to a peak that I have never allowed before. All of a sudden it releases in a wave that flings me onto dry ground, much harder than I like. My body aches and shakes, aches and shakes, and I hug myself for dear life, my arms around my legs drawn up to my chest.

I have finally experienced what is called an orgasm. It hurts. Definitely overrated, I decide. My body is not fulfilled and satisfied. It feels like a limp, torn rag.

Meanwhile, it's winter in the foothills of the Alps. Three feet deep snow surrounds us most of the time, insulating me from people who cannot drive up to see us. And then there is the language. Even when people do visit, since I can't speak Swiss German, I can't join in the conversation. I am alone. I go for long walks in the Alps over the crispy brilliant snow, higher and higher into the lonely peaks where people don't walk even in the summer because there are really no paths and it is too steep. I push myself to climb up snow-covered slopes that are dangerously unstable, in places I don't know. I can easily get lost without trace under an avalanche, or simply wander until I drop, unable to find my way home. Somehow, I always find my way back before the night completely hides the path.

After three months, patches of green grass with blankets of flowers appear through the smooth carpet of white, and the snow gradually fades into nothing more than the occasional white peak in the distance, so that I really have to walk miles to find it. If I had made any money during my stay in Switzerland, I might have pushed myself to go south to Africa, intent as I am on stretching the limits of my endurance, and daring every fate that ever existed. But I have less money than when I arrived.

So I have a good excuse to go north, to Norway where it is easy to earn good money. I will go stay with Kerry, who is spending the summer there without John.

I meet up with Kerry, and suddenly, overnight, a door inside me opens. I fall over its threshold into a landscape radically different from anything I have ever known. I cannot find my feet. I cannot tell up from down, back from front.

She touches me gently at first, stroking my skin with her fingertips. In an instant my smoldering want bursts into a roaring fire. Her lightest touch brings me to a place of burning. I long for her fingers to caress my aching lips, I am desperate for her to run her tongue over my swollen clit and slide her fingers into my wet cunt. My body is constantly reaching out for her touch. She loves to run her tongue and fingers over my body. She's an expert at it and she's not in any hurry. She follows the dance of my body signals. She brings me to that edge of orgasm, and now I even tip over the other side, carried on waves of intensity, so that I don't know what's where or what or why.

Although this new thing—that might be called loving—is wonderful, it's also frightening and confusing. I am at a pitch of tension that is partly sexual and partly just enormous, rock-shaking emotion.

My body has a life of its own, not just in bed. My legs won't always hold me, I stumble and fall. My breathing is irregular, sometimes much too fast. My hands won't always work—I'm constantly dropping things. Often I can't make my lips and tongue form words. Occasional rushes of inexplicable terror are so intense that they literally leave me gasping. I grope for something familiar to anchor me, but my perceptions are strange. Even Kerry looks and acts quite differently from the way I remember her.

We're eating breakfast at the hostel. I want to lift the knife off the table to spread the butter on my toast. All morning I've been feeling like I'm floating ten feet above the floor, and now as I reach out for the knife, I can't work out how far away it is. Reaching and reaching, I finally feel it between my fingers. I close them on it, and the knife lifts off the table. Then my fingers cease to be able to keep their grip, and it drops onto the floor with a clang. I look down at it lying on the floor, wondering how I will ever be able to pick it up. I look over at Kerry, hoping for help. As I watch her lips forming words, I realize she's talking to me. I register that she's smiling and I feel some relief, that she's not angry. Her words seem all jumbled up and distant. It occurs to me that I should ask her to repeat what she just said, and I start to do so, only to find that my mouth won't work. I open and close it several times, trying to make my lips and tongue behave. They won't obey me. I frown with concentration, thinking, surely if I just try hard enough I can do it, I know I can do it. I'm aware of some concern in Kerry's expression. I'm also aware of panic rising in my throat…

I have stumbled upon the connection between love and sex. It requires learning a new way of being.

Kerry didn't bargain for a lover who was such a wreck. After a few weeks she begins to make it clear that I am going to have to pull myself together. I am trying very hard to do that anyway, and failing doesn't make me any happier than it does her.

Any thought of further traveling is clearly out of the question. I need to be somewhere safe where I can rest and put back together all these disparate particles of myself. We return to Wales. Staying at Kerry's place means staying at John's, since they own their property together, and the only dwelling is a small two-bedroom house. We are both anxious about being around John, since neither of us has the slightest desire to sleep with him. I suspect it won't be easy, but there is nowhere else to go.

Kerry tells me, "Chris, I want to leave John. I've known for a long time that he isn't good for me, but he's always been very good at manipulating my reality so that when I'm with him, I forget how much I prefer to be away from him. If I start forgetting, will you remind me that I want to leave him?"

Of course I agree.

When we first arrive, and declare that we want to sleep with each other rather than with him, he is livid with anger. He is a big man, and his fury is tangible. The morning after we arrive, he leans over me with his now habitual scowl, saying, "I need some time alone with Kerry."

"Why can't you say what you have to say with me here?" I ask.

"She's my wife, fuck it, you have no right to interfere in our relationship!"

Kerry interjects, "It's OK, Chris. Why don't you go out for a walk and come back in half an hour?"

I go out to walk around, though I'm nervous about leaving her with him. I know she is easily intimidated. Walking back to the house, I see him through the window, holding her against the wall, his hand around her neck. I run to the door, throwing it open. Grabbing hold of his arm, I pull him away from her. "You leave her alone, you dirty fucking bully!"

In an instant he is towering over me and for a moment I hold my own, but since he is much bigger than me, he very soon has my arm pinned up behind me. "You better shut up and leave us alone or I'm gonna break your arm, you little bitch!"

The weight of his body is crushing me in such a position that his face is close to mine. We lock eyes, the hatred between us like a flow of fire. My upper arm is screaming with pain. I know he could easily break it. I know he wants to, and I'm scared. Trying to swallow my groan of pain, I drop my eyes. Fortunately Kerry intervenes.

"Stop it, you two! What are you doing, for God's sake! Chris, he wasn't hurting me, now just do as he says, leave us alone. John, let go of her!"

He slowly eases off the pressure, taking a step backwards. His voice is like iced water as he hisses, "You're lucky I didn't put an axe through your head last night!"

The screaming in my arm begins to abate. Kerry ushers me out of the door.

Later that day, Kerry and I get some time alone. She says to me, "Poor John, I feel sorry for him."

I look at her with amazement. "*Sorry* for him?"

"Yes, it's not fair that he has to sleep on his own. Maybe I'll sleep with him tonight."

I'm a little frightened at how quickly she has changed her tune. "Kerry, do you remember telling me that you want to leave him?"

She waves her hand dismissively, laughing. "Oh, that was just me being melodramatic! He's a good person. He's just upset right now."

So she sleeps with him that night, and the next night, and every night. John walks around looking pleased with himself. He even smiles down at me now and again from afar.

What can I do? As the days pass, she falls more under his spell. She becomes distant and impatient. She laughs at the many jokes that John makes at my expense and even makes a few of her own. I scream and scream and scream for a gentle touch, for help, for sympathy and understanding. The screams stick in my throat, only emerging as incessant snotty sobs. Somehow I don't die. After two weeks of this hell, I set out with the help of my trusty thumb, to stay with friends two hundred miles away.

Kerry comes to visit. I am desperate for some love in the vast empty hole that is my life. Inevitably, her visit is a disaster. She's such a strange anti-social person. She doesn't know how to relate to any of the other people in this hippie commune where I'm now living, and that's a source of embarrassment for me. She tells me she's happy with John and it's good that she's living with him. My anger and frustration well up. I feel worse than I did before she came, because her presence reminds me of what I don't have. Even making love is not fulfilling. There is no longer a sense of wonder about it. It has become unloving.

We're out for a walk in the woods in an attempt at distraction from our not-getting-along. I'm trying to convey some sense of how I feel, and I'm getting more tangled in the feeling as I talk, which makes me more incoherent. She starts to laugh. In a split second, the long-fanged monster inside me rears up, enormous. All I know is that I want to kill her. It is completely intolerable that she is laughing at me. I must destroy her—it's my only choice. Before I know it, my arm is in motion and I have slapped her, hard enough to stop her in her tracks. Her laughter disappears very abruptly. I am immediately appalled at what I have done. I close my eyes in horror, groaning, "Oh, jesus christ, I'm sorry, I'm sorry!" I reach out to put my arm around her, and she instinctively makes a move to protect herself from the blow she is now expecting. I groan again.

I've blown it now. We will never achieve the intimacy I am seeking while she is afraid of me. The split second joy of letting my muscles express the anger I've been holding for so long is obliterated. I promise her it won't happen again, but why should she believe me?

One thing I now know: I don't want to be sexual with men any more. As I recover from the tidal wave precipitated by my affair with Kerry, I set out on a quest for lesbians. It doesn't prove easy. Everyone around me is very heterosexual. There are only two women at the local meetings of the Campaign for Homosexual Equality, both ardent Christians. I meet a local truck driver who admits she's a lesbian, making it very clear she wishes she were not. Finally, a friend of a friend tells me about a bar in a nearby city, where they have a women-only night once a week. She gives me the phone number of a lesbian couple who sometimes go to this bar. I call them, my words so well rehearsed I might as well be reading them.

"Hallo, I'm sorry to bother you. My name's Chris and I got your phone number from Sharon Turner. She told me there is a women's night on Tuesdays at the King Charles, and I was wondering if it's open to all women?"

"Oh yes, it's open to everyone! New women are very welcome. Do you live in Newcastle?"

"No, I'm from Durham. I'll be able to borrow a car."

"Oh good, because it doesn't really get going until nine or so, and you won't want to be leaving by ten to get the bus home. Pam and I usually get there about nine. Come and find us, just ask anyone for Pam and Marion. They'll know who we are."

Of course I am early, and I force myself to sit in the car biting my nails until it is nine o'clock. Entering the room, I stride up to the bar and seat myself, glancing quickly around as though being in a roomful of lesbians is nothing new or exciting. Ordering a drink, I ask the bartender if Pam and Marion are here. I'm close to hyperventilating and my voice squeaks. She points to a table where four women are seated. Like all the other women in the bar, they have short hair, and they are wearing T-shirts and jeans. Except for my shoulder length hair, I fit the mold. I promise myself I will cut my hair at the next opportunity. Somehow I make my way over to the table.

Pam and Marion are very friendly, and so are the couple they are sitting with. A fifth woman who appears to be single comes to sit with us for a while, and I flirt a little. Other women come by and chat as I watch. In spite of my anxiety, I am deeply relieved to be surrounded by women who are at ease with loving each other. When I leave, as the bar closes, I arrange with Pam and Marion to see them there the following Tuesday.

The week passes slowly. Arriving a little earlier this time, I find the room fairly empty. The woman I flirted with last week is sitting at the bar. I buy her a drink and we make small talk. She has laughing blue eyes that I want to stare into, though I am not bold enough to hold her gaze. A third woman comes over and plants herself between us, ignoring me. Fortunately, Pam and Marion arrive and I go to sit with them. Later in the evening, as the room fills up, I go to the toilets. A tall butch with a very mean expression follows me in. I have previously noticed her as one of a group that dominates the bar. She corners me at the sink.

"This isn't your kind of bar," she says, standing a little too close to me. She takes a deep drag on the cigarette that she holds between the tip of her forefinger and her thumb, blowing smoke in my face. Her eyes never leave me. I am aware of another woman, smaller but just as mean, standing silently behind me.

A cold ache spreads through my body. "What do you mean?"

She drops the cigarette on the floor and takes her eyes off me just long enough to grind it out with the toe of her boot. Then she looks back at me, still expressionless. "You're not welcome here."

Is it my accent that betrays me as *not* one of them? Or should I have refrained from buying a drink for that sweet blue-eyed woman? It would make no difference. This is the old-time butch/femme bar culture, and they see me as a budding feminist with an awareness that undermines the traditional roles, even though I have only just begun to embrace feminism. And I am not working class. It doesn't matter that my only desire is to fit in. Although Pam and Marion tell me to pay no attention, I can't delete the experience from my awareness.

A week or two later, forlorn and lonely, I am thumbing my way idly through a women's periodical, and see an ad for an anarcha-feminist conference in Leeds. I read through the headings of the workshops, finding three that are specifically on lesbianism. Am I brave enough to attend a conference where I know absolutely no one? Considering the state of my self-confidence, that seems like a tall order. What choices do I have? It is not tenable to continue living in such intense isolation, and common sense tells me that somewhere, somehow, there are other lesbians I will be able to relate to. I bite my fingernails for two days before I decide I must give it a shot.

My hands are shaking when I call the number, and I almost put the phone down when I hear a woman's voice at the other end. Somehow I keep my cool. I register to attend and I'm offered a place to stay, sleeping on someone's floor. Will it be a lesbian household?

Arriving at the bleak red brick college on Saturday morning, I make my way immediately to the workshop entitled *The Politics of Lesbianism*. Three women sit chatting and I seat myself near them, wishing both to be visible and invisible. When the room has filled up, a small woman with warm eyes and cropped dark hair introduces the workshop, asking us to say why we have chosen to be there. The discussion gradually picks up and I sit quietly for a long time until, following the line of discussion, I begin to talk about how dissatisfying I have found my relationships with men. When I am done, the butch woman next to me speaks up in an impatient and emphatic tone.

"If you think you are a lesbian because your relationships with men didn't work out, then you need to think again. Real lesbians know they are lesbians because they love women, not because they can't find a man they like." She glances at me, her eyes hard, her lips thin. My eyes slide to the floor, and my heart to my boots. She carries on. "I'm so tired of heterosexual women who are just using lesbians to make themselves feel better. They need to work on their relationships with men and leave lesbians alone!"

The woman who introduced the discussion suggests a break, and people start getting up. Grateful that the hubbub will hide me, I sit very still wanting only to be alone again, and cursing myself that I ever thought of coming here. But a figure stands before me. I look up to see the woman who is running the group. She smiles as she introduces herself.

"Hi, I'm Jan. I'm glad you're here, and I appreciated what you were saying. I just want to say that I think the woman who spoke last was really out of line."

Another woman chimes in, "Yeah, that was real bullshit! Just because a woman doesn't get along with men doesn't mean she isn't a real lesbian!"

A third snorts derisively in agreement, addressing me directly, "Yes, don't pay any attention to her. She has a chip on her shoulder, and that's her problem, not yours!"

Uncertain relief floods through me, washing away some of the pain in my heart. Still smiling, Jan says, "Are you coming to get a cup of tea?" It is clearly an invitation. I stand up, and the four of us walk out of the room together.

Chapter Thirteen

The woman at the counter in the employment office is harried and unfriendly. "Can I help you?" she asks, barely glancing at me.

"Yes, I'd like to apply for one of the government training courses."

"OK, well, here's a list. When you've decided which one you want, I'll help you fill in the form." She hands me two pieces of paper.

I am already sure what I want, so I flip through the brochure till I get to *M*. There is no *mechanics*. I try *A*. No *agricultural*. Running my eyes down the columns, I realize they are all things like hair-dressing, computer skills, typing. This is the brochure for women. I need the one for men. When the harried-looking woman has finished with another applicant, I catch her eye, saying, "Isn't there a course on Agricultural Machinery? That's the one I want."

"You want *what*?"

"I want to do a course on Agricultural Machinery."

Her mouth opens. It's a second or two before she articulates, "Agricultural Machinery?"

"Yes. Agricultural Machinery."

We stare at each other for a long moment. Then she turns away. She picks up another brochure, hands it to me without a word and walks off. I see her lean over another woman's desk, glancing back at me as she talks. She has an unmistakable sneer on her face.

Finding the course I want, I fill in the form and return to the counter. The same woman comes up to me and I hand her the form. She takes it without looking at me, holding it away from her as though it is unclean. As I leave the office, I look back through the plate glass window to see her toss some paper in the bin. I can't be sure that it's my application, and some part of me cannot really believe that she would do that.

So I wait two months before I call up to find the status of my application. They have never received it. I file another at a different office, where they are at least civil, if not actively encouraging. I soon hear that I am to start the training three months later.

Three months to bide my time. A nuclear power station is to be built near the place where I lived in Scotland. This feels like a personal affront to the land that nurtured me as I grew up. I join a group of environmental protestors who are planning to occupy the site. We drive up there with camping supplies and set up a little tent village on a bare field close to the sea beside a small ruined cottage. The infamous Scottish wind whips around us, nipping at any bare skin. We are a motley group, mostly in our twenties and thirties. Although our numbers fluctuate over the ten weeks we stay there, there are approximately twenty of us: half women, half men, with two children under the age of ten. There is one other dyke, and I have a pleasant fling with her, although the other protestors express concern about our image. "It'll reflect badly on the cause," we are told. "People already think we're pretty weird. We need to present an acceptable front."

Various support personnel, who are not present most of the time, do very useful back-up work, like arranging funding. All kinds of people, including my parents, visit on a regular or irregular basis. My father thinks it's quite entertaining, and manages to be fairly pleasant.

We have chaotic meetings in an effort to present a united front, decide who's responsible for what, plan what to say to the media, and organize rotas for who's cooking what and when. The meetings are exhaustingly unproductive, full of arguments that seem to stem from no real basis other than absurd attachment to doing things one way, and *not* doing them another way. I perk up when we decide to renovate the ruined, roofless cottage, with its thick stone walls. Several of the men say they have some building experience so I'm looking forward to learning something.

Weeks pass, with a great deal of talking, plans laid, and some building materials turning up. Nothing actually happens. I gradually realize that the men are afraid of the realities of the project. I decide to start. Choosing a big beam, I recruit a couple of men to help me get it onto the wall. To my delight, the building is soon under way.

After a few more weeks, with plenty of scrambling around high above the ground, the building has a metal roof. It is dark inside, barely retarding the freezing wind that blows off the North Sea, but I am very pleased with it.

All this time, we have neither heard nor seen anything from the authorities, although the date initially set for starting the power plant is long gone. The Scottish weather is becoming unpleasant. So it is a welcome relief when we wake up one morning to find a convoy of machines, accompanied by police, driving across the rough track towards us.

We have talked about this at great length. We know exactly who is willing to be arrested and who will stay behind to make sure our belongings are safe. I clamber up onto the metal roof with five of the men. A few others sit down in the path of the police, who carry them into the waiting van. A man with a bullhorn repeatedly informs us that we are trespassing, and we will be arrested if we don't depart of our own free will. I wait excitedly on the roof, huddled in my jacket, chatting with the long-haired fellow next to me who is clearly nervous. When those on the ground are all locked away in vans, a couple of burly policemen in uniforms attempt to climb up. Their lack of agility and our quick laughter soon deter them. Ladders are brought and placed against the sturdy stone walls, but the policemen slide hopelessly when they step onto the corrugated metal roof. Even when they try to hold onto the stone gable, which is how the five of us got up there, they don't make it very far. I cannot imagine how they will get any of us down unless we go willingly. I have no intention of making it easy for them.

Some longer ladders are brought. These actually reach to the top of the roof, and eventually two of the cops are sitting gingerly astride the ridge. They look uncomfortably out of place. The cops on the ground continue to harangue us with the bullhorn: "Come along now, you've had your fun, it's time to come down!" By this time it's already midday. We have been waiting four hours. I'm quite content to wait till dusk but the others don't seem to feel that way. One by one my companions climb down to the ground where they are led into the still waiting van. Finally, only I am left sitting astride the ridge of the roof. The remaining policeman edges cautiously along the ridge towards me until he can put his hand on my arm. I look at his broad florid face with interest.

"Come along then, there's no need to be difficult," he says.

I smile, cocking my head. "Why not?"

He looks down at his bosses, who are watching us from the safety of the ground. "She won't move!"

One of them impatiently picks up the bullhorn, putting it down again with an expression of disgust. A group of them confer, and shortly another reluctant policeman is dispatched to climb the ladder. Then support turns up from unexpected quarters: one of my fellow campers, who has stayed out of the fray, steps from the group of onlookers, calling up to me, "Come on, Chris, you're not doing any good staying up there."

I sigh. What good was it doing any of the things we did? Why give up now? But it doesn't make sense to prolong the game when my own people are bored with it.

I feel like a horse in a herd of cows.

It's time to start the mechanics course. From eight to five, five days a week, for seven months, I am enclosed in a large windowless building with a thousand men, training in a variety of manual skills.

For my first task, I am given a one inch diameter, three inch long, round steel bar. Using a hammer and chisel, I am required to transform it into a bar with three flat sides. This is not something anyone would ever do in real life—it is part of the testing that occurs in the first three weeks, before the students are definitely accepted on the course. Since I can already tell I am going to learn a lot on this course, I am quite determined I will accomplish this. *Deter-*

mined perhaps isn't the right word, since it indicates some doubt. I have no doubt. I know I will do this.

I set to work with the hammer and chisel. Every ten minutes or so, I miss the bar and hit the knuckle of my thumb on my left hand as it grips the chisel. Since I am wielding the hammer pretty hard, my knuckle is soon a bloody mess. I wrap a rag several times around it, and carry on.

When I have two sides done, and I am just positioning the bar to start on the third side, my instructor comes up beside me. He is a tall soft-spoken man, who has been very respectful of me so far, which cannot be said of anyone else in the building. I look up at him. A pang of anxiety pierces me as I see his frown.

He leans down, speaking quietly, as though he doesn't want anyone else to hear. "Leave it at that."

I'm surprised. "But I still have the third side to do."

"It's good enough, leave it. Come over to the desk, I'll show you how to sharpen drill bits."

He demonstrates how to sharpen a drill bit, and explains the theory, then leaves me with some bits to work on. At first I can't get it right. Suddenly it dawns on me exactly how the angle he talked about corresponds to the piece of steel in my hand. Zipping through the rest of them, I soon turn up at his desk with a handful of sharpened bits. I present them to him, and he says, "You're done already?" I nod. He examines them, and looks at me in puzzlement. "These are the bits I just gave you? You sharpened these?"

"Yes."

He pulls out another handful of bits from a drawer. "Here, a few more."

Is he doubting that I have been able to pick up the method so fast? I take them to the grinding wheel. Now that I've got the knack, it doesn't take me long. This time when I return to his desk, he looks them over and then smiles up at me. "Very good."

Lunch is always excruciating. There are two buildings for the trainees: hairdressing and other traditionally female occupations in one, with carpentry, mechanics and other traditionally male occupations in the other. We share a cafeteria, where the women sit on one side and men on the other. Where does this leave me? I have no desire to sit with the eleven men who are studying agricultural mechanics along with me, but I am hardly likely to feel more at home if I sit with the women, who already think I am very bizarre. I would really like to spend my breaks reading a book. That would be considered antisocial, and I would prefer to blend in.

Today I sit between Harry and Mike. The conversation veers from football to cars, to wives. Harry is telling Jack, across the table from him, about teaching his wife to drive.

"So finally she manages to ge' goin,' and we're off down the road movin' abou' two miles an hour, an' Ah tell 'er to change up, an' what does she do? Tries t' stick the bloody car in reverse! Stupid bitch!"

Laughter echoes round the table. I keep my gaze on my fork, shoveling unappetizing food around my plate.

"You should tell 'er t' stick t' cookin' yer dinner, mate!" is Jack's advice.

Simon, at the end of the table, pipes up, "Yeah, chicks don't know 'ow to drive," and Mike says, "Ah tol' my ol' lady, Ah said, if you think you're ever drivin' ma car, you go' another think comin'! Silly cow, she doesn't know the engine from the gearbox. She'll wreck yer car, 'Arry, mark my words! Ye're a fool fer lettin' 'er anywhere near it."

After a week of listening to them trash women, blacks, Jews, and just about everyone else, I take to sitting at a table on my own and reading a book.

Throughout the course, our instructor treats everyone fairly. He is my one saving grace, my haven of sanity. Then an unfortunate thing happens: he gets sick. Sick enough to be off for a couple of weeks. By a stroke of ill-luck, I qualify as the most senior of the students during his absence, since it is a staggered-entry course and I have been there longest.

The first day he is away, the instructor from next door lets us into the workshop and checks that we all have projects to get on with. With the keys dangling from his fingers, he says, "The most senior person needs make sure all tools are put away, let everyone know when it's break-time, take charge of the keys, lock the doors and bring the keys back to me at the end of the day. So who's the most senior here?"

"I am." A few of the men glance at me and quickly look away.

The instructor is clearly unsure of himself. Addressing the group as a whole, and carefully avoiding my eyes, he says "Well...I'll leave the keys here on the table and I'll be in later. Make sure the room is locked when you go for break."

I keep my eye on the clock. At five minutes to ten I say, "Break-time!" loud enough for everyone in the workshop to hear. Normally the moment this word is spoken everyone stops working. Today is different. Nobody pays any attention, as though I haven't spoken at all. Shrugging, I pack up my own project. I stand by the door with the keys in my hand. I know they won't wait long to go to break. Sure enough, they soon file out, avoiding my eyes, and I follow, locking the door behind me.

So the day goes on. At twenty minutes to five, I call "Time to pack up!" They have developed a different strategy by now; most of them have already packed up. After tidying up my tools, I check around the shop to see that everything is put away, and quickly discover that Harry, who has been working with the welding equipment, has left the oxy-acetylene cylinders out. Walking past him towards my locker, I say casually, "Those cylinders need to be put away." He gives no sign of having heard me. Standing at my locker, making myself busy with nothing, I watch out of the corner of my eye. He is chatting with the other men. I ponder the odds of his attending to the equipment, and go over to do it myself. By the time I am done, it's five, and the last of the men are crowding out the door. I stand still, looking around me, savoring the feeling of having the workshop to myself.

We have already been told our instructor will be away for two weeks. I am wondering how the men and I will manage. The next morning, the instructor from next door resolves the situation. He hands the keys to Simon, who is next in seniority to me. "Here, Mr. Wellington, isn't it? You take care of these."

In the background, I sigh with relief.

During the instructor's absence, we are left to practice on our different projects alone.

I have to wait for Dennis to finish with one of the tractors, before I can work on it. I can see from what he is doing that it will not take him long to finish. I've told him I'm waiting, and as the minutes tick by and he chats idly with some of the other students, I realize I have made a mistake in telling him that. Most of the men are somewhat civil to my face, but Dennis has never even spoken directly to me. His expression is set in narrow-eyed hatred whenever he looks at me, which is rare.

Walking up beside him, I say, "How long are you going to be with that tractor, Dennis?"

His lips tighten as he glances my way, muttering, "Just a while," then carrying on with his conversation.

When the instructor from next door comes in to check on us, the group of men who are chatting quickly disperse to their work. Dennis gets under the tractor, fiddling for a while, with me watching. Two minutes later he gets up again, going off to rummage in some drawers as though he is looking for a tool. I've already exhausted all possibilities of finding some other work to do. Nearly two hours have passed since I first told him I was waiting. He returns, getting under the machine again. It's held up by a jack. As I stand idly and impatiently by the jack, I find my hand reaching out to caress the handle. If I grip it and turn, the jack will fall.

I grip it and turn, the jack falls a couple of inches and holds there as I quickly return the handle to the lock position. Dennis is out from under the tractor in a split second, his face distorted with rage. "What the *fuck* d'y' think you're doing?"

"Just getting you to hurry up," I say, smiling. After six months of working here, my face sometimes feels like a long-dried skull from forcing my muscles into that *fuck you* grin.

"You leave that fucking jack alone!" he spits between his teeth. I take my hand off the handle but I don't move away. Slowly he gets back under the tractor, glaring at me. Within five minutes he is finished.

We get lectures on theory several hours a week. I find it curious that I am the only person who ever asks questions. At first I think this must be because everyone else already understands, and doesn't need to ask questions, but then it becomes apparent from conversations I have with the men afterwards, that they don't always understand.

After our instructor returns from being sick, he is teaching us about electric motors. Five minutes into the lecture I am totally confused. He is using terms I don't understand and referring to concepts I have never heard of. I raise my hand.

"Yes?"

"Uh...I don't understand..." I understand so little of what he has said that I don't know how to phrase my question. "I don't understand the diagram."

"Hmmm..." he glances at the diagram he has drawn on the board, and then back at me. "Let me explain a little more and I think it will become clear."

He carries on talking and I carry on feeling confused. After a few minutes, I raise my hand again to ask, "What is a stator?"

He looks surprised, saying, "Remember in the last lecture I talked about magnetic fields?"

Clearly I am supposed to say yes to this, but the truth is I don't remember. I decide it's best to be honest. So I say, "No."

He is taken aback. He looks around the class. "Does everyone else understand what I'm talking about?"

There is a long silence. "Well?" He is sounding impatient now. "Do you understand or not?"

Someone at the back mutters something that might be no. Jack coughs, and says, very quietly, "No." Someone else murmurs no, and a fourth person echoes him.

The instructor tries another tactic. "Is there anyone who *does* understand?"

He looks from face to face. Silence reigns. He turns back to his diagram and then back again to the class. "You have had the lecture that precedes this, haven't you? You have had the lecture on basic electricity, right?"

More muttered no's around the room. Comprehension dawns on the instructor's face. "Well, that explains it! I must apologize, my mistake. No wonder it was over your heads. Let's begin this lecture again! Good job we caught that before I went too far."

He proceeds with the initial lecture and I follow him every step of the way, to my relief.

After about three months, two or three of the men begin to follow my example and I am not the only person who occasionally asks questions.

I love learning how machinery works, and I am filled with pleasure whenever I take one of the machines apart and put it back together. But every afternoon I leave the workshop with a prayer of thanks that I have survived another day, and that I don't have to have anything to do with men outside the workshop. I spend the evening trying to let go of the tension that has built up in my body from the day. I often wish that I will never have to see a man again in my life. I am deeply, daily, grateful that I am able to be intimate with women, that I can find the physical and emotional fulfillment I need from being with women, and that I am myself a woman. I shudder with relief whenever I think that I will never have to see these idiots again once I finish the course.

My last day arrives. I collect my things from my locker, and wait for the instructor. He has a selection of tools—spanners, files, screwdrivers—laid out on his desk. Everyone who completes the course is given these. He wraps them up in the cloth tool belt that comes with them.

"I wish they'd give you a proper toolbox, but this is all they'll come up with," he says regretfully. He escorts me to the door, where I turn to say goodbye. He shakes my hand formally.

"It's been a pleasure to have you on the course. Nice not to be teaching a blank wall for once. I hope you can get a job. You're smart enough and you're a good mechanic. I wish you the best of luck."

Chapter Fourteen

Debbie is my second woman lover, and being with her has pulled me out of the morass where Kerry left me wallowing. Debbie and I are still in bed after spending the morning making love. Her fingers trail up my belly now, as she lies on her side facing me. I'm sweaty and relaxed from that last fierce orgasm that shook my body, leaving tingles all down my legs and feet. Lying on my back with my hands behind my head, I listen to myself; I'm talking about Tom McFarlane. I haven't thought about Tom for twenty years. I'm telling Debbie about the time John walked into the room, while I was sitting on Tom's knee. This particular incident...I've never thought about it before...I've never remembered it before...it's like recalling a dream. I look up at Debbie in puzzlement as I tell her that he had his hand between my legs. Her face is filled with concern. She puts her arms around me. I feel secure, cushioned by her love. When I've finished describing what I have recalled of that one incident with Tom, I lie still for a moment. There must have been many times when he touched me down there, yet I can't remember them. I remember knowing that was what he wanted, that was always what he wanted. Did he have orgasms when I sat on his knee? Did he push his fingers right inside me? How I hated his scratchy face rubbing against mine! How come my sister managed to avoid being the one who sat on his knee? How come I wasn't able to avoid his groping fingers?

I turn towards Debbie, frowning. "There's something else, that happened when I was about seven, I think...seven or eight. There was an old drunkard who lived down the road..."

In a country area like this part of Scotland, everyone knows everyone else. At the age of eight, I'm still attending the tiny village school. My friends are the shepherd's son next door, and Moira and Lizzie who live down the road. The four of us often roam around in a little gang, making hideouts, playing cowboys and indians, and daring each other to do dangerous things.

There is a row of three cottages near my parents' house. They sit off the road a little, each with a small front garden. The first is well tended, with neat beds of flowers and rows of carrots, cabbages and raspberries. It belongs to a young couple with a baby. He works at the farm. The other two gardens are in disarray, they haven't been worked in years. One of the cottages is abandoned, its windows broken and blank. The last one, although its windows aren't broken, has a similar dilapidated look and so does its inhabitant, Mr. Cockburn. Occasionally when we're playing in the area, usually trying to work out how to break into the empty house, Mr. Cockburn emerges onto his doorstep beckoning to us. Normally we run away when we see him, since there is something vaguely sinister about his unkempt appearance and leering smile. Once, though, he waved a bar of chocolate at me and Moira when we were nearby, and understanding from this gesture that he wasn't going to tell us off, we ventured close enough to take the chocolate. Then it transpired he wanted a kiss. I wasn't surprised; most of the chocolate I have been given in my short life has that kind of price on it. So Moira and I both gave him a very quick peck on his bristly cheek, and ran off as fast as we could.

Today the four of us are at a loss for what to do. As we're walking by the cottages, kicking stones in the road and arguing, Moira says, "Why don't you go and ask Mr. Cockburn for some chocolate?"

I make a face and Lizzie says, "Yuck!"

But Moira doesn't give up. "What's the matter, are you scared of him?" She taunts us. "Go on, I dare you to go ask him if he has any chocolate!"

I look at Lizzie and she looks at me. I consider it to be a weakness to be scared of anything. I am more scared of being seen as scared, than I am of being hurt by Mr. Cockburn. So I say, "I'll go if you go!"

She grins, and says, "All right then!"

Somehow, we all know that Robert has no place in this dare. Mr. Cockburn isn't going to give him a bar of chocolate.

Together we approach from the back so that the couple in the first cottage won't see us, since they've told us off before when we were trying to break into the abandoned cottage. Robert and Moira wait on the corner, in the narrow stone passageway between the two houses.

Lizzie and I walk up to the bare stone doorstep. I reach high to lift the old brass knocker and it drops back down onto the wood with a thud. The two of us stand there nervously giggling and hopping from one foot to the other in front of the door with its peeling red paint. The curtain at the window to our right is lifted, and his unshaven face peers out. We hear his footsteps and the latch lifts on the door. It creaks open and there he stands, reeking of alcohol, his lips parted over his cracked and yellow teeth. At this point Lizzie does the first of her two dirty deeds for the day. She runs away, abandoning me on the doorstep with this ugly smelly old man. Of course I could run away too, and indeed I am poised on the edge of flight. But for some reason I don't run. Perhaps it's because I'm afraid of the consequences of being rude to adults. Perhaps I'm just afraid of being thought a coward. Maybe Lizzie just has a better sense of self-preservation. Whatever the reasons, I stay there on the doorstep, mumbling something about how we were just wondering if he had any chocolate. He opens the door wider and slurs, "Come on in."

Once again I'm very hesitant, but I have been well trained in the importance of being polite, and besides I am curious to see this dark den. So I step inside the living room. He pushes the door closed behind me and grabs me without any warning. He lifts me almost off my feet with one arm and holds me so tightly against his stained and sweaty shirt that I am bent over backwards. I can barely breathe. At the same time he thrusts his free hand down my pants. His fingers are fiddling between my legs. My nostrils are filled with the reek of him. I struggle desperately against his grip, trying to push him away with my fists and my feet. Panic makes me strong. Somehow I manage to wriggle out of his grasp and I race for the door, wrenching it open and running outside, his rasping laughter hideous behind me.

The nightmare isn't over yet, Lizzie still has to play her final part. She returned after he invited me into the house and saw what was happening through the window. As I run down the alley, shaking with terror, she stands in front of me laughing, and shouts so that the others can both hear, "Ha ha, I saw him, he had his hand down your trousers, I saw him!"

Faced with such a taunt what can I do but deny it?

I'm amazed as I listen to my words. This has been stored in my mind for twenty years, yet I never knew it before? The details form like soft snowflakes falling in my mind, making no sound, dropping easily and delicately into place, making a carpet of crystal white, that transforms into the words that are flowing out of my mouth. The memories have no feeling attached to them. I remember being scared, I remember thinking I was going to die, and I remember being deeply ashamed when Lizzie laughed at me. But I don't feel those feelings now. They are over and done with. I'm an adult now and I will never let anything like that happen to me again.

I continue about my life.

This is 1980. I live in Leeds, the city where thousands of male football fans cheer a serial rapist, and the police repeatedly tell women if they don't want to be raped, then they shouldn't go out after dark. This is the city where two white women are raped by black men one week, and two black women by white men in retaliation, the following week. My friends and I don't have to look far to justify feeling angry.

Debbie is the love of my life. I adore her. I have never loved anyone so wholeheartedly. I cannot imagine life without her. However, our relationship is never easy, since she, like many women, wants to talk about feelings, and analyze what is going on between us. Talking about my feelings is virtually impossible for me, since a huge chasm lies between my verbal, intellectual self and my feeling self. I've always kept my feelings firmly at bay when I am with another person.

My conscious self denies it completely when some core part of me starts to push Debbie away. Debbie, however, notices at once, and questions me about it. Of course I can't talk about it, I haven't admitted to myself that I'm withdrawing. Gradually we stop making love and our time together becomes less and less fulfilling. I still love her...I just don't want to be sexual with her. She's angry and upset. Over a period of months, our relationship becomes perfunctory on my part and bitter on hers. I am afraid of her bitterness. But I can't stop myself from looking for someone new. I am craving the excitement and intensity of falling in love again. I have not admitted this to anyone, least of all myself.

I'm with a party of six women in Edinburgh. We're on a trip up here to visit friends and have a good time. We're all gathered round the table drinking pints of beer, everyone laughing and talking about nothing of any importance. It's just another lunchtime at the pub. As usual, we're attracting some attention. The regulars never like us: a bunch of rowdy dykes in jeans and leather jackets, making loud remarks about how gross the men are, and being publicly affectionate with each other. We're all proud of being dykes and we're all far too full of ourselves to hide our disdain for straight society. This pub will probably tolerate us for the short time we're here, as long as we don't get too drunk and as long as none of the men challenge us.

Two of the women present are Jan and Melissa. Jan is a working class dyke with an attitude, known for her fits of rage which often culminate in fist fights. She knows my family background (it's not something I can hide in a country where class pervades everything), and hates me with a vengeance, rarely missing an opportunity to put me down. We only spend any time together because the lesbian community is small. Melissa is her lover. Although I like Melissa, I don't generally try to engage with her.

I'm still not much good at feelings. I know only one way to operate in the world: that is, to protect myself. I might as well be wearing a suit of armor. I choose to be with these particular women because I don't have to be ladylike. I can be loud and obstreperous, which gives me a release valve for the rage that I still cannot name. I want to be the big tough dyke who never gets hurt. If I just try hard enough, I believe I can make the pretense a reality. There's only a small part of myself, hidden away in the center of a ring of high walls and barbed wire, that knows it's not true.

In the center, in that beleaguered place which is the truth of who I am, my rage encapsulates a deep loneliness. So it happens like this: I glance casually across the table and accidentally catch Melissa's eye. Without any warning, I am swallowed up in a deep hole, swirling downwards in a whirlpool of intense desire. It is gorgeously pleasurable to feel something like this, something at least akin to love, something real, some connection with another human being. I'm not alone in the world, after all.

I look down at my beer glass, my hand curled around it. The hubbub in the crowded room seems far away. I am intensely aware of Melissa. I want to be naked next to this woman. I want her to know me for who I truly am. I want to feel my hands stroking her bare skin. I want to float with her in the outer space of our minds and bodies. I want to feel her moving against me. I want to know that she is real. I want my thigh between hers, and her wetness on my fingers, her tears and joy and rage pouring into my open hands. All this I want and more, much much more. I want to know everything about her, and I want to give her everything of me.

All this happens in only a moment of falling into each other's eyes. I know she has felt the moment. It doesn't pass. The woman on my right makes some kind of joke and I laugh, although I'm not listening. Swilling the frothy golden liquid in my glass, I raise it to my lips. I'm trying to pretend that this potential disaster is not looming over us like some huge black cloud on the horizon, or is it like a burst of sunshine as the sun comes out from behind the cloud that is always there? I'm hoping that I imagined it all, but I am holding her inside me now. Has anyone else noticed? I try to act normally. I make a point of joining in the frivolous conversation that's still going on around me. It doesn't make any difference. The moment did occur. For that split second we knew another possibility.

Now I pay the price. In the weeks that follow, our desire for each other is obvious to everyone, despite our repeated denials. I am warned by several women to keep my "hands off Jan's woman." Jan has never been in the habit of smiling at me, but now she glares at me wherever I go, her eyes saying, *I will kill you.* Melissa stays away from me. She is committed to her relationship with Jan. Occasionally we talk, but we never have the luxury of being alone for more than a few minutes. Ostensibly, I try to stay away from her. My desire is stronger than my will. The most I ever get is a long, delightful, deep kiss in the back of someone's car on the way home from the pub, when Jan happens to be away, and I manage to arrange to sit next to Melissa. Every night I go to bed dreaming of her, sweating anguished beads of wanting. Gradually, over the weeks that follow, my flood of unmet desire recedes, leaving me aching and exhausted and stranded.

At least I'm free to repeat a similar experience with someone else.

Chapter Fifteen

At some point in all those years of growing up that are my twenties, I visit my parents for a few days.

One evening, after I have been to the seaside, revisiting those childhood outings, a hare jumps out in front of my car. In the half dusk I see it too late, and although I swerve, I feel the front wheel crushing it. Pulling over, I jump out, hoping to find it dead. No such luck. It stares up at me with liquid brown eyes bleeding pain, its front legs jerking helplessly. I carry it to the side of the road, where I lay it down and find a rock. I smash its head until I know it's dead, its blood mingling with the green grass. Picking up the warm, soft body by its hind legs, I put it in the boot of the car.

"Oh, what have you got there? A hare?" my mother asks enthusiastically as I enter the kitchen. She is standing with her back to the stove, her hands held to her chest and her fingers knotted together anxiously, a stance that has become habitual.

"Yes, it jumped right out in front of me. I thought the cats would like it. Damn, it's dripping blood on the floor." I scoop up its dangling front legs in an attempt to catch the drips.

"Ooh yes, I'm sure they'd love it! Stick it in the larder, and I'll cook it up for them later."

As I exit the larder, I hear a commotion outside, and realize that my father is returning. He's been out shooting. Seconds later, everything is chaos. The two dogs come bounding into the kitchen, closely followed by Arthur, carrying a dead deer, front legs in one hand and hind legs in the other. Its head lolls grotesquely, bouncing as he strides. Blood drips from its nostrils to add to the splodges on the floor from the hare. He's very pleased with himself. "Look what I got! One shot, stone dead!"

My mother is not amused. "Oh, for God's sake, Arthur, can't you leave it outside? I really don't want it in here!"

His eyebrows lift in surprise. "You don't want it in here? All right, very well, then I suppose I'll put it out in the woodshed!" And he turns around to carry the dead body out. The dogs remain, milling around, sniffing here and there and everywhere, looking for their dinner.

Margaret picks up a knife to chop the onions that are waiting for her attention. She grimaces at me. "Honestly, bloody man! So pleased with himself! And we all know who'll be the one that has to skin and gut it! Damn deer!"

She's slicing an onion as she talks, and somehow she is careless with the knife. "Damn!" she says, pausing to look at her finger. I move closer to see, but she carries on chopping. "It's nothing!" she says, and shakes her head. "Honestly, bloody man!" Bloody indeed, I think, as I see the gash on her finger dripping blood onto the chopping board, to match the blood on the floor from the dead animals.

"Here, wait a minute, that's quite a cut!" I am a little appalled that she is trying to ignore it. "You'd better hold it up until it stops bleeding."

She puts down the knife and leans back against the stove, holding her hand up. The blood drips down her arm, and I hurriedly fetch a cloth to wrap around it. A door slams, and a moment later my father enters the room.

"For God's sake, woman, what *have* you done?" His eyebrows draw together in a disapproving stare when he sees her bleeding hand.

She glares back. "None of your business! Don't be so rude!" As she talks, she flicks her wounded hand in a gesture of impatience, as though to push him away. Drops of blood fly across the kitchen. I try to wrap the cloth around it, but she flicks me away as though she doesn't notice, and blood spatters around me. Arthur takes a step towards her, threateningly, reaching out to grab her hand. "Come here, you stupid woman, for God's sake, you need a plaster on that!"

She jerks away from him. "Leave me alone, you horrid beast!"

I step forward between them, facing my father. "Leave her alone! We can deal with this without you! You're just making things worse!"

He glares at us both. "Bloody women! Honestly! Bunch of morons!" He stomps out of the room. I firmly take hold of my mother's wrist and wrap the cloth around the slice on her finger.

As I'm sitting at breakfast, my father enters the room, standing in his usual place, behind the chair at the head of the table with his hands on the backrest. Without any preamble, he addresses me directly.

"So, Chris, what do you think about nymphomaniacs?"

I look up at him in surprise, uncertain I have heard correctly. He repeats himself, with more than a hint of belligerence.

"What do you think about *nymphomaniacs*? Surely you must agree they're just as bad as rapists?"

He waits for just a moment, looking at me intently. Thankfully, the pause is not quite long enough for me to formulate a response. When he continues, his voice is more relaxed, as though he feels reassured. "Well, of course you do, any sane person would agree, they're just as bad as rapists. That kind of behavior is iniquitous, quite unforgivable. They should be prosecuted to the full extent of the law. Only a fool would think otherwise. Of course you agree, there's nothing to discuss!"

He walks out of the room. I look at my bowl of cereal. Have I imagined the whole conversation? When I decide that it was real, I burst out in guffaws of laughter, very relieved that I have not had to argue the point. Much later, I discover that he believes my brother is sick from exhaustion as a result of dating a woman who is supposedly a nymphomaniac.

Soon after I have established to myself that I am a lesbian—or rather a butch dyke—I have a badge on my car dash that says: *any woman can be a lesbian.* I am not sure about the truth of this, but it is a way of stating that I am very happy to be one.

When I am visiting my parents, my father sees this badge. He smiles, making no comment, which is fine by me. I don't want to discuss my lesbianism with him. I've had enough bad experiences trying to discuss feminism. However, I do want my parents to know that I am not on the lookout for a man, and I want to make it clear that my lesbianism is not something I choose to hide, although when I imagine talking about it, I'm alarmed by the size and solidity of the menacing figure in my mind, blocking my way.

I'm determined not to let a phantom deter me. Cornering my mother in the kitchen when my father is out, I take a deep breath. "Margaret, there is something I want to tell you."

"What's that?" she asks, smiling over her shoulder at me as she pulls a bowl out of the cupboard.

"I'm a lesbian." For a fleeting moment my world goes black, as though the faceless figure inside has devoured me. Then there is a sense of freedom at being on the other side of that-which-forbids-speaking-the-unspeakable.

My mother smiles at me again, completely unfazed. "Yes, we thought you were. Your father saw a badge in your car. Well, whatever you do in bed, that's your affair."

I'm peculiarly dissatisfied with this calm response. It's not that I want her to be upset, but...well, being a lesbian has a great deal more to do with my life than just whom I choose to be sexual with. I suck in my lip, wondering how to express this. "It's not just who I sleep with...I have very little to do with men."

She takes this in her stride. "Oh, lucky you! Men are such stupid creatures, I'd love to have nothing to do with them!"

Now I'm flummoxed. Laughing, I inquire if she would like some help cooking dinner.

What I want to communicate to her is how possible and delightful it is to live without needing men, without requiring their help or their approval, tacit or otherwise. Of course, in spite of her flippant comment, my mother is very attached to getting along with men. Like most women she automatically plays the tune that they, the conductors, ordain. She really doesn't want to think about who she might be if she were not trying to fulfill the socially acceptable roles of wife and mother.

Since I was never happy with that particular identity for myself, it's relatively easy for me to embrace lesbianism. Now I no longer have to try to be something that isn't me. And it opens the way for me to express the agonizing frustration and anger that I have been feeling towards men. Although my intolerance of men sometimes gets me into trouble, it is a great relief to live in a community where it is acceptable to express this.

The label *lesbian* doesn't convey all this. Nor, even, does the label *butch dyke*. I am still an individual, dancing my own wild dance, inventing the steps as I go.

My grandmother has a stroke, and dies a long slow death confined to a hospital bed, her mind completely gone. Although she was a very gentle person, with a deep love of nature, I always felt alienated from her in the same way that I felt alienated from all members of my family when I was growing up. In her state of illness, when it is impossible for us to talk, I find myself feeling closer to her than I would have believed possible. I am afraid of the grief that threatens to overwhelm me on the few occasions when I visit her ailing bedridden body in hospital. It's a relief when my father finally calls to say that she has died. I go to Scotland for her funeral.

While I am there, I take the opportunity to look through some of the piles of letters, photos and documents she has left. My parents have already been through them and got rid of the most interesting, but there is one that grabs my attention. I read the following passage in her journal: "Uncle James had been sick for a long time with a series of strokes, and one evening I was sitting in his bedroom sewing, while he lay sleeping in the bed. Jane sat opposite me, reading a book. All of a sudden, something caught my attention and I looked over at the bed to see several incredible golden beings surrounding James. It was the most beautiful sight I had ever seen, beyond anything words can describe, and at the same time I felt the most powerful sensation of love emanating from them. As I stared, transfixed, Jane leapt up with a cry of alarm. She did not see the beings, and had noticed, before I did, that James was having a stroke, his body twisting in the grip of an awful seizure. The contrast between the beauty I was perceiving and the reality of what was happening to his body was so extreme that I could barely make sense of it.

"It was several weeks before he died, but after that experience, I felt much more at peace about his passing, knowing he was loved and attended by angels."

My grandmother was a woman of the utmost integrity, incapable of deceit. I am forced to believe that this *is* what she saw. Unlike my grandmother, I have never had any interest in religion. But now I understand that there is something beyond physical existence. Although I don't believe in angels, as such, the concept of *light beings* stays with me.

I decide that I should re-connect with my Great Aunt Vera, whom I first met when I was four. I visit her farm where she lives, which she has been running organically for forty years. She is the same as I remember from my childhood: a tall, authoritative figure. Is she a lesbian? I don't know, but several people have told me that I take after her. She is certainly a woman who has claimed her personal power, and she shares my concern for the environment. I'm hoping I will have more in common with her than I do with any other members of my family.

She shows me round the farm, and then we go in for tea.

"So, Chris, what are your plans for the future?" She asks in that deep penetrating voice.

"Well, I suppose I will look for work as a farm mechanic. But I'm not really looking forward to the prospect of working in a male environment."

"I'm sure you'll do fine! You've worked with plenty of men before now, haven't you?"

"Yes...let's just say that the experience of working with men hasn't endeared them to me."

"Well, I've always enjoyed working with men myself, I think men are wonderful!"

The last thing I want is to argue about men. I change the subject, and pretty soon we are talking about other aspects of my life. I've just come from London, and she asks what I was doing there.

"I went to a workshop on class and race. It was run by a friend of mine. She's doing a series of them." Although previous experience makes me hesitant to bring this up with any member of my family, I'm not going to pretend I was doing something else.

"Class? Hmmm...I can't imagine you would find that very useful!" She laughs, with the slightest air of condescension, so that I bristle inwardly. She continues: "Really, class is no longer an issue in this country."

I glance at my watch, thinking it's nearly time for me to go.

Chapter Sixteen

Inspired by an increasing sense of alienation from almost everyone around me, I've been considering moving to the United States for a couple of years. By the time I'm thirty, I'm forced to acknowledge that I will never be acceptably British in any circles. I've heard that there are 30,000 lesbians in the San Francisco Bay Area. Very few of them will know about my upper class upbringing, and perhaps they won't mind if I am not politically correct. So I arrive, with only a backpack and a few hundred dollars to my name, lonely and anxious, but determined.

Another country, another culture, leaving everything familiar behind. As always, things work out. Since there are far more available forests and hills in California than in Britain, an opportunity to move out of the city soon arises. The piece of land I caretake belongs to a woman who lives in San Francisco. She comes up on weekends. The land is beautiful, rolling hills and meadows with a creek flowing seasonally in the valley, and acres of wild woodland. Snakes, deer, raccoons, possums, lizards, foxes, coyotes, bobcats, hawks, owls and turkey vultures share the wilderness with me. There are bears and cougars too, though I rarely see or hear them.

Life is not easy here. Without electricity, everything must be done by hand. A water pump is installed down the hill to provide water to the trailer, which is the only dwelling on the property. The engine that runs the water pump is very temperamental. Sometimes it just won't start. In the summer, when the heat is harsh and unfor-giving, being without running water is not fun. In the winter, when it rains, the road up to the trailer is often impassible.

I love living here. I love getting up in the morning to the silence. I love my huge garden. I love the unspoiled wildness and the lack of artificial light. I enjoy all the physical challenges. Staying busy keeps me from having to feel my feelings, after all. I start a small organic market garden, selling my produce in San Francisco.

Although at first I am pleased to have human visitors, I get dis-illusioned with them. Friends who come to stay, full of enthusiasm for life in the country, quickly become disgruntled with the summer heat or the winter rain, the hard work, the isolation, the lack of amenities, and my short temper. If they would just leave when they find that life in the country doesn't measure up to their ideals, it might be OK. But they don't like to have their ideals shattered. They resent the fact that I am not (apparently) fazed by the difficulties. When they look around for someone to blame, I am the obvious cul-prit.

Impatient though I am with them, I am not impervious to their accusations. Although I like my time alone, I don't like to be hated. I experience a raw ache that is only partially mitigated when the dis-illusioned and angry women depart.

I see an ad in the local paper: *Psychic readings: Caryn McCloskey is an experienced reader who can offer insights and help to clarify life goals.*

I'm desperate. And perhaps the fact that this woman doesn't know me at all will give her a clearer perspective.

She is about my age, but, as I would expect, very different from me: long skirt, long hair, warm friendly brown eyes, with depth and penetration to them.

I sit on the sofa in her office as she settles herself in a chair opposite me. "Do you have specific questions?"

"Well, I've been having a very hard time recently with women who visit the land where I live...and it seems to be a pattern that repeats itself in my life. Whenever things go wrong, I seem to get blamed...I can see some ways that I invite that, but I can't seem to change it."

"OK. I'm going to go into trance and then I'll talk for a while. Feel free to ask questions at the end."

She closes her eyes and breathes deeply. In only a few moments, her eyes flash open and she leans forward. "You're not making good choices for friends. These people are taking advantage of you and then trashing you. You don't have to put up with that, you know. There are good people out there who will love you for who you are, and forgive your failings—perhaps not even see them as failings. You think you have to be perfect, but it's not so. You just have to be you. If you can start believing in yourself, and being kind to yourself, you will attract people who will treat you well. Be discriminating. You don't have to be friends with everyone who wants to be friends with you, or says they do. You don't have to isolate yourself in order to avoid the people you want to avoid, you can just tell them you don't want them in your life. You're entitled to do that, you know."

Hmmm. I've always felt grateful to people who act as though they like me. Can I really afford to be choosey about my friends?

Her eyes flutter shut. "You have some major issues with your father..." she shakes her head slightly, and there is long pause. "Your father controls you in your third chakra." She touches her belly. "He has you corded there and he really doesn't want to let go. He is a very frustrated and unhappy man. I think you know that!"

Her eyes fly open again, and she leans towards me, taking my hands in hers. Now there is an urgency and intensity to her. "You are still living your father's version of reality. He hurt you deeply and then told you that he wasn't hurting you, and you believed him, because you were a little child. You didn't know any better. So you don't know what emotional pain is. But you're *in* pain! It's OK to acknowledge that. You *need* to acknowledge that, in order to heal it. You need to address that pain. And you need help. You also don't know that it's OK to ask for help—that's another thing your father taught you."

I've never had any concept of myself as someone who experiences pain, or is motivated by pain. I have always assumed that the need to push my lovers away, or the constant underlying anger that I work so hard to keep in check, are merely character flaws that I need to overcome. I am functional, after all—at least, I walk around, and get things done.

If there is one person I love and trust in this world it is Nancy. I know that she loves me and even though I have not always been good to her, she thinks I'm wonderful. She says that to me sometimes, her lovely blue eyes crinkled and laughing with pleasure. And I think she is beautiful. I adore the dimples that make her face so very individual, that dance on her cheeks when she smiles.

We were lovers for about a year—no, less, because of course I did my pulling back thing. I didn't want to let go of our closeness even when we weren't sexual any more, and so we still spend a lot of time together. Now that I've moved away to California, she's come to visit me. We're off on a trip together to Death Valley, camping out in the truck. We snuggle and cuddle together, and it feels good. One night we start to kiss, and I suddenly become hyper-aware of what I have always known, that Nancy still feels sexual towards me.

In the same instant I am almost overcome with a fury that takes my breath away and leaves me rigid with tension. I want to kill her. I want to kill Nancy, this woman that I love, because she desires me, even when I know perfectly well that I only need say one word, and she will pull back at once. She's already picked up that I have withdrawn, and she puts her arm around me, a gesture of love to indicate that what she wants most of all is just to be close with me, and she will always be prepared to put her sexual feelings aside if they jeopardize our closeness. I lie motionless next to her, saying nothing, barely breathing. I am afraid of the rage that swirls around inside me. I am afraid of the way it constricts my throat. I am afraid I won't be able to control it. I am afraid of hurting my friend. Most of all I am afraid because I have just realized that this swirling torrent is what I always end up feeling towards the people I am sexual with.

I've kept a tight leash on this rage. More than a leash, I've kept my rage locked up in a dungeon inside myself. No ray of light could filter its way down through the thick layers of cold damp stone. In past relationships with women, I have been bored and sometimes deeply uneasy, and sometimes I have even been vitally aware that I need to do something other than what is being done. I have been very good at slipping out of relationships after a few months, but it's always seemed like there were many good reasons for doing so. It has never occurred to me that the most compelling reason for getting out of a relationship was my potential inability to hide my anger. Most of the time, I have simply not thought about what was choking me, about the beast that was trying to claw its way out from inside.

I've been publicly angry, yes, but there are so many reasons for being angry in a world where so many people are oppressed, that I had my feelings neatly politicized and rationalized. My trust of Nancy lulled me into a sense of safety, and now, my very personal, very politically *in*correct, and completely irrational rage has seized the opportunity to make itself known. As I lie there, acknowledging it for the first time, I'm actually able to look at it without being engulfed. I see that my body is tired of holding this rage inside. It wants to be free of it.

I can no longer pretend it is justifiable. What will I do with it? What will it do with me?

The pump wouldn't start this morning, so we're nearly out of water, and I'm in a bad mood, which is not at all uncommon even when the pump works fine. I walk up the hill with my usual fast stride. One of the ranch visitors is in the trailer cooking breakfast.

"Good morning!" she says cheerfully.

"Morning," I mumble with my back turned. I'm trying to ignore her so that I can get on with things. Then I realize I'm going to need her help. I turn towards her decisively. "I need you to help me lift the pump into the truck."

"Oh, OK! When do you want to do it?"

"Right now." She looks down at her plate of scrambled eggs. I stare at her impassively. The thought of her not getting any breakfast is somehow pleasing to me.

"OK, well...I'll just gulp this down and I'll be right there."

"I'll be waiting outside." I'm vaguely aware that there is something threatening in my tone. I'm not sure she picks it up.

When she's ready, we walk down the hill to the pump. I stride way ahead of her so that she has almost to run to keep up, and she's still slightly behind me. This too, gives me a perverse pleasure.

We arrive at the pump. "Hold this while I undo the bolts," I order, and she obeys me. I quickly undo the four bolts and nearly hit her with the wrench as I spin round to return it to the toolbox. "Sorry," I say. My tone makes it somehow clear that I'm not sorry, and she's the one who should be sorry for getting in my way. "Now you take that end."

We lift together and heave it almost all the way into the bed of the waiting truck, when it catches on a piece of wire. "Lift your end higher!" I command her. She's doing her best, anyone can see that, and she can't quite make it. I shift my body so that I can get a little more purchase, and it slides reluctantly in. We both lean on the tail-gate, panting.

"That thing's heavy!" she exclaims.

"Yes." I force my facial muscles to form a smile. She probably picks up on what I'm thinking, which is: *it's not heavy, you're just weak.*

I drive off without thanking her.

A few weeks later, when fall arrives and I am less busy, I start seeing a therapist who is recommended to me by Caryn, the psychic. My first few visits are agonizing since I have no idea how to talk about myself. Still, the process of healing has begun.

One day when I am visiting San Francisco, I'm walking along Guerrero Street when a man and a woman catch my eye. He's tall, classically good-looking, short dark hair. He's propelling her along the sidewalk at quite a lick, his hand around her upper arm. It's obvious even from a distance that she doesn't want to go with him, although she's not shouting for help. He's staring intently ahead as he strides, not looking at her, though she is talking to him. I trot across the street to intercept them, and when I get closer I can hear her words: "John, leave me alone, I don't want to go, let go of me. John, what are you doing, don't be stupid, come on, let go of me, I don't want to go..." On and on in the same quiet but insistent tone, and he paying no attention, his face set and staring straight ahead.

She's beautiful, not that it matters in the slightest. I concentrate on him, almost running along beside him to keep up. I stay very close to him, and start talking too, looking up at him all the time. "Hey, come on, sonny boy, she doesn't want to go with you, let go of her. There's gonna be trouble, you know, just let go of her. Take your hand off her arm. You're gonna have to let go of her, you know, so you might just as well do it now, she doesn't want to go with you..." and on and on, a little louder than her. He stares grimly ahead, barely even looking right or left as we cross 25th Street. For a whole block we go on like this, me on one side running to keep up, and her on the other dragging back. He never even glances at me, never alters his pace, and his grim expression never changes, but I know he must be aware of me, I am almost brushing his arm as we stride.

By the time we reach 26th Street, I decide more drastic measures are necessary. So I put my hand on his arm, pulling back on him a little. It's pure bluff, since I've had enough training in martial arts to know that I am not likely to be effective in defending myself against someone his size. But it works. In a sudden explosion of energy, he lets go of the woman's arm, and turns on me, his face now twisted in fury. "You fucking dyke bitch, it's none of your business, you stay out of it! I'll fucking teach you a lesson!" As I back away from him and he bears down on me, I see the woman out of the corner of my eye making her way back down towards 25th Street at a very fast walk. I've achieved my objective and now I am going to be turned to pulp. Before I can even register the inevitability of this, my assailant departs, as suddenly as he turned on me, striding furiously away—in the opposite direction from the woman he was so intent on abducting.

I too depart speedily, glancing nervously behind me. My adrenaline carries me several blocks before I slow down, allowing myself to shake. Later it occurs to me that I could have got myself killed. After all, this is America, where people carry guns.

Chapter Seventeen

I'm visiting Scotland, staying with my parents, for the first time in the three years since I moved to California. They both seem quite pleased to see me in their restrained British upper-class fashion, and my father hasn't spent the whole of the last three days haranguing me. He doesn't appear to be obsessed with shaping me into an acceptable member of the upper classes any more.

This is my last evening: tomorrow I'm off to London to fly home. I'm in the sitting room with my father, while my mother's in the kitchen preparing dinner. My father is wandering round the room, drink in hand, reminiscing about my childhood. He seems almost ill at ease, which is unusual. I sense that something's up, and I don't like it.

"You always were so determined to do your own thing, never would listen to anyone else," he says. I feel my body tense.

I try to change the subject by asking about his brother, who lives in London. "How's Uncle John? I haven't seen him in twenty years. Does he ever come up to visit?"

"Oh, he's fine, same old fool," he shrugs off my question. "The trouble with you was you were so convinced that no one else understood you. But we were all just trying to help, you know. You just...well..." He runs his hand through his thinning hair and swills his drink a little more vigorously. He's winding up to something. I make another attempt to avert what I am diagnosing as potential disaster.

"Do you think Margaret's all right in the kitchen on her own? Maybe I should go and help." I start towards the door.

"Now wait a minute, for God's sake, I'm trying to tell you something! Can't you listen for a second?" I know that tone, irritation thinly layered over lashing fury. I turn back to lean against the mantelpiece above the fireplace, the muscles of my face carefully arranged, as he taught me years ago. Anyone watching would assume I was amused and a little bored, certainly not anxious.

"If only we'd had enough money, we'd have sent you to a boarding school in England. I think you'd have done much better...I'm really sorry we didn't do that..." This is an old theme of his. He bumbles on about my childhood for a few minutes more. What *is* he getting at? "And that awful red brick university you went to, that was a big mistake. Great shame you didn't get into Cambridge. You'd have met some good people there, I think."

"I met some good people at York." *Better than any I'd have met at Cambridge*, I think.

"Yes, well...but you get my drift?"

I return his stare blankly, wishing I could say yes, and get this ridiculous conversation over with. "Uh...no."

He snorts, glaring belligerently. "Oh, for God's sake, I'm just trying to say I'm sorry for being such a lousy father!"

I am completely taken aback. In all the thirty-three years I have known this man, he has never apologized for anything, never even admitted he was wrong.

The class system on which he once based so much of his value is crumbling. Is my father learning some humility as a result of losing his standing in the local community?

I decide it's more likely that my mother has been flinging the past in his face.

In spite of his apology, I still don't like being around him. My parents' lives are too weird for me. I don't see them for several more years, then I'm in Britain with Liz, my lover, and we visit for a few days.

Liz's presence helps. She's so very likeable, a good choice in a lover, if what I want is social acceptability. When I'm with her, I am forgiven for things I don't normally get away with.

We're sitting at lunch: the same polished oak dining room table from my childhood, with my father at one end and my mother at the other. My uncle is here, and one of my nephews, John, a handsome and precocious ten-year-old. He's sitting in the place where I sat as a child, on my father's right.

I'm chatting about the garden with my uncle and my mother. My father is annoyed at being ignored. He starts haranguing my nephew, his grandson. I begin to lose track of the conversation with my mother as I watch my father out of the corner of my eye. He's leaning over John with that look on his face, that look I remember so well from my childhood. One bushy eyebrow is raised, giving him that familiar expression of ferocity.

"Come on then, boy, I'll say it one more time. A man is standing looking at a picture, and he says, 'this man's father is my father's son.' Who is the man in the picture? Come on, it's easy, haven't you worked it out yet? What's the matter with you? It's easy, just *think* about it! Use your brain!"

I glance at John. He's cringing a little. The riddle is well known to me, it's one my father tormented me with as a child. I feel a kind of hardness rising up inside me, something with a steel edge to it.

I say to my father, "Oh, for God's sake, you're not still harping on about that stupid riddle, are you?" He stops and looks at me, a little surprised. Without waiting for him to recover, I turn to John with a smile and say, "Don't bother your head trying to work out the answer, it isn't worth your while thinking about!"

From the end of the table my, mother pipes up, "It's himself, isn't it?"

My father was poised to deliver some crushing remark in my direction, but now he turns on her with scorn. "Oh for God's sake, woman, no, it's not! Good God, haven't you got a brain in your head? It's his son! He's looking at his son!"

He hasn't changed at all. The hard edge inside me slices through everything. "Don't be such a bully! You and your stupid riddle! I don't want to hear any more about it!" I meet his eyes, my face carefully set in a casually amused smile. I turn away to continue the conversation with my mother.

Out of the corner of my eye I see him raise the eyebrow again, and he directs his next comment at me. "You! You're such a humbug! Just because you couldn't work it out, you won't let anyone else have a go! You're such a humbug!"

I get up to help myself to some soup from the side-table. He continues to harass me, saying I'm a humbug again and again.

I feel the hard edge of steel filling up my body, leaving no space for anything else. I put down my plate as I turn towards him. Our eyes meet, the steel glinting in mine.

"That's enough," I say, interrupting the flow of abuse. I turn away just as his eyebrows rise up together in surprise.

There is a brief pause, long enough for me to take a ladelful of soup. Then he says, "Honestly! How did I manage to beget such a humbug for a daughter?"

Before the sentence is done, I have turned back towards him. This time I feel the surge of cold unforgiving steel flow down my arms, out of my hands. I know that if he continues, I will hit him. Now I raise my voice, just a little. "I said, that'll do!"

Again the commanding tone makes his eyebrows fly up. I wait, looking at him. The steel has filled my mind. I will do whatever it takes to silence him. Will he dare to continue? Clearly taken aback, he pauses for a few seconds. Then he opens his mouth again, to say, "What's the matter, can't you—"

Steel pours out of me, filling the room. I take a single step forward, one finger raised, pointing at him. "Shut up."

I am aware of the taut electricity, everything stretched out and still in this moment of truth when my refusal to allow his abuse meets his refusal to be silenced. He stares at me blankly before looking down at his plate, rubbing his head and muttering under his breath.

I turn away to pick up my soup bowl, walking back to the table. Realizing that everyone else is sitting very rigid, staring at their plates, I'm suddenly alarmed.

"This is very good soup, Margaret," I say in a hearty tone. Without looking around, I feel the atmosphere relax. I glance at my mother. Will she be angry? Though her face maintains its now habitual tension, her mouth forms into the smile she has been wearing for years.

"I'm so glad you like it," she says. Then she leans forward and adds, in a conspiratorial tone, "You shouldn't let him get to you, you know!" Her false smile broadens, outlining the strained facial muscles. I experience a flicker of anxiety. What parts of herself has she had to destroy in order to be able to maintain that smile? What price has she paid for pretending he doesn't get to her? Why didn't she leave him when there was still time for her to reclaim herself?

Chapter Eighteen

I didn't really fancy her when I first met her. It's often like that for me, I meet someone and I don't see her as attractive until I start to get to know her. Gradually a rapport develops between us, and suddenly there's sexual tension that slices the air. I love it, that zing passing like a current of warm sweetness between me and another woman. The warmth in my belly when I think about her. The certainty of being wanted. The knowledge of our mutual power, and its possibilities. The game of to and fro, yes, no and maybe, sometime; never spoken, even if verbally acknowledged. In reality it's not something that can be spoken, it's a body language.

She meets Liz and me in the spring, before Liz leaves to spend the summer in Europe. Someone told her I had horses, so she suggests we ride together. It's great for me to have someone to ride with. When Liz leaves to spend the summer in England, Rosie and I start spending more time together. I figure out pretty quickly that she is interested in me, but I know she won't push it because she doesn't want to jeopardize her friendship with Liz. She is the kind of woman who would see it as unethical to pursue a romantic interest in someone who is already attached. Liz is that kind of woman too. I'm not sure what kind of woman I am: I believe that our intellects are frequently unwise advisors, and what the body desires is not to be lightly denied. And I am not at all sure that monogamous relationships are a preferable option.

One day she turns to me as she's getting into the car to leave, saying shyly, "You know I'm very attracted to you, don't you?"

She makes a slight movement with her shoulders as she says it, that indicates her embarrassment and makes me want to put my arms around her. I say, smiling, "Yeah, I'd kinda picked that up."

"Well, I just want to let you know that I know nothing's going to come of it, and that's fine by me. I would never want to mess with your relationship with Liz."

I nod seriously. "Yes, my relationship with Liz is really important to me." I don't choose this moment to tell her that Liz and I have an agreement to leave our relationship open while we are several thousand miles apart.

She smiles, more relaxed now it's out in the open. "OK, well, I'm glad I said something anyway. I didn't want it to be a big thing between us. I'll see you next week. Take care."

We continue to go riding together once a week. One day we are riding along together, when she suddenly breaks into a canter. The next moment we are flying along beside each other, our horses vying for the lead, veering around the bends in the trail, racing neck and neck. It's one of those truly exhilarating rides, when you feel completely in tune with your horse, like you're a part of her. Finally slowing to a walk, we are both laughing with pure joy.

"Hey, that was great! We should do that more often!" I say gleefully.

"Yes, we should," Rosie grins back at me over her shoulder. And watching her slight form astride the horse just ahead of me, I suddenly realize that I want to kiss her and stroke her skin. I want to feel her moaning and moving under my hands.

So that's the beginning of it for me. From then on I think about her almost constantly, imagining her body naked next to mine, taking her face between my hands, running my tongue gently over her skin, sliding my hands down her sides and over her breasts...and so on. I try not to think about it too graphically, because I really don't want to get involved with her. Not just because an affair with her might be a problem when Liz returns, but also because I know Rosie well enough by now to know that a relationship between us wouldn't work. She is too dependent, she would want too much of me, and I would begin to hate her, as I have so many of my lovers in the past. I would end up pushing her away, and she would feel hurt, and that would enrage me, and the more I pushed her away the more she would try to get close to me. She is too sweet for me. She doesn't have a tough edge.

Knowing this in my head makes no difference at all to my body's desire, which grows daily. It is soon sweet agony to have to keep her at a distance. Not for the first time, my head and the rest of my body are in disagreement about the correct course of action. I go to sleep thinking of her and wake up thinking of her, imagining how she would feel to my fingers, how she would respond when we kissed, how her body would dance to my touch, how her voice would sing to our lovemaking.

Scared that it will reinforce them, I don't talk to Rosie about my feelings. I fight my desire with every weapon I know. I hold those disobedient muscles taut to stop them jumping when I watch her move, or when she touches me. I refuse to let the goose bumps rise on my skin. I rein in my desire with gritted teeth, and keep myself very busy with practical things. I give myself sternly worded pep talks.

Nothing works. The truth is, my body loves to feel this way.

One day when I've been over at her place and I am getting ready to go home, I say, "It's getting harder and harder to leave you."

She makes a face, and puts her arms around me, saying, "Yes, it is. I wish you could stay. But..." she steps back, shrugging, "this is the way it has to be."

"Yeah." I agree unenthusiastically. "It does have to be this way. But I don't like it." And I leave, feeling very bad tempered.

Things don't get any better. I begin to feel like we might as well be lovers anyway. We are spending more and more time together. I know that my desire will probably subside faster if I indulge it than if I deny it. I consider not seeing her at all. But that, I know, will make me feel angry with Liz, because I'd only be doing it for her, and it would make me very miserable. Anger is not a logical emotion.

Rosie and I go to a concert together. The music is excellent and leaves me feeling very high, bouncing with life. At the intermission,

I want to kiss Rosie so badly that I can't even look at her. She is staying at my place tonight, because driving back to her house would be
too far, too late. I know that I won't be able to sleep a wink with her
nearby, and I certainly wouldn't be able to keep my hands off her if
we were sleeping in the same bed. All through the second half of the
concert I am strategizing busily in my head. Not about how to stay
away from her, I have pretty much given up on that. Not about how
to seduce her. That, I know, will be easy. I am fretting about how to
deal with the situation when Liz returns. She is due back in eight
weeks. Could Rosie and I have just one night together? Two nights?
A week? Two weeks? Eight weeks?

I sit on my hands, hardly looking Rosie in the eye, except for
sideways grins, until we get in the car to go home. I am driving, and
fortunately it is a nice straight empty stretch of road, because I don't
pay much attention to it. I still haven't decided what I am going to
do, but I've dismissed the idea that one night might be enough.

We talk about the concert for a while, and then I say, "Rosie. I
think we ought to have an affair."

She turns to look at me, laughing, and flicks a strand of hair off
her forehead with her hand, a movement that seems indescribably
sexy to me. I can see her eyes gleaming in the darkness. The muscles
of my sex ache so badly it hurts. "Well, you know I want that...but
what about Liz? I really don't want to do anything that would hurt
her."

"Well, here's my idea. It's eight weeks until she comes home.
We could have an affair for six weeks, and make an agreement right
now that we'll stop sleeping together two weeks before Liz returns."
I know myself well enough to figure that my passion will probably
run its course in six weeks. Her passion for me might last forever if
I let it. Is this discrepancy my concern? I am concerned about it,
since I really don't want to hurt her. On the other hand, she is an
adult, she can make her own decisions.

I glance over at her. She's staring straight ahead, running her
fingers up and down the seat belt. I swallow.

"How do you think she'll feel about that?" She asks.

"Since it would be over before she knew about it, she wouldn't
have any say. She might be a little pissed, but we agreed before she

left that we were both free agents. And it's quite possible she's having an affair over there. She mentioned she was going away for the weekend with Karen in her last letter. She's never mentioned anyone called Karen before, so that was a little suspicious. Anyway, she'll get over you and me."

"Hmmm..."

"I don't know about you, but I don't think I can sleep in the same house as you and keep my hands off your gorgeous body."

She laughs again, and shivers run down my spine. I try to concentrate on the road, but the idea of touching her has risen from belly to throat, and I can hardly draw a breath. One thing keeps going through my mind: *I'm not going to be able to get all the way home without kissing you, I'm not going to be able to get all the way home without kissing you, I'm not going to be able to get all the way home without*...I try to pull myself together but I am dizzy with exhilaration, and my resistance is worn down to a bare thread. I know that this is going to be a kiss in a million, it will be tender and deep and long and orgasmic, and her lips will be soft as silk, and she will taste as sweet as the sweetest nectar, and we will both die a long slow delightful death in the endless moment when our lips touch. I am going to pull over to the side of the road, and I am going to undo my seat belt and lean over towards her, and take her face in my hands and...I blink and blink again, trying to breathe. My body is already in ecstasy, because it knows it has won over my mind, and the rushes of joy radiate all the way to my toes and my fingertips so that my skin feels electric and I think I am floating several inches above the seat.

I don't know how far I have driven. We don't talk any more, although my mind is scolding me, saying that I really should negotiate with her some more about all this, because once we kiss, it's a done deal—I know that as a certainty—and she is the one who stands to get hurt, not me. But I can't make my vocal chords work. And anyway...I know she will agree to anything I want. I am beyond any moral reasoning, and way too unsure that it is a moral issue anyway.

I can feel my heart beating, regular and calm, strangely clear. A bead of sweat rolls from my armpit down my side under my shirt. It feels gloriously sensual.

At some point I begin to slow down—perhaps not on purpose, maybe my foot just won't keep the accelerator depressed. When I realize we are only going at about forty miles an hour, I turn onto the hard shoulder and apply my foot successfully to the brake. We come to a halt. Rosie looks at me, a little surprised.

"Is something the matter?"

I don't trust myself to answer her question. Pulling the emergency brake on, I switch off the engine. I undo my seatbelt, and lean over to her. The electricity thrums through my body.

I take her face in my hands.

My passion wanes in a timely fashion, as I guessed it would. It's replaced by the rage that I have always previously denied. Now that I am gingerly allowing myself to feel my feelings, my rage is unpleasantly visible, at least to me. Although I still have some control over the way it expresses itself, the clarity of its intensity appalls me.

You want me to tell the truth about my feelings? You want to know about my desire to destroy you, to take your body and tear it apart until there are no more recognizable parts anywhere, just blood and pieces of torn flesh, just blood dripping red, and the edges of flesh splayed out, ripped? You think I love you? Oh how laughable! I loathe you, the smell of you makes me cringe with hatred, the sight of you makes my lips curl with scorn.

I have already destroyed you, on an energy level. I take your mind, using words to twist your comprehension of reality, and then I use my body to make you desire me so that you lose touch with your rational mind. This is the power of sex, of the body's desire. This is what happens when people fall in love. Love is an ugly sham, it's a con, and we are con-people, tricksters, those of us who play the game called love.

You think you don't know about the game, but you too are playing it. I know that you want to reach inside me, seeing all that is there, so that you can use it and mold it and ultimately destroy me. Saying you love me immediately alerts me to the fact that you have decided that I am the one who will be your slave, your savior, the one who will die for you. If I allow it, eventually you will suck the life out of me until I am a desiccated shell, and you are full and fat.

The wild beast inside me will never allow that. It needs to play this game, delighting in the hunt. I keep my beast well hidden. If it could be seen in all its ugliness— its pointed teeth dripping with saliva, so desperate to taste blood, lips bared and snarling, eyes glowing with hatred— if this beast was visible, no one would be foolish enough to come near me.

Once the game has lost its charm, then I want it to be over quickly, I want to stop messing around and go straight in for the kill. When your body is strewn to the four winds, just a few pieces of bone and drops of blood remaining at my feet, I will dance a dance of victory, singing my pleasure over your departure, your gone-ness, the nothing of you that is all that is left.

If you only would go when it's time to end the game, you might avoid some of the pain. I have even tried to warn you, as I feel the head of my fierce beast rising from its den, uncontainable any longer, howling with hunger, desperate to feed, straining at its feeble leash, eager for the taste of your blood. You aren't wise enough to depart until long after it is too late, long after I know the leash will not hold.

Maybe the truth is I have spun the web that entraps you. I have spun it carefully and skillfully so that you cannot choose to leave, because I must feed the beast.

I grew up ensnared in someone else's web, knowing each moment that I might die in this web, that I was at the whim of the web makers, who were all around me. So now I spin my own web in return. I am sorry that you must die for them, it surely wasn't your fault that they did that to me. But they did, and now someone must pay.

The beast was bred and raised with the knowledge of the joy of the taste of blood. Now that I am adult, it is also adult, and it has adult tastes, and must be fed. The judgment is already made, the payment must be exacted. Love is a fantasy invented by the makers of the game, to make the game more fun, to give it intricacies, to confuse the players.

This monster is my life force, after all. Her fierceness nourishes me. Sometimes I must unleash her, and let her have her way.

Chapter Nineteen

Dealing with my stuff is hard work. Now I'm becoming aware of the fear that is underneath the rage. I'm driving along, thinking busily, when I suddenly realize that I'm in a state of anxiety. I'm afraid I'll be late, or I'll forget something, or...whatever. My mind is capable of finding many excuses for being uptight, and it always believes if only I can just fix whatever it is that I'm currently worrying over, then everything will be all right. Believing that for years, I got very good at fixing things. When I stop long enough to feel what is real, I am sometimes afraid I'm going to die any minute.

In this moment, in my life as an adult, there's nothing to watch out for, nothing to be late for, no schedule but my own that I have to stick to, no one but me to be upset if things don't go right. I have worked hard to set my life up like this. Yet I can't enjoy it, because my child-mind doesn't believe it's safe. That child part of me is convinced that I have to be in absolute control of everything around me all the time.

Or I'm preparing to go out and I feel weighted down with lead, because I am afraid of being seen. Sometimes it requires every ounce of willpower I have to walk into a room full of people, when I have no logical reason at all to be afraid of any one of them.

So I get to the place of remembering. It goes like this: I've been seeing Sue every couple of weeks for several months. I really like Sue—she's a deeply compassionate, intuitive and gifted therapist.

She takes me on guided journeys, and has me do breathing techniques that put me in touch with those feelings I so desperately want to be on the other side of.

I hate this. I have to lie down and breathe, let what comes up come up, and not push it away. I have to feel what I'm feeling. Yuck. The part of me that is the watcher sits to one side making sarcastic remarks and trying to involve me in what I'm going to be doing tomorrow, which won't be what I am doing right now.

Unpleasant things come up when I'm lying there. Hard to say what they really are: mostly rage, and fear, and something absolutely un-nameable, unthinkable, which might be terror. I grind my teeth and clench my jaw and sweat and moan and roll around on Sue's blanketed floor, trying to escape.

In spite of all my resistance, clear pictures sometimes form: of my mother, or my father, or the most common picture of all, a raised clenched fist, and blood, red blood flowing and flowing. The image of blood gives me some sense of satisfaction. The blood is what I want. I want to make blood flow. I want to lash out, I want to be the fist, the propeller of the fist, the power behind it. I am terrified of being the helpless recipient of that fist, smashing into my face, making my blood flow, distorting my already distorted face.

Sometimes I have images of the house where I lived till I was six. These images are always shrouded in a strange mist, like they are out of a horror movie. Over the months I've been working with Sue, I've come to think that maybe something bad happened in that house, something I have never remembered, which set the tone for the rest of my life.

Today a specific image is clear and eerie: it's the image of a man's upper body, naked, thick and solid and powerful, with coarse black hair. The *me* in this picture is very small: I say hesitantly, in answer to Sue's query, maybe three or four. The man seems very big and he's pressing down on the little me. Sue asks if I have any idea who the man might be. I shake my head. Certainly not my father's body, he doesn't have thick black hair. Not Tom, since I can't imagine any occasion when he would have been naked with me. Not Mr. Cockburn since there was only that one occasion with him, and neither of us were naked, and I was much older.

I go home feeling distant and anxious. I want to know who the man is, yet I don't have any way of finding out. Anyway I don't really believe any of this stuff. Surely it was enough to have been molested by two men.

This is all going on at a period in my life when Liz is away for months at a time. Tonight I am on my own. I sleep deeply and wake in the morning remembering nothing of my dreams. At the moment of awakening, there is a single word in my mind: Alec. I lie in bed staring at the ceiling, rolling the name around my mind.

Alec is a small stocky Scotsman with a mass of black curly hair and a Scottish brogue. A photographer who works with my father on his books, he soon becomes a friend of the family, a regular visitor who often stays the night. He loves children. He rarely arrives without sweeties or some little trinket for us. When we hear his car pull up in the driveway, my sister and I run to meet him, and he scoops my four-year-old body into his arms to carry me into the house.

To begin with, I am always delighted to see him, delighted to find a grownup who will play with us. Alec gives me piggy backs, running around on the lawn with my little body attached to his back, my short arms pinned around his neck and my skinny little-girl legs wrapped around his waist, bouncing to and fro, and screaming with elation, until he unlaces my clamped fingers, panting and laughing, and lets me slide to the grass. He throws me up, and stands below me with his arms outstretched, as I soar through the air, breathless and thrilled, until he catches me deftly, his hands under my armpits breaking my fall. He swings me in circles, gripping one wrist and one ankle, while I squeal with elation to feel myself flying, everything whirling unforgivingly around me. Then he gently sets me down, and I fall helplessly about on the cold grass, my legs like water.

He never tells me to be quiet and behave myself like most adults do. He is never angry with me, he never tells me off. I adore him.

In the evenings when it is my bedtime, and my older sister is allowed to stay up longer, he makes it bearable for me being sent to bed by carrying me upstairs and telling me bedtime stories. He sits by me when I am in the bath and makes sure I wash all the appro-

*priate places. He helps me to pull on my pajamas, and reads to me
as I lie in bed.*

*As the hands that hold and tickle me begin to wander to parts
of my body that I am not used to having touched, I become uneasy,
though I am also intrigued by how it feels. Alec reassures me. This is
a game that people who love each other play, he says, it is a very
special game, that he will only play with me. It is our little secret and
I shouldn't tell anyone else. It's fun, he says, and when I frown, he
tells me not to be so silly. And he laughs, to show me that everything's fine. I decide that if he thinks it's OK, it must be OK, because
he loves me. I try to ignore my anxiety.*

*One of the initial results of Alec's interest in my body is that I
become intrigued by what is down there between my legs. So one
day, as I am playing in the bath, I investigate that part of my body.
It does feel kinda good. When Nanny comes in to get me ready for
bed, and sees what I am doing, she is outraged. "What do you think
you are doing, you dirty little girl! Don't you ever let me see you
doing that again! That's dirty!" She slaps my hands away, hauling
me unceremoniously out of the bath.*

*I make one shot at defending myself. "Alec touched me down
there when I was saying my prayers," I protest, trying to squirm out
of her grasp.*

*Immediately I realize I have made a mistake, but it is too late.
Her eyes get big, and her mouth drops open. Then both her eyes and
mouth get very small and tight. She puts her face close to mine as
she hisses, "You are a very bad girl! Don't you ever tell stories like
that again! You need a good spanking, and that is exactly what you
are going to get!"*

*She drags me to my room to administer the spanking with thin-
lipped fury.*

*Now I know that Alec was right when he said not to tell anyone.
He doesn't seem to be as afraid of Nanny as I am; he continues to
touch me down there. One night, when the house is still and dark, I
wake groggily from a deep sleep to feel the smell and warmth of him
hovering over me, his alcoholic breath hot on my face, as he whispers, "Hello poppet, it's only me. Stay quiet, we mustn't wake anyone."*

Sliding under the bedclothes next to me, he holds me very tightly against the length of his big hairy body. His hand makes its way under my pajamas and fiddles between my legs, like he's done before, but now there is a clumsiness and an urgency to his movements that scares me. I begin to whimper, and he quickly leans over me so that my face is scrunched against his hairy chest, and I can barely breathe, much less make a sound. Then his hard body begins to rub and push with an intensity that grows and grows. He is panting into the pillow, crushing me against the bed, driven by some force far more powerful than me. I think I will die.

After one long shudder, he lies still, breathing hard. I am able to drag air into my lungs, and I begin to sob. Immediately he puts his hand over my mouth and I hear his words in my ear: "Shhhh, it's all right, don't cry, you must be quiet!"

I am silent, afraid now of his disapproval. As his breathing returns to normal, he whispers, "Now, you mustn't tell anyone about this, OK? Or you'll get into trouble!"

He slowly lifts himself off me. I stare up at the faint outline of his face in the gloom, waiting for some comfort. What has just happened? What is wrong with him? He glides out of the room into the darkness.

He comes back the next weekend, and the weekend after that, and the weekend after that. As soon as he arrives, I remove myself to the ceiling of the room, becoming very familiar with the pattern of the wallpaper. Before he leaves, he always whispers, "Now, remember, this is our secret! If you tell anyone, they'll be very angry!"

I believe him. Clearly, the world is a dangerous place, where no one can be trusted.

I tell Nanny I don't like him any more and she tells me not to be so silly.

Gradually, as the weeks and then the months pass, I stop running to meet him when he arrives, and I scream when he wants to carry me upstairs to bed. My parents are angry with me for making a scene.

For a period of weeks, I have trouble differentiating present day reality from my past reality. The form this takes is an extreme wariness of the people around me.

Liz, who has just come back from a trip to Europe, bears the brunt of it. Every morning I jump out of bed and make myself very busy, so she won't notice I am avoiding her. If she notices, she will want an explanation and I am terrified of having to explain myself.

I am constantly suspicious of her. I am sure she is going to ask me to do things I don't want to do. When she asks me the simplest question, like, "Shall I buy some bread?" I suspect some underlying motive. I wait for her to make demands and accusations. As the day wears on and she treats me lovingly, asking for nothing in return, I lower my defenses and by the evening, I am feeling almost warm towards her. Then we go to sleep, and in the morning the cycle begins again, as though the bitter and mistrustful child has taken over while I slept.

She has given up asking me to talk about my feelings, but she does ask me why I am being so guarded. I'm surprised. I hadn't realized I was being that way. It seemed there was no other way to be, and it requires great effort to imagine being any other way. I hesitantly acknowledge that I may feel guarded. I cannot explain why, and when she questions me further, I stare out of the window in intense discomfort. I simply cannot find words, cannot make words come out of my mouth, cannot relate words to the reality of what I am feeling. I just want her to leave me alone to think about the shed I am building.

One morning when, once again, I react belligerently to some innocent suggestion on her part, she looks me straight in the eye, directly engaging me, and saying very calmly, "Chris, I'm not your enemy."

What a novel concept. A wave of powerful energy washes through me as I stare at her, digesting this vital piece of information.

Something inside falls away.

I dream that I'm at my parents' house, where I grew up. I'm looking for something, the thing that I have been wanting for so long that I hardly know it's missing any more. I'm drawn to the aviary where Pablo the pigeon lived for one summer. When I go to look, I see a golden glow, and there—right there in the aviary—is a huge pile of priceless treasure.

Visits to Britain have become a two-yearly event, and I generally stay with my parents for three or four days. They always seem happy to see me. They try to make me feel at home, and don't purposefully bring up any difficult subjects. Although we still disagree on everything important, we manage to make an appearance of getting along for a short period.

There was a time when I wanted only to obliterate the past, but now that I perceive how much it holds me, I'm interested in ferreting out some truth. I'm trying to elicit my parents' help. Alas, they have very mangled and selective memories. Today I'm chopping onions in the kitchen for my mother, and my agenda is Alec.

"Margaret, I was just thinking about Alec Brown the other day. How did you get to know him?" I turn round to look at her, and she puts down the dishcloth she's holding, leaning back against the stove, folding her arms over her chest.

"Oh yes, Alec Brown. Nice young chap. He was a photographer, helped your father with several of his books. He lived in Edinburgh. He loved you three, he used to take you out all the time." Her eyes widen a little as the memories fall into place. "You adored him."

"Did he stay often?"

"Yes, he often spent the night. He had long photo sessions out on the shoot with your father and the dogs. Goodness me, that was a long time ago. Why were you thinking about him?"

"Oh, I was just trying to remember living at Gleninnes. My memories of that time are so vague. What happened to Alec? Why aren't you in touch with him any more?"

"Oh, I don't remember what happened to him. I have no idea where he is now. He just stopped visiting and we lost touch...actually he was pretty messed up." She lowers her voice a little and her lips purse. "You know, I think he was probably homosexual."

Despite the fact that my mother knows I am a lesbian, and shows no apparent disapproval of me, she frequently refers to homosexuals in a very disparaging fashion. This time I don't trust myself to pursue it, though I wonder what made her think that about Alec.

Later, I try again on a related subject. We're in the kitchen, which is the only place where my father isn't constantly present. I've just finished washing up. "Margaret, do you remember me telling you about Tom when I was about six years old?"

She looks puzzled. "What about Tom? Old Tom McFarlane, you mean?"

"Yes. He used to put his hand down my pants."

Now she's shocked. "Tom McFarlane? How awful! My God, I'm so sorry! I didn't know anything about it!"

"You don't remember me telling you?"

"No, I don't remember! Really, Chris, I'm so sorry!" She crosses her arms over her chest, that familiar protective gesture. Her face is the picture of shocked distress. "I'm so sorry! Really, I don't know..." she shakes her head as though to rid herself of the image, then she turns away and takes a jar down off the shelf. Not looking at me any more, she says, "Really, I'm afraid we weren't very good parents."

I don't want to get into this. I'm not interested in her guilt. I say, "It wasn't your fault," and then I wonder if I really believe that. We discuss what we will have for dinner.

Visiting my Aunt Kay is a pleasure. She is beautiful, with her shining white hair and her small round face, twinkling eyes set in ever deeper wrinkles of laughter. How has she managed to maintain such a zest for life when my mother, her sister, seems to perceive living only as a chore? She gives me a warm hug. "Oh darling, it's so wonderful to see you! Come in, let's put the kettle on, and then we'll sit down and have a cup of tea, and you can tell me all your news!"

So we do. I tell her some of what's going on in my life. (Even my aunt doesn't get to hear it all). Soon we get round to discussing my parents. She and her husband Frank recently stayed with my parents for New Year.

"I don't know what we were thinking, it was a terrible mistake, and we'll certainly never do it again," she says with a rueful smile. "As soon as midnight struck, we set off to go first footing. Have you met the Grindells?" I shake my head. "They're the people who own Easthaugh now—I don't know them well, but they seem nice enough. So we went into the sitting room, and there was another couple, and of course we're all hanging around with drinks, very boring really, though I did have an interesting conversation with one

of the women. Anyhow, Arthur was standing around drinking, looking at the pictures on the wall, some kind of landscape by some
famous artist or other, and there were various little eats on the table,
including a bowl of walnuts. So he picked up a walnut and said to
Frank, 'Do you know that if you throw a walnut at a framed picture,
the walnut will crack open without breaking the picture glass?' So
Frank said, 'Oh, come on, Arthur, don't be silly, of course it will break
the glass!' Well, you know what Arthur's like, he threw the walnut at
the picture to prove his point, and the glass broke. Well, that was bad
enough, I was so embarrassed. He was very apologetic, and helping—
or pretending to help—our poor hostess clean up the glass, but then,
you'll never believe it—well, you probably will, since you know
him—he said to Frank, 'That's extraordinary, there must have been
something wrong with that walnut!' And he did it again! I was so mor-
tified, I couldn't wait to get out of there. I couldn't very well pretend
I didn't know him, but I certainly wanted to!"

When we have both stopped laughing, she says, "Really, he is
an extraordinary man."

"Yes," I nod. "And a difficult one to grow up with."

"Surely you didn't take him seriously?"

I look at her questioning face, full of character accentuated by
middle age creases. "Well, yes. He was my father. Of course I took
him seriously."

"Oh...yes...yes, of course you did." She tightens her lips, staring
out of the window.

I bring up the subject that's uppermost on my mind. "Kay, did
you visit us often when we were living at Gleninnes?"

"No, not really, I wasn't very close with your family at that
time. Arthur was so overbearing and he was always being rude about
Father. And although I loved to see you and your brother and sister,
I really didn't like the way you were treated. I didn't like Nanny at
all. Not at all." Her brow creases into disapproving lines. "Your parents loved her, of course, because she did manage to keep you all in
order."

"Why didn't you like her? How long was she with us?"

"Well, let me see...she must have lived with you for about four
years, because I think she came when you were about one, and then

she left just before you moved from Gleninnes, and that was when you were five. Or six, maybe, I'm not sure. I didn't like her because I thought she was far too strict with you. She was into corporal punishment. I don't think young children need to be hit. She hit you far too often. I really disapproved. Your parents never made any attempt to prevent it."

Her face is set in anger now. She turns away to attend to something on the stove, and there is a moment's silence. I don't remember being hit, only occasionally spanked, by my father as well as Nanny. But then, I don't remember much about that house. Vague shadowy recollections of Alec's body, a pervasive sense of fear. No, more than fear, a sense of horror.

There is something specific that I want to know. "Kay, where was my bedroom in relation to Elizabeth's?"

"Your room was next to Nanny's at the end of the corridor, and you had to go through Nanny's room to get to your sister's. When you got to the head of the stairs, Grandpa's room was on your right, then the bathroom, then the guest room, then your parents' room, then yours, then Nanny's, then Elizabeth's. David's was downstairs."

As she speaks, a perfect map of the layout forms in my mind. Yes, I remember climbing those stairs with the red patterned carpet, my short legs stretching to make each step in one. The polished wooden banister rail, taller than me, and far too wide for my little hand to go around. I remember the stool in the bathroom flying from under my little feet and my chin splitting open as it hit the sink. I remember running through Nanny's room into my sister's. I remember leaning on my bed with my eyes closed and my hands clasped in front of me, saying my prayers. I remember hands behind me reaching under my nightie as I knelt there...I remember Alec's cajoling voice with his broad Scottish burr...

And now I understand why Elizabeth's experience of our childhood might have been so different from mine. An accident of geography made her less accessible.

I bring myself back into the present. My aunt is talking. "Why are you asking about Gleninnes?" Her brow is still furrowed though her voice is no longer angry.

I take a deep breath. "Do you remember Alec Brown?"

She purses her lips, looking off into the corner. "Alec Brown...wasn't he a photographer? Yes, I think I met him once."

"I recently had a memory of him coming into my room at night."

"He came into your room at night? You mean, to molest you?" She looks horrified and her tone is indignant. "Oh my God, Chris, how horrible! Did he do that often or was it only once?"

"I'm fairly certain it happened a number of times."

"What triggered you to remember it?"

I talk a little about being in therapy, about working with Sue. "She's really a wonderful woman. You know, about fifteen years ago I remembered being molested by Tom McFarlane. He used to put his hand down my pants when we were visiting him."

"He did? My God, what a nasty old man. What a horrible thing. Well, but you know, it doesn't totally surprise me. He was always putting his hand on my knee when he was teaching me to drive. I really had to push him off a few times, he was very insistent. And, you know, that was bad enough, but then he did the most incredible thing, I can't believe how inappropriate this was..." she pauses, her eyes very wide, "he actually came on to Mother a few times!"

I almost laugh.

She carries on. "You know, Father had a theory that it was TV. It never started happening until he was retired, and then he used to just sit and watch those sexy women on TV all the time. I think it completely turned his head. He couldn't handle it. Because, you know, he never did any of that stuff before. He was a model employee."

I shift uneasily in my chair, realizing I've been holding myself quite rigid. I want to change the conversation. "Well, you know, an awful lot of children are molested. It's very common."

Pausing in her vigorous stirring of some dinner dish, my aunt looks at me earnestly. "Well, some children do make up stories in order to get attention. They really do."

Chapter Twenty

oday I cut down a tree for my friend Jill: a huge old madrone, three or four feet in diameter, its magnificent gnarled limbs reaching upwards, heavy with thick green foliage hiding the deep red-orange bark.

I start with a V on the downward side of the oblong trunk, cutting into it unforgivingly with my saw, the ear protectors tight over my ears, insulating me into a world where there is only me and the saw and the tree, the roar of the saw surrounding me and holding me, the feel of it thrumming in my fingers, the muscles of my neck and arms aching as I hold it tenaciously in place, cutting down at an angle through the wood, slicing out the life of several hundred years, the chips flying down around me, filling my boots and the cuffs of my pants. Not dust, but chips of wood, little neat chips diced mercilessly by the chain that I keep so sharp that sometimes I feel like I am cutting through a big chunk of butter. The vibrating machine draws me into the wood, into the heart of the tree, into the center of the life I am destroying.

I finish one arm of the V, and as I adjust my hold on the saw, the engine dies. I put my foot through the handle to hold it in place, while I give the starter rope a determined tug. The little engine roars to noisy life immediately. Inwardly I smile. I'm always pleased that the saw will start like that for me. Years of working with engines of various kinds has left me with a deep appreciation of the miracle of metal moving inside metal, fired by a fuel that gives it dangerous power, and all attached to some kind of mechanism that enables me to utilize it to defy what is natural: to cut a tree, to pump water against gravity, to go somewhere at remarkable speeds, to charge a battery, to produce electricity. I know what magic this is, I don't take it for granted. I know that the metal is working with me when it lets me start it up like this. I know that the three women watching would not have the touch to do this. I have worked to earn the magic of this touch, I have sweated and cried and bled to earn this privilege. This is my saw, it answers to me, and works with me, and I know how to relate to it to get what we both need. Occasionally women will remark how impressed they are at my handling of it, and then I glow with pride, though I try to hide my pleasure. To gloat would be to court being taken down a peg. I won't invite that.

I am always jealous of my older sister. She is beautiful and charming, finds it easy to say the right thing, never asks awkward questions, and is normally sweet and helpful. Photos of our child-hood usually show her with a wide glowing smile, while I stand to one side, glaring or frowning with a concentration that seems to say, if only I try hard enough, surely I will be able to understand. *I never do understand, while my sister apparently never has to try.*

Today I have made the mistake of boasting to my sister that I am better at schoolwork than her. I only say this in response to some remark that she has made concerning the fact that I rarely clean up my side of our shared bedroom. Hurt, she runs off crying and tells my father. He comes up to our bedroom where I am sitting at the table doing my homework. I listen with dread to his big feet clumping up the stairs. I'm shrinking inside. He opens the door, filling the space of the doorway. I glance up and quickly look away. His expression is one of complete disdain, his lips set into a sneer, his eyebrows drawn down over his angry eyes.

"You stupid little brat, don't ever imagine that your doing well at school means anything to me, or to anyone else for that matter. You're just a silly sniveling little good-for-nothing. Your sister will always be worth twenty of you, do you hear me? Don't ever let me hear you boasting like that ever again, it's pathetic and ridiculous

and it brands you for the useless idiot you are. You think pleasing your teachers at school is going to get you anywhere? More fool you! Your classmates must be complete idiots. When are you going to grow up? Your sister will always be smarter than you. You don't understand anything, do you? You may have your school teacher wrapped around your little finger, but when you get out in the real world, you're not going to be able to pull those tricks any more. People are going to see you for who you really are, and none of them are going to be any more impressed than I am. You make me sick!"

He snorts with disgust as he leaves.

I've finished the V. Letting the saw die, I stand back a little to make sure that I have cut it the right depth and the right angle. It's hard to tell with such a big tree. I walk around to either side, looking upwards at the lean of it. Satisfied, I walk round to the back of the tree and start up the saw. Once again it thrills me with the surge of its power. I am also overwhelmed with the magnificence of the tree, with the inevitability of its death that will come now very soon. I feel the knowledge of that and the knowledge of the possibility of it taking me as it goes. Maybe it will fall to one side, and I won't be quick enough to jump away. Unlikely, but always possible; sometimes trees do strange things. You can do everything right and still get unlucky. This tree is so majestic and old, imbued with power and beauty. I am very aware of the sadness of its passing and I feel some guilt that I am instrumental in that, I and my vibrating saw, roaring away at this very second, slicing through the core of the tree with such little effort, guided by my strong female hands, big and powerful like my mother's, so unladylike. I am nothing else right now but this, these strong hands and arms, the veins bulging in my wrists, blue against the skin powdered with the heart of the wood eaten into by the slivers of metal on the chain, rotating so fast you cannot see them, sharpened each to a fine point by these same competent hands holding a file. There is nothing now but me and my machine, this metal moving faster than sight, and this tree who has been here so many hundreds of years, growing from a little red berry that once dropped here and sprouted roots and leaves, long before any white person ever came here. Did Native American people live here and watch it grow?

When Jill came here twenty years ago, this tree was already old and full of wisdom. Over the years that it took her to build her house, starting with one room and then gradually adding, she kept looking out her window and thinking of the mountains that were hidden by the leaves of this great old tree. All those years of deliberation leading up to this one day, now, when she finally decided that it would go. As I lean over slightly to get a better purchase with my roaring saw, I feel the ancient, timeless spirits of this tree entering me, the destroyer, speaking to me, feeling me and letting me feel them. We are somewhere else together, and I am aware of their timelessness, their being in a place beyond any of this, and their desire to be with us, with humans, to reach me in my place, us in our place. The saw roars and the tiny regular chips of madrone wood shoot out in a regular stream from behind the bar as it eats away at the interior of this huge trunk, and I feel blessed and honored, and tiny and huge, and grateful that I can experience this communion with these other existences, that I can cross into this other place, even while I am wielding this instrument of destruction, that devours the solidity of this old being. I know that in the whole scheme of things this tree falling is just as it is meant to be, and that the sadness of it is the sadness of being human in a world where all things must pass: me, you, and this tree. All that remains forever is this other knowledge, this being in another place, that is not a place but a state, a reality of energy without physical form.

I'm almost through the tree now. I pull the whirring blade out of the slice it has eaten, walk half way round the tree and replace it, trying to make sure that I cut evenly from both sides, since my saw is not long enough to go all the way through from one side. I'm carefully watching the quarter inch slice my blade has made. As soon as I see it start to widen, I step back, removing the saw and letting it die, holding it away from me. The quarter inch becomes one inch, two inches, six inches, as the bulk of the tree arcs down in its slow inevitable falling. A massive crashing shakes the ground and branches are splintering. Then everything is still, the sound of the saw dying away with the sound of the tree dying. I stare at the huge shape lying on the forest floor. I'm overawed, not just by its hugeness, not just by the fact that I was the one who did this (me and my saw), but by the sense of a new presence in my life; the entities that were the tree are now with me, residing in me. I look up at the sky that has been revealed, studded with gray clouds. I look at the tops of the other trees still towering around me and see how they have more room now to reach for the sunlight with their hungry branches. I look at the three women standing nearby surveying the wreckage. What have they been thinking as they watched me? I look at the incredible rich deep pink of the stump, filling my eyes with the glory of this newly exposed beauty. I feel like a new person, like it's a new day and I just woke up.

Sometimes I feel like this after good sex.

My grief, the rage of my heart, has always dripped steadily, each drop gathering with the next behind the dam, until it squeezes its way through tiny, invisible rips. It's real, like blood. It is the pain of a dozen generations, of centuries of lies. It's the pain of greed and blindness, the pain of padlocks and chains. It clanks in the night, waking me from sleep in dread. It peeps through cracks in armor, wells up through unseen openings without warning. I've been afraid its deep dark ruby redness will burn my skin, leaving marks like scars. I've been afraid of the torrent that might eventually wash away everything I know, leaving me stranded in the unknown.

But now, nothing can stem its flow. Those years of pushing against it, sweating with the weight of it, straining my muscles to contain it, bleeding with the pain that came from resisting it, all that is ineffective now.

What vast relief.

Loving, real unconditional acceptance, true love from someone who sees me and doesn't try to change me, that is what frees me from this leaden weight I've carried for forty years. My lover says that loving me is the biggest thing that ever happened to her. I hold that honor in my heart, and delight in the tears of my grief, even as I fly by at full speed, looking the other way busily.

Every now and then, I have a recurring nightmare, where I am being chased by a man who is laughing at me. The closer he gets, the more maniacal his laughter becomes, and the more terrified I am. I always wake in a panic just before he catches me.

Thinking about this in the daytime, I realize that I need to turn and confront my pursuer instead of trying to get away from him.

One night, waking from this dream sweating and panting, I sleepily recall my daytime decision. Instead of waking myself up enough to erase the sensation of terror, I order myself to fall back into it. There he is behind me, laughing with horrible glee. For the first time, I turn around, ready to defend myself. It's not necessary. He melts away to nothing as soon as I face him fully.

I never have that dream again. I have ceased to be a victim.

I have always been wary of the people who say, *I love you.* What do they mean? Alec said, *I love you.* And, at first, I loved him, simply because he was attentive and kind to me, in an atmosphere that was markedly short on kindness, in an environment where children were mostly ignored. I had no idea that when he said, *I love you,* he meant, *my sexual desire is out of control, and I must use your body in this fashion whatever the cost. If you love me, which you should, you will let me do these things to you without resistance or complaint, and you will forgive me, and you will never tell anyone.*

Later, in my teens, when boys said, *I love you,* they meant, *you're mine, I own you, and when we appear in public together you will behave in an appropriate manner. I'll have sex with you when-ever I want, and you must at least make an appearance of enjoying what I do to you.* Or sometimes, they just meant, *I'm really horny right now, give me access to your body so that I can come.*

When my father said, *I love you,* he meant, *I'm sorry you seem to be hurt by the things I do and say, but I need to have someone to bear the brunt of my frustrated rage, and so I'm going to continue to do and say whatever I want to you, and you'd better just endure it without making a scene.*

When my mother said, *I love you,* she meant, *I'm sorry I'm not able to protect you like good mothers should, and I haven't ade-quately been able to hide the fact that I never wanted to have you, and I really need your forgiveness.*

When my female lovers said, *I love you*, they meant, *I admire who you are and I want to have access to you whenever I desire so that your qualities will be mine too. I want to control everything you do, so that you will never leave me.*

What do I mean when I say, *I love you*? I certainly mean, *please don't hurt me*. I go around saying that to everyone (nonverbally of course, because in everyday reality I don't easily admit that I am capable of feeling hurt). I mean, *please help me*. I feel the need for help really acutely, but I don't know *how* I need it, so I get really frustrated with my lovers, because no matter how hard they try, they don't really manage to help me in any real way. I mean, *life is too hard, please make it easier for me*. I mean, *please forgive me for all the wrong I do to you, for all my faults*. I mean, *please overlook all the times I nag and bitch at you*. I mean, *please see more of me than the tough exterior I present, and please love that other side of me, or, at least, please don't make fun of me*.

I want *I love you* to mean, *I see the wholeness of all that you are in this moment, and I accept you without judgment, honoring your unique, infinite beauty. In this moment my heart is joined with yours and I know that we are not separate beings. I support you absolutely in being fully who you are, even if that means that you will go away and I will never see you again.*

And this kind of love without judgment is not something I want to be exclusive. I want to be able to feel this kind of love with my close friends as well as with my lovers.

Jo eases her big body into a more comfortable position, tucking one of her legs underneath her on the armchair. She leans towards me, with her curly, non-Caucasian hair framing her impossibly loveable face (which is very Caucasian). Her expressive brown-green eyes are delightfully sweet. Jo is one of those people whom everyone likes, though she does not give herself away in order to be seen as nice. I enjoy her from the moment I meet her, wanting her intelligent comments and her unique, insightful points of view to be part of my everyday life.

Now something different is happening, something inexorable, something I want so badly I dare not admit it. Liz knows it is happening, and so does Jo's lover. Both of them are very displeased. I myself am dismayed, since on a superficial level I am not ready to give up Liz—she is an ideal girlfriend in so many ways, so easily acceptable. It's hard to acknowledge that she does not feed my inner self in the way I so badly need, and that Jo can offer much more of the kind of intimacy I am looking for. She is the radical thinker who will both challenge and accept me. The break-up with Liz looms like a monster on the horizon, no matter which way I turn.

Like all the other things in my life that I have resisted out of fear, its unfolding only becomes more unpleasant the more I resist. At last Liz finds another lover and with great relief I stop trying to take care of her. I embrace my relationship with Jo in all its glory, facing the new growth that will result, along with the inevitable growing pains.

Chapter Twenty One

It starts with a sow that the owner of the land I'm caretaking buys for pork. A wild boar turns up. Handsome and ferocious in his powerful black body, he appears out of nowhere to fuck the sow when she comes into heat. So she has babies—ten little squirmy things, some striped, some black and white, some all white like her. They are born eyes wide open, and in no time at all they have progressed from staggering on uncertain legs to running around at high speed with astounding agility. They move as though a single force motivates all of them, like puppets. One moment they are rooting around, carefree and casual, the next moment something startles them and they all stand perfectly still, looking, smelling, listening. Then, in one concerted wave, they take off. They are small enough to get through any fence, and within a week they are everywhere, endlessly curious, racing back to mother whenever they get scared, quickly venturing out to investigate the world again.

I discover that pigs are remarkable animals, with very distinct, individual characters, and a delightful tendency to playfulness. So we get another couple of sows, and I'm in the pig business.

As with any business, the problem is selling what you produce, or rather, what the sows produce. After raising some of the piglets and selling them at six months old, I progress to slaughtering them myself and selling the pork. The slaughter is the part that never gets easier, the part that, no matter how hard I try, I can never quite come to terms with. I advertise them for sale as piglets, when I can still pretend that they will be allowed to live beyond their teenage years. One of the people who buys from me is a local woman called Anne. She is not your average pig farmer. She is a married middle class woman, with a very well paid job designing computer systems. Every summer she raises eight or ten pigs, because she loves them, because she adores their antics, delights in the diversity of their characters, and revels in their playful energy, just as I do. She also likes to eat them.

One spring, just after the first Gulf War has been declared, she pulls up in her truck. As we walk down to look at the pigs, I ask her how she is doing.

"Oh, I'd be doing better if I hadn't just heard that my son is going off to the Gulf on Tuesday!"

I look at her in horror. "Oh, my God! You must be terrified!"

"Yes, I am. I can't believe he's really doing it. He thinks he's doing his duty for his country!"

I roll my eyes, and so we embark on a conversation about politics. Seems like we agree on a lot of things. Before she leaves, she says, "My friend Sarah and I are starting a monthly women's empowerment group. You should come along! It'll be fun, there are some good women coming to it. First meeting's on Thursday at my place, at seven."

I nod and smile, thinking it will be a bunch of heterosexual women, and I would just feel very out of place. I have no intention of going.

Then Anne leaves a message on my machine reminding me about it, and I start to think it might be interesting after all. It might broaden my horizons. In the eight years I have lived in this country, I have met very few heterosexual women, and socialized with precisely none. I have no idea what they are like. It would be a new cultural experience to hang out with a bunch of them.

Perhaps the truth is that I need to see if I will be accepted in heterosexual circles. I have lived full-time on the very edge of the fringe for so long that I feel alienated from mainstream society. I am not prepared to compromise myself or my beliefs in order to be accepted, but I want to get over my sense of estrangement. I will never feel quite like a woman, in the way that most women seem to, so it's not that I want to be accepted as a woman. I want to be like my Great Aunt Vera, some kind of well-respected third gender.

One problem I face when I go out to socialize is looking clean and presentable. There is always something to attend to: I have to pick up restaurant garbage for the pigs while I am in town, or the truck misbehaves and I get oily when I mess with the engine, or the pigs need attention as I'm leaving home, and I get muddy. Somehow mud and dust stick to me more than they do to other people. My friends are accustomed to seeing me streaked with dirt, but it doesn't create a good impression on people who are not used to me. It's a particular problem with the pigs, because the smell of pig-shit is very pervasive.

I feel awkward in situations where everyone else looks clean, and smells of soap or perfume. I feel particularly awkward when they all look conspicuously heterosexual, and I look, as always, like a dyke.

So I'm nervous when I arrive at Anne's, wearing jeans as usual (I don't have anything else to wear). I am as clean as I can manage, considering that on my way out I had to feed the pigs and check on a sow who is just about to give birth. Anne is very welcoming, and so are the other women. Although I don't find myself inspired to join in the conversation much, it's interesting to listen to them talking about their lives, especially since two of them are in the process of divorce.

I go to the next meeting, and the next one, and the next one. I never quite feel like I am one of them—they are all so…respectable? Lady-like? Well-behaved? Neat and clean? Well-off? Middle class? Maybe they are just being women, and I am being something else. Still, they are very accepting of me and, in return, I am of them. I gradually learn that I can trust them to treat me respectfully.

Sometimes, when I listen to them complain, for the n-th time, how hard it is to find a good man, I wonder why they keep on looking.

"You know, every time we meet, I hear you all complaining that there are incredibly few good men around. I don't understand why you don't consider relationships with women."

Anne says, "I'm just not turned on by women. They just don't do it for me, they don't smell right or something. I'd love to be a lesbian, I think it's the answer to a lot of problems! But I guess I'm just not wired that way."

Sarah says, "I had sex with my girlfriends when I was in college in the seventies, when everyone was having sex with everyone." We all laugh. "But, I don't know, it just really doesn't occur to me now. I'm interested in men."

Margaret says, "I don't know really...I don't think of women that way."

The other three don't say anything.

I take a class with Caryn, the psychic. The class, which involves four very intense weekends throughout the year, is based on Angeles Arrien's *Four Fold Way*. It utilizes shamanic methods to develop a spiritual path that is integrated into our daily lives. Other classes I've taken with Caryn have been very validating—she is so compassionate and nonjudgmental that it is very easy to trust her. I feel like she sees who I really am, and thinks I'm just fine. That is amazing, to be seen; and the fact that she is *not* a lesbian makes it all the more affirming.

Nevertheless, this class is difficult. It demands an honesty and a presence that brings up a lot of resistance. It is the also the first class I have done with Caryn where there are men: four men and eight women. Three of the men seem likable. One is silent and, though clearly intelligent and thoughtful, he is a little awkward in social situations, which endears him to me. One is handsome, smart and very self-possessed. I might dislike him if I spent much time with him, since I think his air of competence probably conceals a typical male arrogance, but within the class he does not impinge on my sensibilities. The third, Peter, is gangly, whitehaired and amusing, with an expressive face and body. He emanates a gentle, unobtrusive and interesting energy.

The fourth man, John, is the bane of the class, at least for me. Loud and insensitive, he seems quite out of touch with the effect he has on others. Constantly wishing he had the sense to shut up, I dismiss him as stupid.

By this time I have done enough classes with Caryn to know that no group comes together by accident. The people who bring up my judgments are often my most important teachers.

There is one other dyke. Although she seems to find it easier to be presentable than I do, still, it means I don't stand out quite so transparently as the strange one with short hair, always wearing odd socks and looking a little scruffy.

Part of the class agenda is looking at the authentic and the false selves. We spend a day identifying the false self, making an image of it, and then burying the image. Caryn cautions us not to despise the false self, it has been with us for a reason, and it may have served a very important purpose. Now we have outgrown it.

The false self motivates us to actions that are not our soul's desire. It is that part which holds shame and guilt, that says and does things that are not truthful, out of fear or habit. In order to help us identify it, Caryn has us stand up in front of the class, one by one, and make a simple statement about something we have done, or something about ourselves, that we are ashamed of. We are not allowed to respond in any way to anything anyone else chooses to reveal.

Naturally, I am appalled (and I suspect, from the groans and horrified faces, that everyone else is too). Caryn begins by saying something she is ashamed of. Various people follow suit. I cannot remember what any of them say, although every time someone says something, I think, "That's nothing! Why on earth is s/he ashamed of *that*?" My mind is spinning off in all directions. Thinking of a dozen things I *could* say, I dismiss them all as not serious enough. Finally, I stand up and stutter that I once did a scam with a friend's checkbook, without letting her know that I was responsible for its disappearance.

I sit down, but I am not deeply relieved that my turn is over. My mind is still spinning. I want to explain that I did not consider it wrong to have stolen from the bank, I only consider it wrong to have deceived my friend. I want to tell the group about all the other things I have done that I am ashamed of: all the times I have lied, all the times I have broken someone's trust, all the times I have been deceitful, all the times I put myself and my safety before truth. My mind won't let go of it. I remain confused and uncomfortable for the rest of the day.

In the evening, when the class is over, my mind is still going nineteen to the dozen as I drive home. I feel more and more confused, to the point where I cannot recall why I am doing this class at all. I cannot remember why we are doing this work. It just seems really foolish and masochistic. By the time I get home, a large part of me has decided that I am not going back the next day. The small part that is not in support of this decision keeps piping up in a squeaky voice: "Wait a minute! There is something you are forgetting! I don't know what it is, but I know there is a very good reason for you to go to this class! You really wanted to go yesterday, and the day before that, and the day before that! You've just forgotten it right now!" Then it is drowned out by the louder voice that keeps saying, "Stop being so stupid! The class is a complete waste of time!"

Although I feel exhausted by this compelling internal argument, I realize that I will not be able to sleep a wink with these voices so loud in my head, and I consider calling Caryn. Perhaps she will be able to tell me why I should go to the class. Initially I dismiss this option, since it seems unfair to Caryn to bother her late in the evening. Besides, since she is teaching the class, obviously she has an investment in me attending it, so she can't be trusted to be honest.

But the desire to call keeps pulling at me. Finally I dial her number, ignoring the voice inside that yells, "You idiot! You know what you want, you don't have to ask other people! You're just being a weakling! What are you going to say to her, anyway?"

Caryn picks up the phone.

"Hi Caryn, it's Chris. I'm sorry to bother you so late, I'm just in such a tizz, and I'm hoping you can help me out. I...I can't work out...I can't remember why we're doing this class...I can't work out what it's all for..."

She interrupts, her words soft and warm over the line, but very decisive. "Chris, it's your father. It's your father's voice, trying to control you."

Abruptly, the voice of doubt and scorn inside falls away. The silence inside is delightfully peaceful. She carries on, "You don't have to listen to his voice." After a long pause, during which I am savoring the silence, she says, "OK?"

"Yes...I got it now...thanks."

"OK, then, you sleep well, and I'll see you tomorrow."

"OK...thanks, Caryn...that was very helpful."

Putting down the phone, I sit there for a few minutes, crying quiet tears of relief and gratitude, for the absence of the derisive voice, and for Caryn's clarity and wisdom.

It becomes a problem in the group that some people want to wander casually back after lunch, happy to start whenever we all happen to be there, while others want to stick to a strict schedule. One day Caryn is clearly fed up with waiting. She gets to the point without preamble. "It's now 2.30, and we agreed before we left for lunch that we would be back here at 2. This happens regularly. It's a group issue, and I would like the group to resolve it. Does anyone have anything to say about it?"

Silence. I am always one of the on-time people. I hate sitting around waiting, and I'd love to say this to those who are always late, but I figure that, for once, it would be good for me to remain an observer. I sit back on my cushion, leaning against the wall.

One of the women speaks up, obviously sincere. "Well, I want to apologize if I kept people waiting, I just didn't realize what the time was."

Silence. Then John, who is always late, and has never shown any sign of repentance about it, says, "Well, really, it doesn't matter when we start, there is no need for anyone to get uptight about it—"

Before I can stop myself, a single word explodes out of me: "Bullshit!"

John stops in his tracks, and we lock eyes.

"That's bullshit, John! It may not matter to you when we start, but it does to me, and I don't like waiting while others dawdle!"

Looking discomfited, he mutters, "Well, I didn't realize anyone felt so strongly about it…"

My initial instinctive reaction over, a voice inside says, *Oh, for God's sake, Chris, can't you* ever *keep your mouth shut?* I glance around the circle to see what effect my bluntness has had. No one is really looking at anyone. I suspect there may be a shadow of a smile on Caryn's face, which comforts me.

Andrew, the silent man, speaks up.

"I feel exactly the same way as Chris does. I find it really irritating that some people are so lackadaisical at getting here on time, and I don't want to have to wait for them." His tone reflects his annoyance, and I smile, grateful.

In the course of the class we are required to talk about the difficult things in our pasts, the areas where we need healing. Of course, for me, this is about my father and my negative experiences with men. I speak of this, just as everyone else speaks about their issues. One day at lunch break, Peter follows me as I go out into the garden with my plate.

"May I have lunch with you? I'd like to talk with you."

"Sure."

"Let's go and sit by the pond."

We make ourselves comfortable on a small deck by the pond, and he begins. He is a slow speaker, as though he finds language inadequate to convey what he would like to say.

"I want to tell you...I have heard what you said in there," he waves his arm back at the house. "I want to acknowledge that you have had a very hard time in your life...and it is because you were born a woman, that you were treated so badly. You have been treated very badly by men."

He pauses, staring at the water, and I wait. He looks at me again, his blue eyes deeply sincere. "It is very hard to listen to the stories you tell...it hurts me here." He puts his hand over his heart. "I know that I am not personally responsible for any of it, and if I had my way I would like to...well, never mind about that..." He laughs a little, and then is immediately serious again. "I would do something awful to those men who hurt you. But really, that is beside the point, because of course there is nothing anyone can do now but try to move beyond it."

He shrugs, sighing. "Anyway, so, I just want to say, as a man, I am sorry for what happened to you. I want to apologize for what happened to you and for what happens to many women. And I want to say, if ever there is anything I can do to make it better for you, let me know. I would like to be your friend...I would like to be a brother to you. I want to show you that not all men are like the ones you have known. Some of us *do* know how to love."

Later, thinking about this conversation, I wonder how it is to be a man like him. How alone he must feel, one amongst so many who are not willing to allow themselves to be real and vulnerable. I could consider myself alone for the same reasons, but I don't think I am alone in the same way as Peter. I have a family of women around me. True, the world does not generally recognize the full power and value of the feminine, nor does it generally recognize my femininity. Nevertheless, I am very sure of both. To be a *man* of integrity in this world must require constant vigilance, dealing with layers of guilt and alienation. Where can men go for support in trying to change the standard way of being a man?

I am very grateful that I have experienced first hand all the gifts and trials associated with being born a woman. I have been given exactly the lessons I need, to learn that true power grows out of the heart, from the fertile soils of compassion and acceptance. It is never about exerting will over others.

Peter's apology stays with me, although it is a year or two before I come to trust that this man might have something to offer me. Eventually I decide to take a weekly meditation class taught by him. It seems a little farcical, trying to still my mind—I have a very loquacious voice in there, forever telling stories, working out what I have to do tomorrow and what I forgot to do yesterday, and what would happen if this, and what would happen if that. It thinks it has to be on guard all the time, and when I tell it to shut up, it thinks I am deluded, so it just *pretends* to shut up, and then the next time I notice, there it is, carrying on the same as usual.

In spite of this, I feel it is a laudable, if lofty, aim, to quieten my mind, so here I am in this class, staring at candles, and lying on the floor imagining I am made of golden light. Occasionally I feel peaceful enough to fall asleep, which is embarrassing, but a lot of the time I am simply anxious about doing it right.

During one of the classes, Peter places a Tibetan singing bowl on the floor near my head. When he hits it, the bowl resonates with powerful reverberating notes, that cycle again and again, penetrating and deep, yet incredibly gentle. The sound emanates from the bowl around my head and over my body. It is like water flowing, and when I let it surround me, it fills me up, finding every nook and cranny of my being. He takes a second bowl, placing it on my abdomen. Now when he hits it, the sound is inside me, it is in my flesh and my blood and my bones. It flows into my heart and my belly, washing out all the skuzz that's there. I want to laugh out loud with the pleasure of it.

Then the most astounding thing happens: I become the sound. Or does the sound become me? We are not separate. The sound is singing my body into existence.

Words, understood by the intellect, cannot communicate the magnificence of this experience.

During the next class he uses the bowls again. It happens to be a day when I am feeling sad, and this time the sound facilitates the tears overflowing out of my eyes and rolling down my cheeks. It's rare that I can allow this to happen, and these days I am always grateful. So I try to stay with the sensation of sadness, just allowing it to be. What is it I am crying for? I don't know. My grief seems to encompass the whole world. There is so much that is not right. I ask Peter what he does when he feels overwhelmed by the wrongdoing in the world. He says, "I cry. And then I look for the golden light."

His words catapult me into a dream place. I find myself in a huge room in an old ruined castle, the cold gray stone (huge hunks of it forming three-feet thick walls) all around me, the windows empty with mist. The wood is all rotted and gone. The stones stand, as they do, timeless, patient and enduring, silent witness to all manner of horrors. Ahead of me, slicing through the dullness, a shaft of bright light shines in through one window, casting a powerful beam onto a patch of floor. I try to go towards the light but it is too bright. The sorrow has to be acknowledged and the stones sung awake before I can go there. I turn back into the big room. Tears rise in my throat, sliding down my face, and I realize that this is the Hall of Sorrow. It feels fine to be there. I meander slowly around, allowing space for the sorrow that I normally carry bundled up inside. I feel the gray sadness of the blank still stones, solid and impermeable, yet soaked in grief, thick and hard and stuffed with grief, with deep unending grief; the legacy of my ancestors, centuries of pain compressed into shame by the demand for secrecy and silence, by the denial of any sign of vulnerability.

Thus the silent stones hold their unheard message, waiting for the sound of a compassionate heartbeat to waken them, to allow them to unburden themselves. They are waiting for one who is willing to embrace pain. I lay my cheek against their surface: cold as ice, hard and gray, smooth and solid, containing, absorbing, oozing the heartless silent pain in which they were carved. I feel as though my heart is walled in by this ancient unforgiving stone.

I realize that the castle is a shell, containing the shell of the house where I lived when I was a young child. My five-year-old self still lives here, when she is not cuddled in my arms. She grew up playing in the ruined castles that pepper Scotland—statues to a history where ramparts and dungeons played very real roles.

The bowls have been singing, and I hear the sound of them arising from within the walls. Its volume is growing, echoing around me. The waves of sound vibrate through the stone like a shaft of light carried on the mist, like waves of warmth. Gradually the stones are awakening. We are singing an end to the cruelty and shame. The light and the song and the warmth meld with the stone, melting it. Unseen lungs fill, and hearts beat, imperceptibly at first. The song brings life, so that the hallways that have been dead and dark for centuries (even when they gave an appearance of life) are penetrated by shafts of light carried on undulating sound, breathing in love.

The time is here, this is all as it should be, and I am honored to be a participant.

Chapter Twenty Two

I've noticed a derelict house beside the road that I take when I am visiting Jo. I scope it out with the idea of pulling it down and re-using the wood to build my own house. It looks easy enough to demolish. I stop one day with my hammer and crowbars, leaving an hour later with a very nice load on my truck. Demolition is one of my favorite things to do, and I am very efficient at it.

A couple of days later, I return with Jo, setting to work while she wanders off looking for plants in the long forgotten garden. I'm wrestling with a couple of beams when I spy a jeep drive up. It skids to a stop in a cloud of dust.

"Uh oh," I say to myself, "maybe I should have found out who this place belonged to."

Two people jump out of the jeep—a small woman and a tall man, both wearing fatigues, both looking very purposeful. As they stride towards the house, I step out into full view, not wanting to appear to be hiding.

"Put down those tools!" barks the woman. "You know what happens to people who steal, they go to jail! And that's where you're going!"

"I'm sorry, I thought the house was abandoned," I say, projecting as much innocence as I can muster. I am careful to meet her eyes, although her glare is fit to fry me on the spot.

"Where's your partner? Come on, we know you're not here on your own!"

How do you know that, I wonder, as Jo strolls over. Pointing at her, the woman shouts, "You, get over here at once! What do you think you're doing?"

Jo has a sweet and love-able face, and now she puts on a smile that would melt a murderer's heart. "I was just looking at the old garden over there." She is an inveterate gardener. "Look, I found a sprouted walnut!" She holds out the nut in her hand.

The woman growls. She turns to the man. "You keep an eye on them, I'll go and get the cops. See you in a while." Scowling, she glances back at us as she strides towards the jeep, saying, "Don't think you're gonna get away with this!"

I'm relieved it is the woman who has left, rather than the guy— I know he will be easier to handle. And it is so. In no time at all, Jo and I have thawed his anger with our ingenuity. We have both lived on the fringes of what is acceptable for long enough that we know how to sweet-talk our way out of fixes, even when we are caught red-handed.

Pretty soon, Jo has discovered that they live near her, and they're chatting away about the neighborhood. He says they had a barn smashed up and a bunch of stuff stolen. "As a matter of fact, we thought you were the ones who did that," he tells us. He laughs and shakes his head. "We were all set to beat the shit out of you, and then it turns out you're ladies! What a waste of an adrenaline rush!"

Jo and I both laugh too. My own adrenaline is only just beginning to settle down. "I'm sorry," I say, "I know what that's like, you get all geared up for something and then it doesn't happen. But I certainly didn't smash up your barn, and I'm very glad you didn't beat us up!"

"Well, we'd have put you in the hospital if you'd been guys. We're both black belts in kenpo karate. So, was it you that smashed the windows over there?" He points at the other building nearby.

Jo scoffs, "Chris break windows? She might take the pane out whole so she can re-use it, but she'd never deliberately break a good pane of glass!"

I nod. "I'm not interested in smashing things up for the sake of it. I wanted the wood from this building so I can build my own house. There's some good lumber here. Were you planning to use it?"

He shakes his head. "We were going to call the fire department in to burn it."

I raise my eyebrows. "Hmmm!"

By the time the woman returns with a policeman in tow, the three of us are getting along fine. As the woman strides up, her face set in a glare, he turns towards her, and I hear him say, "These two are too nice to go to jail."

The three of them go off to have a conference, leaving Jo and me under the tree.

"I'm sorry," I say to her, "I seem to have got you in a bit of a mess."

She shrugs, smiling. "I don't think they'll put us in jail."

"No, we're too nice!"

"And we're not in the hospital because we're ladies!"

We both crack up.

In a while the cop comes over. He's a little guy in his fifties, with a friendly face. I stand up and introduce myself, saying, "You know, Jo really didn't have anything to do with this, she wasn't taking any of the wood, it was just me."

He nods, "So you're our culprit, eh? What were you going to do with the wood?"

"Build my house! There's some good lumber there. It's a shame to burn it."

Setting his face in a stern expression, he puts a fatherly hand on my shoulder. "Well now, you listen to me, this is what I tell my kids, you gotta *ask* first! You can't just go taking things! Things don't sprout out of the ground, they belong to someone. You gotta ask before you take them! You understand me?"

Biting my lip to stop myself laughing, I manage to nod seriously. "Yes, you're right, I should have asked first."

Breaking out in a smile, he says, "Well, you go over there and talk to them. I think they want to make you a deal."

Feeling like a schoolkid, I walk over to where they are standing on the porch of the other building. The woman addresses me much more civilly than previously. "So we'll forget about this if you bring back the wood you took and leave it all neat and tidy."

Bring it back? So they can burn it? "What are you going to do with it?"

"Burn it."

I almost wince. What a waste of good lumber, while the forests are being chopped down around us. "OK, I'll make *you* a deal. You need to get rid of that building, it's been condemned, right? So, I'll get rid of it and leave everything nice and tidy. I'll take the lumber and use it."

"How long will it take you?"

"Hmmm…two weeks."

She glances at the guy and he nods. "OK, it's a deal. But if you don't keep to your side of the bargain, we'll have the cops back!"

I grin. "Don't worry, I want that wood!"

Using this wood, along with other lumber that I have gleaned over the years, I build my house on the edge of a promontory, overlooking the valley. Since I never get around to finishing it inside, it's not quite like other people's houses, but it has an unrestricted view of mountains and forests so that I cannot fail to remember what a beautiful world I live in.

There's a new guy at the scrap yard today. He looks at me suspiciously as I come in carrying my tools. When I start to walk on through, explaining briefly what I've come for, he says, "Uh…just a minute, I gotta check with the boss." I wait, hoping there isn't some new policy along with the new guy. I always use that scrap yard specifically because they let me take off my own parts. I hate having to wait for someone to take them off for me. Once I waited all day for a part, until just before five, when the guy finally admitted he didn't know how to do it, and allowed me to show him.

The boss comes out of the back room, and the new guy says, "Can she go out and get the windshield wiper motor out of that '83 Toyota Tercel?"

He barks a laugh in response. "'Course she can, and she'll do it in half the time it would take you!"

I stroll out the back door, with my tools in my hand and a grin on my face. Although I am a little alarmed at how the new guy might retaliate to being told in public that he's not as good as a woman, I am glowing inside. Not so much at the compliment—I know I can work faster than most male mechanics. What makes me glow is that the boss enjoys making a public statement about me being a good mechanic. True, he probably enjoys putting the other guy down. Still, this kind of thing makes up for a great deal of the way it was when I started doing mechanics in Britain.

Now I'm home, I've installed the windshield wiper motor, and I'm replacing the starter motor. I'm lying on my back on the ground with my arms entangled in the machinery over my head. In my right hand I have a ratchet, and in my left hand an open-ended spanner. I'm muttering under my breath as I struggle to undo a nut and bolt. It's a common mantra for a female car mechanic. It goes like this: "Idiots! Only a man would design something like this that you can't get at! Idiots!"

I can't get a purchase on the ratchet. I use my feet to walk myself round, rotating on my shoulders. The wheel of the car is in the way of my legs, but I manage to wriggle them where they need to go by bending them at an impossible angle, banging my knee in the process. Metal is so hard and unforgiving.

I haul on the ratchet. Nothing happens. I shift my body just a little. My neck aches from holding my head up, but I manage to prop it on the tire behind me. I take a deep breath and pull down with my right hand while I push up with my left, using all the weight of my body so that my butt lifts off the ground. Every muscle in my body takes part in this effort. My face is twisted in a grimace, my eyes are squeezed shut and some strange involuntary sound comes out of my mouth. My hands are aching from my grip on the tools. I'm praying that neither of the tools will slip off, because if they slip off while I'm putting this kind of weight on them, it will surely mess up the head of the nut, and then it will be a two or three hour job to get the nut undone.

All of a sudden, it gives with a crack, and the knuckles of my left hand, clenched around the spanner, meet the chassis of the car with some force. I grunt with a mixture of satisfaction and pain. Letting go of the spanner, I look at my knuckles. Like the rest of my hand, they are black with oil—there must be an engine leak, I think, and make a mental note to take a look the next time I'm vertical. The black skin is bulging off two of my knuckles and blood is beginning to ooze. Knowing from experience that distraction is the best method of pain management, I return my attention to the nut and bolt. There isn't much room to move the ratchet, and so my tender knuckles get banged on the chassis again, but I soon have the nut and bolt off.

I glance up at the sky. Only another half hour or so and it'll be too dark to work. Should I stop now? I decide to carry on while I'm on a roll. I pick up the wrench I need and lie down again, wishing Jo was here with a cup of tea, thinking that I'll go work in my garden tomorrow. I need to prune the fruit trees.

Chapter Twenty Three

I **am beginning to understand** that there is no goal to reach for. Given that everything is in a constant state of flux, everything is just as it should be right in this moment. And in the next, and the next. There is no better way to be. What does better mean? Better than what? Better than I have been in the past? Better according to whose dictates? I can only be me: fiercely, proudly, wildly, me.

But my past selves still litter my life. Whenever I look back, I see them: living husks, hovering just out of sight, desperate ghosts seeking absolution, begging for deliverance.

Sometimes I hate them. I want to tread them underfoot, crush them into oblivion, destroy them for once and for all. Or at the very least, pretend they never existed. But if I am to be truthful, I cannot deny them. They have lives of their own. So how do I integrate them? How do I give peace to the ten-year-old girl who lives in such a world of horror, wracked with shame? To the stubborn fourteen-year-old who hates everyone?

I ask for Sue's help, and she takes me on a guided visualization back to the house where Alec molested me. Soon after we have begun, I find myself taking over from her, taking charge of my own journey. I am in the house at Gleninnis. I walk up the stairs, thinking how big I am now. I walk tall and I am strong and independent, more powerful than anyone else in this house.

I am standing in front of the bed where little Chris lies, and Alec comes into the room. My eyes are flashing fire. I find a shining sword in my hand. I slice him to pieces. Then I run rampage through the house, wielding my sword. Pull the tablecloth off the table so all the china smashes onto the floor. Knock things down and break them. Slice up the furniture in the sitting room. Hold the point of the sword to Nanny's throat, telling her she will never be allowed to maltreat little children any more. Her reign is over. Cut her to pieces.

I slice up my parents, tears in my own eyes now because I really don't want to hurt them, yet what else can I do? I am most sorry for my father, seeing the always-hidden fear in his face as I stand over him with my sword raised. I become aware of the young boy that he was once, who stands next to him now, trying to dodge the blows that are not meant for a child. They are all so frightened, I don't like to look at the fear on their faces. I don't want to perpetuate fear. I want to create something new and wonderful, a new way of being. I want to be able to protect other children from these horrors.

But some things have to be finished. I go to Mr. Cockburn's house. I have no qualms about slicing him to pieces. I slice Tom Mac-Farlane to pieces too. My shining sword in hand, I stride on up the lane and as I reach the gate to the house where I grew up, I look around: there is an army of children behind me. They include all the wounded children who became the adults whom I have cut into pieces. I am overwhelmed: how can I take care of them all? And how can I possibly teach them all to live compassionately and proudly, without perpetuating the old damaging patterns?

In spite of my initial overwhelm, I am deeply pleased at this demonstration of the universal desire to heal. I know that these souls will all find the help they need, because we all do.

I can no longer continue, uninterrupted, in my old familiar ways. Now, even as I look everywhere else, the black cat of my glorious grief entwines itself around my leg and trips me up. Now I am aware that the door inside me is creaking open with a groan. Carefully, I look the other way, waiting breathlessly in the wings, not wanting to close it, but knowing that I might easily (by accident, or on purpose, in order to be in order) slam it shut. Through the door pads the black cat, graceful and flowing, wanting to be wild. It has been unseen in the moonless blackness of my past, pacing to and fro in the confines of my fear. It's free now to race across open meadows in the light of day.

Loving women, our loving, dissolves the cold metal bars that I created long ago. Padlocks melt in the heat of our passion like candles in the midday sun. Every time we ride our desire, every time we are carried to that place of truth and vulnerability that lies in the center between us, that is the two of us sharing the innermost songs of our souls. The door glides open, less noisily now that its hinges are in use. Still, I wonder, what will emerge? Again and again, I have turned the other way, not wanting to look for fear of ugliness. Again and again, I have prepared to leave. Now something pads proudly across the room to rub against my ankle, demanding attention and love. I bend down to stroke the gorgeous black cat of my glorious grief.

One summer I find myself with some money. I have always known that when I have cash, I will use it to search for that mysterious missing element whose absence was so obvious to me as a child. Caryn and her classes have been offering me some pointers. I consider going on a two-week retreat about tuning into one's personal spirituality. It is facilitated by Brooke Medicine Eagle, who has been one of Caryn's teachers, and takes place on a huge ranch in a remote part of Montana. The decision to go is an anxiety ridden process, since there will be at least thirty women at this retreat, and that seems like a lot of people to be spending a lot of time with, for a recluse like me. I don't know any of them.

Various interesting things happen on the retreat. Being alone in the wilderness for three days doing a vision quest is a vital experience that shows me how much I dislike having to listen to those damn voices in my head. No wonder I stay busy all the time. I need to be distracted from them.

On the morning of the tenth day, Brooke informs us that we are going to meet with Dayana Jon, who channels a group of entities called Amag.

After lunch, we file into the big tipi, and make ourselves comfortable. Brooke and Dayana are seated up front. Dayana seems like a regular sort of person, with strong, interesting features, and a very sweet, gentle smile. When we are all gathered and ready, she addresses us. "I'm very glad you're all here, and I just want to say thank you so much for coming. Amag is a large group of spirit beings who have been speaking through me for several years now. It's easy to be intimidated by them, but please remember they like to chat just like all of the rest of us, and it really is fine to ask any questions you want. They like to talk about all kinds of things. So we're just going to have a regular conversation."

With that, she closes her eyes, breathing deeply for a minute or so. Then she leans forward a little with her head down, taking a particularly deep breath. Her arms sweep around in a slow graceful circular motion, and she sits up straight with her hands resting on her thighs. An extraordinary transformation has occurred. This is not Dayana any more, although I can still recognize her if I look hard. The primary impression I have is of a regal presence. The atmosphere in the room has tangibly altered. A powerful sensation of wisdom and compassion flows around me, riveting me with delight.

The being that is not-Dayana speaks in a relaxed masculine voice with what could be a Russian accent, saying, "Yes, we are here, it is a pleasure to be with you." It looks around the room with half closed eyes, and continues, "What would you like to talk about today?"

We are all somewhat overawed, and there is a long silence, before I reply, "Love!" I say it simply because that is what I am feeling.

They respond, "Ah, love! That is a *huge* subject. That is all there is. You think of yourselves sometimes as falling in love, but truthfully you are never out of love, so you cannot very well fall into it."

They speak a little more on the subject and then there is a long pause. They ask again, "What would you like to talk about? We can tell that you have many thoughts you want to discuss!" In the silence that follows, we hear the birds singing outside, and Amag says, "The birds seem to have some ideas!" Our laughter eases the tension, and soon other people begin to ask questions.

After this introduction, I stay in touch with Dayana, visiting her every once in a while. Over the next ten years, she and Amag become good friends and an invaluable resource.

As I enter my forties, I develop a desire to revisit my past, and see it with the vision of the present. Perhaps it is an effort to forgive myself for failing to be truthful and kind.

I get in touch with some British friends from the days when I was a barefoot hippie. John, Lucy and their son are all that remain of the commune where ten of us once lived, built a business and shared our money. It's strange to see the remaining house so nicely finished and neatly furnished now. John is pleasant enough, just as I remember him, while Lucy is just as opinionated and pushy. Their eight-year-old son harangues me mercilessly about my American accent until Lucy finally orders him to stop being so rude.

Some things haven't changed. As we are sitting there drinking cups of thick black tea with milk, John pulls out cigarette papers and rolls a joint. He passes it to me and I politely refuse—I really haven't had any desire to get stoned for years now. I can get high just looking at a tree dancing in the wind. Lucy offers me a glass of wine instead, and I refuse that too, although I'm tempted to have some just so they won't assume I've turned into some kind of purist.

They have both been involved in training with a Native American spiritual teacher. Lucy talks about this at length, and although I find it interesting, I feel slightly uneasy. I have begun to identify myself as someone on a spiritual path, simply because I have begun to comprehend that life *is* a spiritual path. My concept of the meaning of the word *spiritual* has evolved out of my personal healing work, the self-examination that I have been through. I don't see any sign of John or Lucy doing that kind of personal work. These are the people I knew when I first developed a political awareness, and they are still political activists. Whereas I now believe that changing the world has to start with me changing myself, they still seem to see change as something that has to be forced to occur externally.

I wonder, am I judging them as *less than*, because I secretly wish I had a spiritual teacher like theirs, and a path set out like they do? Being who I am seems to preclude having a *master* to lead me. I am unable to learn the steps of someone else's dance. I am mastering the art of self-mastery.

I am celebrating the winter equinox with Jo and a few friends. It is a clear cold evening, a billion tiny specks of light overhead making the blanket of darkness look threadbare and worn. This is the time of the longest night, when we look within, deciding what it is we want to leave behind as the days begin to lengthen and we move again into the light.

I start by calling in the directions. We stand in a circle around our small fire, facing first to the east. I raise my arms, speaking in a loud clear voice. The words are a conglomeration of concepts from all the various traditions I have known. They spill out of me from some place beyond my rational brain.

"Aho, powers of the East, new beginnings, all winged beings, whose element is air: hawk who soars, swallow who flits, raven who croaks, lark who sings! You and all your sisters and brothers, we who are gathered here this evening call upon you. Each new dawn, each sun that rises from a hue of golden-red, we call upon you. The clarity of the sky at the moment of light dawning, we call upon you. The new growth of spring, the start of a new year, of a new day, a new week, a new world, a new moment, we call upon you. We ask for all your energies to support us now in this time of rebirth. We honor you, and we are grateful for your presence here."

I turn towards the south, the group turning with me.

"Aho, powers of the South, the bright light of the midday sun that blinds us that we may better see, we call upon you, we welcome your energy. May your fire burn out what is no longer needed. Lizards and snakes, all who love the desert's heat, all who shed their skins, all who bask on rocks, we who are gathered here call upon you. Help us to allow the passion of being-ness to flow freely through us, so that we may create what we have chosen. Help us to find shelter from the unforgiving heat when we need it. The flowering of plants at the prime of life, the stillness of a lizard basking, the speed of a snake striking, help us to integrate all these gifts. Powers of the South, we ask for all your energies to support us in this time of rebirth. We honor you, and we are deeply grateful for your presence here with us."

We turn to the west.

"Aho, powers of the West, the time of dusk, the mighty oceans, waves that crash on the shore in constant crests of white, streams that trickle, rivers that roar. May all creatures of the seas and the rivers be with us. May your wisdom, the wisdom of feeling, flow through us freely. All of the whales and dolphins who know the pleasure of the ocean, we ask for your presence here to help us in this time of rebirth. All fish who swim, and crabs who crawl, shellfish that live in the sand, we call upon you. May we know the power of life-giving water, of tears flowing down our cheeks, of sweat dripping down our skin, of long cold drinks, of e-motions that flow. Powers of the West, water that cleanses us, we ask for your presence here this evening. We honor you, and we are deeply grateful."

The north.

"Aho, powers of the North, the time of darkness, we call upon you, the grandmothers, all who ride the red dragons of fire and ice, who bring us the clarity of the night sky, showering us with stars. You who offer us the silver moonlight that casts deep shadows, we call upon you. All the fourleggeds that walk and run, we ask for your presence here to help us so that we may know the sleekness of a wild cat stalking, a deer running, a monkey swinging through the forest from branch to branch. We call upon you, we ask that we may integrate your wisdom into our being at this time of rebirth. May we know the vastness of our being as we know the vastness of the night sky above. And may the wisdom of the Earth, from which we are born, flow through us."

Now we all turn to face the center and I reach upwards into the darkness. "Oh Grandfather Sky, we embrace you as we are embraced by you! Be with us always, as we are with you."

I kneel down to touch the soil, and the others follow suit.

"And you, Mother Earth, from whom we all arise, we honor you, we adore you, and we will serve you always, as we hope you too will serve us."

We all stand, facing the center. I put my hands on my chest, looking round the circle.

"And last, we call in that-which-lies-in-the center, the circle of our own hearts. May we all be fully present together this evening."

We have all prepared short lists of things we want to let go of, and now we each speak about them in turn before consigning them to the fire. As the red flames greedily lick at our paper offerings, we appreciate their warmth.

Sometimes I use the drum to take people on drum journeys in these ceremonies. I have learned to journey in other realms like this from Caryn's classes. Doing a number of guided visualizations in my work with Sue, I see that they are just different ways of journeying. I meet a shamanic practitioner from Seattle, who uses the drum in a lot of her healing work. She asks me to help her write a book about her life and her work, so I follow her around for months, which is a great learning experience. This shamanic work makes lots of sense to me.

In the long run, I become disillusioned doing ceremonies in a group, because I find that people either don't focus on the power, which is an essential element of any ritual, or they take it too seriously. Humor, for me, is an important ingredient.

My friend Peter is a Sufi. Sufis are the mystics of Islam, and although that is not a religion that I want to embrace, since I cannot condone its view of women, I am interested. I go along with him one day to *zikr*, a Sufi meeting that happens once a week. A small group of us sit chanting for an hour or so. The words and phrases are in the ancient Aramaic language. I feel quite blissful afterwards. I go to other Sufi ceremonies that involve dancing as well. They are a delight, bringing me to a reverential understanding of the power of movement and sound.

Rumi, the fourteenth century Persian poet, was a Sufi, and many of his disciples were whirling dervishes—they whirled round and round for hours, which took them into a state of ecstasy. In time, I start to whirl as a form of meditation. I find it centers me. Of course.

I've looked at other religions. Although I'm beginning to perceive that kindness is very important to me, I still think I am not *nice* enough to be a Buddhist. A friend who has studied Buddhism in a Zen monastery tells me, "One of the women living there was really violent. She attacked a number of people."

"Well, don't you think that's bound to happen when an institution places such an emphasis on people being peaceful and loving? You're going to get someone manifesting the hidden shadow that everyone is trying to deny. I'd probably be the person in that role if I took up Buddhism seriously."

She shrugs. "Well, they certainly didn't want to deal with it at the monastery. She went after me in the kitchen with a frying pan! When I went to the Abbess to complain, she said, 'There's no need to make a fuss, and it's better if you don't tell anyone about this. It wouldn't be good for our image.' And that was that!"

I roll my eyes. "There you have it."

Chapter Twenty Four

Jo and I are not getting along as well as we used to. Sometimes it seems like our relationship is mired down in a morass of feelings that won't go away, can't be explained, and don't come from anywhere rational. Today I'm over at Jo's and I can tell she's unhappy. So I ask her what's wrong.

She shrugs, looking away uncomfortably. Then she looks back at me sadly. "Just the usual."

The usual means it's the same thing we've been talking about for weeks now, or so it seems to me. It's an incident that occurred some time ago where I said something that was hurtful to Jo.

"Is there anything I can do to make you feel better?" I ask, solicitously. I'm aware of a knot of anxiety sitting in my belly. I hate this going over and over the same thing. I always feel like I have to come up with the right thing to say. And of course I never manage. But sometimes it does seem to make Jo feel better when we talk, and I very much want her to feel better. I hate it when she's so depressed, when her energy is like a heavy wet blanket suffocating both of us.

I sit on the sofa next to her, holding her hand while she talks. I try to make sense of what she's saying and I try to find the appropriate response in me. But I can't really apply what she says to my reality. It just doesn't go together. She's silent for a while and I stare into the fire, feeling sad and frustrated, wishing for some way to make our realities converge. Becoming aware that she's crying quietly, I look at her face. Big tears are rolling down her cheeks. Mixed emotions roil around inside me. To my immense relief, compassion triumphs and I reach up to put my arms around her. She puts her head on my shoulder. In the short run, I know that my being able to do this will ease the tension between us. In the long run, I think perhaps we are too different to be spending a lot of time together, because I don't seem to be able to give her what she needs in order to feel at ease with me. Whatever our differences, I certainly love and value her, as she does me.

As I sit there holding her, I carefully investigate some of the other feelings I'm having, besides compassion for her pain. A part of me is furious, wanting to slap her and order her to stop being so juvenile. Are these the internal voices of the adults who couldn't tolerate my childhood tantrums?

Another part is jealous, because she can cry at all. So often I feel the tears stuck just behind my eyes, a sob like a sharp lump lodged in my throat. I want to let the tears flow and the sob rise, but something always blocks me. The same voices, telling me not to be so weak and stupid?

Yet another part, the knot in my belly, is very anxious, to the point of being quite afraid. I am afraid of Jo's grief. It reminds me of my own grief, which is pressing against the firmly closed gates that hold it confined.

And Jo's grief reminds me of my mother's grief, which was as ever-present in my childhood as the grass and the trees, although it was never openly acknowledged. My child mind knew it was there, and knew it was dangerous. My child mind knew that my mother didn't want to be alive. Her grief was like a fog that constantly crept and swirled its way around the house. I knew that I must take care of my mother, to help prevent her grief getting the better of her. Any needs of mine were always secondary.

I have a very vivid dream. I'm looking at my mother, who is smiling at me in the false way that she does. She says, "It's a good thing you've come home, because it's not fair that there's no one else to feed the big black birds when you're not here."

I wake from this dream crying deep, gut-wrenching sobs.

My mother. My mother.

How can I say what is true about this woman who has lived such a lie? She hides under a mask that has become a disgusting distortion of that once handsome face staring haughtily unsmiling, and slightly drunkenly, from her wedding photo. She has large full lips like me, with the same tendency to move outside of her conscious volition. When I was growing up she held them stiff and still, but nowadays they are constantly twisting and pursing, and she holds her hands over her mouth as though to hide them.

When I was a child, I only saw the carefully manicured facade. I imagine the kernel of resentment that she nursed in her closed, broken heart—broken by the same kind of horrors that broke my heart, and by other horrors too, by the nightmares of a boarding school in one of the coldest areas of Scotland, where the girls were forbidden to have more than two blankets apiece at night, in an unheated dormitory. This I cannot imagine: to lie in bed each freezing night huddled against the cold. Did her body get used to it? What other kinds of torment were they forced to suffer (these privileged daughters of the aristocracy) that she has not even told me about, that she probably cannot afford to remember?

I imagine the fear that must have tugged at her belly when her period was late for the third time. She must have woken each morning hoping and hoping that she would start bleeding. Finally she would have to admit the horrible truth: that another child (yes, me) was growing inside her, sucking the life out of her. I imagine her crying every morning as she went to the bathroom to throw up. I imagine her struggling to contain the errant tears, to contain the distress that must never be shown. I imagine how she must have forced her face into a smile when delighted relatives congratulated her on being an excellent producer of children, which is a woman's basic duty after all. My mother admits now that she hated being pregnant and, to this day, hates babies.

How could she survive being married to my brute of a father for so many years? How many times did she regret those moments of passion with him that led to the first pregnancy, that led then to their marriage? Why didn't she leave him for someone who would have treated her better? *Why didn't she leave him?*

She knows that for all her efforts, she was never really good at being a wife and mother. How I hate those generations of dragon women—my ancestors—that instilled that sense of duty into her, so that in spite of the massive sacrifices she made, she still feels like a failure. She tells me that now. That she has done nothing worthwhile with her life. That she might as well never have been alive. She wishes she'd never been born, and now she wishes she were dead. All these things she says with a smile, her lips twisting awkwardly. I watch the kernel of resentment, that walnut-sized kernel filled with the most potent dynamite in the world. I watch it twist and turn inside of her, looking for a way to escape, and I am frightened. She is no weakling, she is a strong desperate woman. And now the kernel of resentment is a roaring river of dis-ease that can't be contained. It has been nursed inside her for so long, kept warm in the confines of her poor heart, that it has turned rotten, and seeps out all round the edges. People who come near her are appalled at the stink of it, so she has few friends anymore.

I've joined a group for incest survivors. I keep telling myself I don't need to be in this group. I've thought about these issues inside out and upside down for years. I've discussed them ad infinitum with my friends. I've been in therapy for years. I could be running this group. I know all the right things to say.

So why am I not running this group, I ask myself. Why are Selina and June running it? I have to listen to them giving me advice, when they have far less idea of what I need than many of my friends.

I tell myself that I need to be in this group because I want to learn that it is safe for me to be vulnerable. Many of my friends don't want me to cry in front of them. They wouldn't know what to do with me, even though they love me dearly. It's true that Selina and June also don't really know what to do with me, but at least they think they do. I want to learn to feel safe even when I'm surrounded by unhappy people in varying states of deep pain. I want to learn that it's OK for me to show my pain in a group. Here, we don't have to pretend to be other than our deeply hurt selves.

But…I am not so sure that I am deeply hurt. Yes, I have my fears and my anxieties, but I function. I understand, I see, I hear, I love. I wasn't blinded or otherwise permanently injured by the trauma of my childhood. I see my life in a positive light, I am able to appreciate the beauty of the world around me. And I know I am a powerful person.

I've been to watch the movie *Braveheart*. The consistent betrayal that is so vividly illustrated in the movie is too much for me. I cannot, with any semblance of equanimity, watch the shallow, power-hungry Scottish aristocracy casually condemning working class lads to horrible deaths. I have too much personal experience of their callous presumption of superiority, their lack of integrity. It hurts my heart. I talk of this in the group, as unchecked tears pour down my face. June and Selina try to get me to talk about the inner child that feels so abandoned by her parents. That isn't relevant to me right now. What I am feeling is a kind of existential loneliness that arises because of the state of the human species.

I don't return to the group—I realize I am too different from these women. But I'm pleased, because I have touched into some very real truth for myself. Now I am able to cry much more easily, releasing some very old grief, that is both deeply personal and surprisingly impersonal.

Chapter Twenty Five

I am not singlemindedly monogamous. I tend to have a roving eye (or is it an open heart?) even though I may not always act on it. I love women, I love to watch them dance and work and walk and talk and move and play. I am most of all seduced by a woman who shows me her strengths and her weaknesses, who is willing to be real with me, who can talk to me about who she is and what she thinks, who can allow her feelings to flow through her without apology. I love to be caught in the intensity of the web that is spun between me and another woman when we choose to focus on each other, when we open our beings to each other, painting our desires and our passions on the canvas of the empty air between us.

Although, on an intellectual level, Jo is very encouraging of me doing what I want, she is still vulnerable to fits of jealousy when I engage in this kind of interchange with other women. So I turn away from someone when I feel that potential, when I feel that doorway beginning to open up. I don't really speak with Jo of my turning away. It is a restriction I put on myself because I have learned in past relationships that I will suffer, in one way or another, if I let my interests and attractions be too apparent.

When Jo shows interest in another woman, I am not pleased. If I am not allowed to do that, how come she is doing it? After many long and heated discussions, I realize that she did not intend to restrict me in my attractions to other women. She feels like I made that choice myself. And she is right, because on a verbal level she always encouraged me to be open to other women. I limited myself, as I had done all my life, for my parents, my teachers, my friends, my lovers. It was an unspoken bargain I made in order to fit in, in order to gain acceptance, in order to be loved, in order to make life easier.

Later—too late—when I really sit back and examine the ramifications of my having made that restriction, which was a compromise of who I am, I realize that it bled slowly and inexorably through our relationship, like salt on steel, wearing away at the integrity and trust that had been the foundation our relationship. Have you ever seen what salt does to steel? It eats away at the smart smooth shiny surface, leaving it rough and rusty and peeling off in flakey layers. Eventually the metal becomes so flimsy that you can rip it apart in your hands.

That is what happened to our relationship, because truthfully, the compromise I was making was intolerable to me.

No amount of appreciation from her could ever make up for the way my heart hurts when I am not being me. Little by little, the walls around my heart closed in, as they had done in all my relationships. They were silent in their closing, so I barely noticed. With my heart locked away, my body ceased to respond to Jo's loving hands, long before she got involved with another woman.

Jo says she still wants to be with me, but I am not sure. I am twisted inside and torn apart with jealousy. How can Jo prefer this woman to me? When I ask Jo, she insists that she does not prefer Jean to me. I question this. Our struggles push us further apart, and when we're together we only talk round and round in circles, in adversarial, unhelpful, horrible circles. I am not often as jealous as this. I feel betrayed, and I cannot distract myself from the feeling.

Still, I am relieved to be abandoned for once, instead of being always the one to do the abandoning.

Gradually the ocean of agony that clouds my days and blinds me to beauty begins to recede, though a red mist of pain and rage still occasionally drowns me. Things slowly get easier between me and Jo. But something has changed. The differences between us are more vivid. I can no longer gloss over them. I don't spend much time with her any more.

Lena, a friend of a friend from Britain, comes to California for six weeks. She's a very attractive woman. I don't really imagine she will be too interested in me, but I'm wrong. She's very interested in me.

How strange life is. Jo being with Jean rips me open. Me being with Lena rips me open too. It's the same thing, but one is awful and the other is wonderful. The one makes me want to close in on myself and hide away, and the other makes my heart burst open with delight. I am consciously aware of my essence as love, of vibrating with that energy called love.

I am aware that for most people, love is possessive, singular, and conditional, focused on a particular person. The love I'm feeling now isn't like that. It's more generic. And it encompasses the whole world. I probably will never see Lena again after this passionate week we spend together. I'll still be in this place of open-ness.

I won't be feeding the big black birds. I am fed by the life force of love.

The property that Liz, Rosie and I have bought is in the middle of nowhere, with a creek running through it, and forests of madrone, fir, oak and pine. It's my dream to own land like this. But it isn't always easy to work things out with my land partners. Right now, Liz and I are pissed at Rosie because she brought a trailer on the property, when we had an agreement not to do so. We're having one of our monthly business meetings, sitting around the table in Liz's kitchen.

Liz pours tea out of her fat brown English teapot into three flowery mugs, as she broaches the tricky subject. "I noticed you have a trailer." She is tactful, maintaining her tone at an acceptable level, so that her disapproval is only just discernible.

Rosie knows she is in trouble: her voice is stiff and slightly awkward. "Yes, I got it really cheap, I thought it would be great for my sister and her family when they come in the summer."

"You know, we did agree we wouldn't have any trailers on the land."

"Yes…I didn't remember that when I bought it. I can't see what difference it makes to either of you, you are never going to see it."

"Well, that's not true, you can see it when you drive down the road."

They argue to and fro, politely. I throw in a few comments to show I agree with Liz, trying to keep my tone neutral. Rosie bridles, sitting forward a little, shifting her shoulders awkwardly. "Well, I need to be able to do what I want here, it is one third my land, after all."

The tension is thick, with Liz unwilling to back down, and Rosie feeling she is up against the wall. I'm aware that she is afraid of our disapproval, or maybe mine in particular—she's been in my line of fire before.

I don't like her being afraid of me. Suddenly I don't care about the trailer. Clearly, she's got the message that we are not pleased about it. She doesn't need to be made to explain herself further.

I lean forward, putting my hand over hers on the table. "Rosie." As she looks up to meet my eyes, I read her defensiveness in them. "You're right, you do need to be able to do what you want here. I want all of us to be able to have what we want, all three of us. If you need to do something that Liz and I don't like, then we can talk about it, and work out a way of making it happen so we all feel OK. It's just I would prefer you not to go ahead and do something that we have agreed not to do, without talking to us first. If you talk about it, we can always work it out. I really believe that, because I really believe that we all love each other, and we want the best for each other."

She looks down at the table, hiding her tears. Her voice is soft as she replies, "I know you're right, and I appreciate you saying that. I do love you both, and I know that you love me. Sometimes I forget. I know I need to communicate with you more, and I will try to do so."

We move on to the next topic on the agenda.

I'm down the hill from Liz's house, working on the water line, which was damaged in a recent frost. It is a beautiful winter afternoon, the sun shining down out of a clear blue sky, although the air is sharp and cold in the shade. Out of breath from walking up the steep slope, I pause a moment to sit on the red soil, stony and bare here where only scrub grows, maroon and green manzanita bushes.

The sun feels so good on my face, I lie down and close my eyes, soaking up the warmth. After a short rest, I open my eyes and stand up. There is a moment—or is it several minutes?—when I see everything silver. The naked branches of the oaks, austere in their leaflessness, their strange shapes unmasked, are coated in silver, dripping silver. And I am aware of their kinship to me, the earth beneath us, our roots reaching downwards, silver threads running through us into the earth, who is the mother of all beings on this planet. I am aware of the trees singing to me, singing to all beings, singing the song of life, singing the song that echoes in my bones. I am aware of my feet on the ground, on the soil that is my body in a different form, and I am aware of my one-ness with this Earth, who is the giver of all, the beginning and end of everything, whose body is mine.

The small chestnut mare is standing in the shade with the other horses, and she flicks her ears as she hears me, then turns her head towards me. She's part Arab, part Welsh pony, a good mix for an inexperienced rider—I didn't learn to ride till I was thirty-three, and this is the horse who taught me. She's small enough that it's not far to fall, and she's not so strong that I can't pull her head round.

Opening the gate, I walk up to her and run my hand under her thick mane, scratching her neck just the way she likes it. I slip the halter over her soft nose. She lifts her head to make it more difficult, and I say, "Come on, sweetheart, don't do that!"

It's a token resistance. Buckling the halter behind her ears, I lead her out of the field. We walk up the short hill side by side and I tie her lead rope to the tree trunk that serves as a hitching post. I brush her down in long even strokes, starting at her head. Her red-brown mane is thick and tangle-free but her coat is a little matted with mud, and I brush hard to get her smooth and clean.

"Look at you, you dirty horse, you've been rolling in the mud," I mutter affectionately. As I brush, I admire the powerful muscles of her back, the perfect solid slope of her shoulders, the roundness of her butt, the way the bones of her upper legs give way to the finer bones below her hocks, and the way the hair on her legs forms a neat fringe over the top of her hooves, as if trimmed just so.

"Hey, pretty girl, you're so beautiful." I am murmuring sweet things to her, hardly aware of what I am saying.

Soon her coat is smooth and soft. I slip the saddle over her back. She looks round at me, tossing her head, as I do up the cinch, as though to say "Not too tight, please!" I slip the bridle up her head and slide my thumb into her mouth behind her front teeth, so she opens her mouth for the bit. I stroke the white blaze that is painted between her eyes, down the hard bony part of her face to the place where it turns so soft and warm and damp, her wide black nostrils fringed in long fine hairs.

Putting the reins over her head, I unclip the lead rope. Then I gather a handful of her mane, put my left foot in the stirrup and hoist myself onto her back. As usual, she wants to go right away without giving me time to get settled, so I pull back on the reins, saying sharply, "Ho!"

Then I'm ready and we're off down the road.

Pretty soon she wants to run, so we canter for a little while. Then there is a long downhill, and we walk, picking our way carefully. I watch the tops of the trees, the hill stretching upwards on my left with scrub growing out of bare red earth, falling away on my right into thick tall forest. The orange branches of the madrones wend their way towards the sky, interspersed with leafy oaks and a few tall pines, whose sparse trunks reach straight towards the sunlight, in contrast to the twisting and turning of the other trees.

We cross the rushing of a little creek, still full of the joys of a wet spring, and then we are at the beginning of a long flat stretch. I feel her legs gather under her, as she puts all her power into a full gallop. We are flying, and the wind is stretching my eyes back into my head, my hair streaming back off my face. I strain forward with her a little, lifting myself off the saddle to avoid being thrown around, as her long mane lashes me in the face. Sitting up straighter, I follow her quick swerve round a bend. Her power and her joy in the running surge through me. I let the reins hang loose. I am perfectly balanced on her back and we are moving as one being.

She slows to a canter, and then to a trot, tossing her head from side to side. Her sides are heaving, but her step is still vigorous and I know she will be ready to go again in a minute. I laugh, exhilarated.

A vulture makes a low lazy sweep overhead, effortlessly catching the breeze under its long black wings to lift itself gracefully up and away, after checking us out. The trees have opened up, and ahead, perfectly framed by closer wooded hills on either side, is a vista of a snow-capped mountain. Wisps of cloud float around it, slightly tinged with sunset's early pink.

Again and again, I am deeply grateful.

Chapter Twenty Six

These days I talk about sex with lots of women, which has given me plenty of insight into women's sexuality, quite apart from my own. When I am introduced to a woman who is a successful literary agent, I ask her how a book on women and orgasm would sell. Her eyes get big.

I spend six months interviewing women and writing about sex. The book is published by a reputable firm in the San Francisco Bay area. I have a delightful time going to book stores, like Barnes and Noble, where I talk about sex in a loud voice in front of a group of people who are genuinely interested in what I have to say. The veils of secrecy that surrounded sex when I was growing up are truly in shreds.

At one of these readings, a woman asks me, "How did you get to be so wise?"

A day or so later, I realize that the correct answer to that question is, "We all have access to an infinite source of wisdom. It's a matter of learning how to let it flow through you."

One by one, I call a list of radio interviewers around the country, arranging phone interviews. Almost all the people who interview me are men, and I am prepared for them to refuse to address sex seriously. To my great pleasure, the majority of them treat it as an important, interesting subject with far-reaching implications.

One day I call a number in the Midwest, saying my bit. "Hallo, my name is Chris Brixton, and I've written a book about women's sexuality. If you think you'd like to do an interview, give me your address and I'll send you a copy."

After a short pause, the faceless male voice replies, "Is this a *joke*?"

Annoyed, I respond, "No, it's not a joke! I've written a book about sex, and I'd like you to review it!"

"OK, well, send me the book then!"

I send it off, although I don't expect to hear from him again. Two weeks later he calls me, saying, "I read your book and I'd like to interview you."

So we set up a time. These interviews always depend on the interviewer asking intelligent, leading questions, and this man's questions are excellent. The following day I receive an email from him, which reads, "I want you to know that your book has changed my relationship with my wife beyond my wildest expectations. I never knew that such loving intimacy was possible, and your book made it so for us, after twenty-five years of marriage. Thank you from the depth of my heart."

With such good feedback around this book, I am thinking maybe I will become one of San Francisco's sexperts. I teach a class for women who have trouble reaching orgasm, and quickly discover that what I have said in the book is true—when women start to address sexual issues, their unexpressed feelings come to the surface, and it's often unpleasant. They are angry. I have tremendous sympathy for them—and I don't want to put myself in the line of fire.

I start an ongoing class on sexuality and spirituality for women at the Metropolitan Community Church, which is very alternative. At the beginning of the class, a woman questions me about privilege, and I freely acknowledge that I consider myself a privileged person. It would be stupid to pretend otherwise, considering that I am white, I'm a citizen of the USA, and I own my own house. I refuse to discuss the concept of privilege any further within the framework of a class that is specifically designed *not* to be an intellectual exercise. "I'd be happy to discuss it later," I tell my questioner firmly. She doesn't want to talk about it afterwards. They fire me after the first class.

A man who has read my book emails me, wanting help in his relationships with women. After talking on the phone for five or ten minutes, I know we are not on the same planet, and probably never will be. This happens several times.

The fact that I feel genuine compassion for these people's situations makes no difference. Most people want me to tell them how to have good sex, and I can't tell anyone that. Sex is a metaphor for life. Having good sex is like leading a good life. It's an individual thing, and no one else can dictate what you need to do in order to make it happen.

Whenever I'm in Britain, I visit my friend Nancy, who's known me many years. She reckons I'm not cut out to be any kind of counselor. "You don't have enough patience with people's fears," she says, with that beautiful twinkling smile. "And that's your gift. But nowadays, anyone who wants to be a teacher has to be very concerned about everyone's safety."

"Hmmm…" I frown. "If people don't move through their fears at some point, they'll never change."

"Yes, and you know that, and you can help people to do that. Mostly as a role model, though, not in an established capacity as a teacher."

"Hmm, you're probably right. I love helping people, but truthfully, the times when I am able to help seem to occur by accident. And I feel that it's arrogant to *assume* that I can actually help anyone. I don't have the right to make judgments about what people ought to be doing or how they ought to be doing it."

"You just have to be you, and people will be inspired by your example."

"Yes, I just have to do what I love, and when it helps someone else, then it's an added bonus. I love the idea that I inspire others. I've always wanted to do that."

I meet a woman, Kassie, in San Francisco. I watch the way she touches her lover, and my skin craves the feel of those hands. As time passes, we become lovers. My initial interest was well-founded—she is one of those rare people who really understand the art of touch, knowing exactly how to communicate what a million words cannot express. Like me, she isn't the monogamous type, and since we live two hundred miles apart, our relationship works well. I have the space that I need to be me. She has the space to play around with other women.

We've been at the beach with some friends, climbing on the rocks, watching the waves smash themselves ceaselessly, flinging tireless spray in the air, again and again and again. I'm invigorated by the boundless energy of the ocean. I watch my lover as she walks up the path in front of me. I admire the way her ass moves, outlined by her jeans, the curve of her leg, the way her arm swings and her fingers brush her thigh. When we get in the car, I lean over and put one hand on her cheek, turning her head towards me. Very gently I run my lips across hers, and then across her face until I reach her ear. My tongue lightly flicks the lobe of her ear and then I take it between my teeth, biting down momentarily so she gasps. I tip her head up with my thumb under her jaw. She doesn't resist. Her throat is bared to my teeth now as her head is tilted back, and I tease the skin with my lips, my tongue, my teeth, enough to arouse but not hurt. I pull back just a little and let her feel my breath caressing her neck. Slowly I remove the pressure of my thumb from the point of her jaw and let her head drop until her face is level with mine. We look into each other's eyes for a long time, as I hold the palm of my hand against her cheek. Then I sit back, and we both smile. She starts the car.

Sex is such an easy way to reach altered states of awareness, to experience the unlimited ecstasy of the spirit beings that we are. The boundless joy of relating so intimately to another person reminds me that we are so much more than flesh and blood. It reminds me why we are alive.

I love to use sex to give voice to those forbidden shadows that lurk in my subconscious. I can express the innocent and maybe angry schoolgirl who doesn't want anyone to touch her, the abusive domineering part who just takes what s/he wants, the sexy teenager who flirts only on her own terms. I can play with these roles, my very own archetypes, with all the intensity that a sexual charge will bring to any situation. To have fun with my worst inner demons—that is a delight! And then, to play foil to my partner doing the same thing, that is the tastiest icing on the tastiest cake I ever ate.

I carry in two bags of the groceries and set them down on the counter. I'm about to go out and get the rest when Kassie steps in my path, putting her arms around me. I relax into her embrace; it feels so good. She strokes my head and runs her fingers through my hair, giving a little tug and pulling my head up so I meet her gaze. She has that look in her eyes. I feel a rush of desire, as though an electric current has passed between us. We kiss, hard, and I feel her fingers tight in my hair now, pulling my face into her. My hands are under her jacket and I stroke her back, just where I know it is most sensitive. She jerks and groans, and I smile, enjoying my power. Abruptly, in one adroit movement, she has me turned around so that my back is against the kitchen counter, and she thrusts one knee between my legs. Now it's my turn to groan. One hand still controls my head, now the other is between my legs, kneading me through my jeans. She knows just where to put just the right amount of pressure, pushing up into me with the knuckle of her thumb. Then she's using both hands to pull my shirt out of my jeans and she has her hands on my skin, both nipples between thumbs and fingers, stroking them just right, then running the palm of her hand across them and back, watching my face. I feel the muscles around my mouth flexing, almost as though my lips swell. Then somehow she is on her knees in front of me, holding my wrists by my sides. I push my hips into her face as she pushes her face into me. "I want to feel your skin on mine, I need to feel your skin on mine …" I realize I am saying it aloud. Letting go of my wrists, she slides her hands up under my shirt, grazing my belly and squeezing my breasts, her forearms stroking my sides.

I am suddenly completely amazed that I can allow myself to be overwhelmed in this way, that I can let go and delight in our wild animal wanting.

Kassie isn't the intellectual type. Although I enjoy mental tasks in general, I don't miss the endless analytical discussions about what's wrong. Kassie and I seem to be able to communicate on a gut level, with remarkably little use of words. We don't try to hide anything from each other. We couldn't do so. We *feel* each other. I trust her implicitly, not because I know she will never leave me, but because I know she will never be able to deceive me, nor I her. In fact, I know she *will* leave me at some point—in spite of our love for each other, our goals in life are too far apart.

Chapter Twenty Seven

Now, I go to Montana every year to see Dayana, and talk with Amag. It has become a necessary pilgrimage, since their wisdom speaks to me in a way nothing else does. It fills me with joy.

I am sitting on the sofa, totally focused on an intense conversation with Amag. As always, they answer my questions with questions that make me think beyond thought. Most of the time, I understand everything perfectly and wordlessly as I sit here in front of them. Later, when I try to use my brain to compute what I've been told, it all seems to be incomprehensible riddles, and I often feel deeply confused. My brain just isn't the right tool to grasp these concepts.

When we are done, and Dayana comes back into her own body, I somersault off the back of the sofa in delight.

The next morning, I leave to go to Seattle, a six hour drive. I feel deeply pleased with the world and myself. At some point, this sensation of pleasure becomes all that I am, all that is. I stop the car and get out, turning round and round, staring in astonishment at the trees, the road, the passing cars, the sky. Something truly indescribable (existence itself, perhaps) is occurring.

Now, of course, I am going to try to describe it.

Everything around me is breathtakingly beautiful. The air is suffused with golden light, and I am lit up by that light. I am breathing it, as it breathes me. I feel it filling me up, creating me. I am transported, de-lighted, and completely at peace. I desire nothing. The vastness of this moment, which is always, is all I could possibly need or want. I understand that *all is well*. Whatever I might have thought to be the meaning of those words, I had not understood them before this moment. There is no possibility that anything could be wrong. Even if there were a major accident and bodies were strewn all over the road, I would still know that all is well. This knowing astounds me. It moves me in a way I have never been touched before, in some very deep place where I am beyond human.

This is how it always has been and always will be.

Like that blissful aftermath of orgasm, the knowing fades over a few days. I do what we humans are so good at: I fall into a kind of sleep where I layer reality with an illusion that is delightful, appalling, terrifying, compelling, and above all, familiar. It's called daily life.

What I do remember is this: that no matter how I might feel in any given moment, there is the possibility of existing in a place of peace that is far beyond any concept of peace and war. When I am in that place of awareness that all is well, I am more powerful than I could ever know, without even caring about the concept of power. Anyone who comes into contact with me is bound to experience my vastness.

No *having* or *doing* can be as profoundly effective as being in that place of peace.

One day I'm driving down to San Francisco, maneuvering my truck through the traffic, trying not to feel enraged with the drivers who won't get out of the way, when I find myself thinking, *there must be an easier way to get from A to B.* It is a vivid thought that stays with me. A month or two later I'm in Montana, and I ask Amag this question. Their response is immediate: "Well, you have thought yourself here, you can certainly think yourself somewhere else! You believe that you require muscular or mechanical means to move yourself around, but in fact all movement occurs because you think it, because you desire it."

A long conversation ensues, leaving my mind reeling. Much of what they say is fascinating, though I can't grasp it on a mental level.

"The personality gives the impression of a *who* but in fact you are more of a *where* than you are a *who*. It requires more awareness to be a *where*." I'm very intrigued by this, although I cannot formulate questions that will facilitate my understanding further.

What I do understand is that my body, and everything else I experience, are thought forms, created by me. Therefore, what I think, or what I believe—which, surely, is just a thought that becomes so automatic I don't notice I'm thinking it—is very important. And not static, but changeable.

I want to learn how to utilize this magnificent power of thought very consciously.

I take another class with Caryn. It illustrates how far my process of healing has taken me. I am out on the far edge of the wisdom seekers. Once, I believed that love or creativity would bring me happiness, and I just needed to find the right outlet. Now I see that there is a much larger force at work. Neither Caryn nor Peter, not any other human being I have met, nor anything I read, is able to give me satisfactory answers.

In spite of the fact that I no longer subscribe to the belief that the world is a dangerous place, I still catch myself falling into those old habits of anxiety. I've changed on some levels, but not as deeply and completely as I want.

When I ask Amag how to reach a deeper level, they tell me, "You only have to choose it."

Hmmmm. Perhaps I haven't been one hundred percent committed to change. Perhaps it's time to get really serious. I make a decisive commitment, to whomever one makes such commitments: I will do *whatever* it takes to let go of all my old limiting belief systems. I am nearly fifty, I've tried many things in my life, and now I want something absolutely different.

Soon after this, I am riding my horse late on a December afternoon. I have no memory of what occurs. The following day we find my helmet, cracked, in the road. I must have been lying unconscious for an hour or two. Gradually, piece by piece, I become aware of physical reality. It's completely dark, I'm very very cold, and excruciating pain is emanating from the area of my head. I can't make my body work properly. I don't have any awareness of who I am, why I am there, or where I am. That stuff isn't important. I just know that this body feels very bad, and needs help. Making out the shape of a vehicle parked close to where I'm lying, I figure that means there will be people nearby who can help me. I manage to crawl over to the vehicle and pull myself upright. When I open the door, a smell of mold hits me and I suddenly remember who and where I am. I know that this vehicle is the old abandoned truck parked down my driveway, which means the closest inhabited house is half a mile away by road, or a very steep walk through the woods. Both are impossible on a dark, moonless night, considering I can't stand up without support. Even with all my faculties in place, I've never been able to make my way through the woods in this kind of darkness, devoid of a flashlight, without getting thoroughly scratched and bruised.

The next thing I remember is waking up—slowly again—on the floor in the house that is half a mile from where I fell. The owner has covered me with blankets and called an ambulance. Later, she tells me I fell in the door of the house and crashed to the floor. How did I get there? Since I have not a scratch or a bruise on me, it's impossible that I walked or crawled. Did I create this whole scenario because I wanted to have the experience of moving myself by the power of thought, and I could only do that when I'd hit my head hard enough to displace all the old belief systems about needing muscles or mechanics to get from A to B?

Whichever way you look, it's a miracle, along the lines of a mother who is suddenly able to pick up a car because her child is trapped underneath it. And now I *really* want to do it again, without having to hit my head first.

In the meantime, an ambulance takes me to the hospital. Once I'm warm enough, and I have ingested a painkiller to calm my throbbing head, I feel quite happy, in a way that is very unfamiliar to me. It is a perfect kind of contentment. For the next few days, I simply sit, observing and appreciating what is around me. I'm not at all bothered about anything. The list of things-to-do that normally starts my day doesn't even cross my mind.

Other people, however, are very anxious. I have fairly serious concussion, and at the hospital, they tell my friends that I'm not to be left on my own for three days because I may die if my brain starts bleeding, or some such thing. I don't notice that I can't finish a sentence, and I don't care anyway. Only one thing seems important to me, and that is that I do what feels right from moment to moment.

The first night I stay at Liz's house. When I wake in the morning, I'm feeling fairly OK, so I walk up to my house—only a few hundred yards through the woods—and hang out on my sofa. A couple of friends stay with me most of the day to make sure I don't die. The next night Liz wants me to come and sleep at her house again. I walk down there and have dinner with her. I can talk almost normally now. But when I lie down to sleep I find myself wanting to be back in my own house. So I get up and walk home without waking Liz.

The next morning Liz calls. She's furious. "You could have died in the night!" she rails at me.

I'm not even consciously aware of the anger that surges out of me in response. "I don't care if I die in the night, just leave me alone!" Liz later tells me that I was shouting so loudly, she had to hold the phone well away from her ear.

At that moment, avoiding death is not a motivation that carries any clout with me whatsoever. I am only concerned about enjoying life.

Three days later, I'm back to my normal active physical state, making lists about what I need to do. I'm restored to my civilized self, being reasonably polite to the people around me. One thing doesn't change: I am really not worried about dying.

For three months I carry on with my life the same old way. I'm in the process of writing the book about Char, a shamanic practitioner living in Seattle, and I fly up there for ten days. The day before I leave, I get what seems to be flu. Arriving in Seattle, I am really sick. For nine days I lie in bed, alternating between such a high temperature that I soak the sheets in seconds, and such a low temperature that I can't get warm with ten thick blankets on the bed. I refuse to go to hospital—my experience with the doctors when I fell on my head has convinced me that they don't relate to what I perceive as my best interests. I know that what I am going through is a result of my decision to change my life. It is a healing crisis, a cleansing of old outmoded stuff. It needs to be allowed. Char feels the same way about western medicine as I do. She and a friend do some shamanic work to help move things along.

By the tenth day I am just well enough to return home, though I feel pretty groggy. I visit a friend who is studying acupuncture, and she takes my pulses. I can tell she's worried. She gives me some herbs, instructing me to come back in a few days. When I do so, and she checks my pulses again, she looks relieved. She explains that when I had first seen her, my yin and my yang were about to separate. If that had happened, I'd have gone into a coma. She tells me it will be six months before I'm back to normal. She's right—it is six months almost to the day before I wake up one morning and leap out of bed filled with energy.

So I spend a lot of the spring and summer lying around. Mostly it's OK, since I want to learn how to *be* instead of *do* all the time, and I appreciate watching the infinite, constantly changing variety of beauty around me. However, I am hounded by questions such as, *who or what am I, that I can create myself through the power of thought? What are the limits on this potential?*

I manage to get myself to Montana to talk with Amag. "The illness you have created is a little like an incinerator which is used to dispose of thoughts and feelings that are no longer useful, or healthy, so that *the you* that you are and have always been, emerges. You may benefit from looking at your eyes in a mirror, so that you can feel who is looking back at you."

When the reading with Dayana is over, I go into the bathroom and look in the mirror, thinking I will stare soulfully at myself for a few minutes. As I glance into my own brown-green eyes, surrounded with wrinkles, I meet myself, again. I am so intensely shocked that I actually jump backwards. In that instant, the last time I met myself—an occasion that I had remembered and dismissed as a nightmare—comes vividly back to memory.

I was seven years old, lying in bed one night, when I became aware of the air in the room vibrating. At first it was quite slow, then the vibration gradually speeded up. As it became faster and faster, I found myself having trouble breathing. Soon I could barely make my lungs expand. My breath got shorter and shorter until I was gasping for air, thinking I would certainly die. Just as the terrifying feeling of suffocation engulfed me, I managed to make myself leap up and dash for the window. I thrust my head outside, taking great gulps of air, which somehow brought back the ability to breathe normally, although the air outside was no different from the air inside.

Shaken though I am by this memory, I continue to look into those eyes. The being I see looking back at me is certainly not human and not the kind of being you would want to mess with. It is all-powerful, all-knowing, and vast beyond any mental comprehension. It is implacable, determined, absolutely focused, and quite unmoved by considerations of pain or grief. How do I know this? The same way I knew peace on the drive to Seattle. The same way I know my name. The same way we know all things.

After a minute or two, the sensation of this unthinkable presence fades away, and I'm just looking at myself in the mirror.

But isn't that what I was doing all along? I'm reeling. I could never have expected this.

It takes me weeks to process the magnitude of this experience. The word that comes to me, to describe the being-that-is-me, is *ruthless.* An interesting word—it literally means *without rue,* which means *without regret.*

Now I have the answer to the question that has hounded me, *who am I?* And I know that there is never the slightest reason for me to be afraid of anything, since that's the kind of being I am.

Later, Amag tells me that the experience of dying for a human is often one of suffocation, because it requires concentration on the part of spirit to pump air into lungs, and when spirit removes that focus, then the physical being cannot get enough oxygen to continue living. The *dream* that I had at the age of seven occurred because I had begun to let go of my human identity/body, intending to die. Then I met my Self and understood the vastness of being, which made me decide to continue in human form after all.

Chapter Twenty Eight

Every morning I walk down the hill to feed the horses. If he is in the mood, Joey, my feline Hollywood boy, accompanies me. He flies in front of me at high speed, leaping over ruts and puddles with carefree abandon. Sometimes he goes so fast, the breeze created by his movement flattens the long black fur on his back and his tail, and he looks like a skunk with a stripe. If he can't see where I am, he calls to me, a plaintive little miaow that just about breaks my heart. Then I call his name and he comes running to find me, with a chirrup as he reaches me. Alive and alert he stands, his black-slitted yellow eyes big and open. He's looking expectantly about, as though to say *OK world! What have you got to offer me today?* He crouches, his eyes getting big and very round. He darts away, a wild thing in the woods, flying up a tree trunk, twenty feet directly upwards, with no apparent effort, as though he has wings. Hanging there, hugging the trunk, he looks around. Then he backs down a little way and walks out along a horizontal branch, checking that I am watching. Seeing that I am, he starts to rub his face and body, strutting proudly on the thin branch.

I want to be like him and strut my stuff proudly, unselfconsciously.

He gets distracted, a little too pleased with himself, rubs too hard and falls sideways. I screech in terror but he catches himself by wrapping his front paws around the branch. For a few precarious seconds he hangs there, the weight of his body held only by his front legs. He looks down at me uncertainly, almost pleadingly, but he is twenty feet above me. His back feet reach out to find a purchase, and he manages to swing his body upright. I'm standing underneath, tearing my hair out, while now he acts as if nothing happened, continuing to strut and rub. I walk on, hoping this will encourage him to return to ground level. I glance behind to see him backing down the tree. Moments later he dashes past me with his tail straight up in the air.

I want to be like him, a wild uncontrollable animal racing through the woods.

Later in the day, he comes into the house to say hallo and get some food. Some days he hassles me mercilessly for attention; other days he is mellow and tired after his adventures, chasing and being chased out in the big wide world. Today he jumps up on the chair next to me where I am working on the computer, and purrs, although I do not have a spare hand to stroke him. He seems perfectly happy to sit there purring, his yellow eyes half closed. After a while he curls up in a ball, wraps one white-socked front paw over his black nose and goes to sleep. I get up for something to eat, and when I come back, I say his name: "Joey!" He wakes and chirps, raising his head sleepily. I rub between his ears, admiring his long white whiskers. He purrs, and rolls on his back, stretching out his legs, exposing his belly for me to rub. I oblige him, reveling in the thick softness of his luxuriant fur.

I want to be like him and roll over easily, trustingly, for a belly rub.

I'm standing outside my house, staring at the vista of hills on the other side of the valley where the creek flows, hidden from sight by the trees and the geography of the land. The occasional grassy meadow, dried golden in the heat of the summer sun, peeks through the dark green carpet of the firs and the yellow green of the autumnal oaks. A break in the hills reveals a distant peak, one of the mountains that must be more than seven thousand feet high. To my left, beyond a grove of orange-trunked madrone, the red ground rises up, covered in scrub, dotted with occasional pines, ideal terrain for cougars and bears.

I have been dissatisfied for months, perhaps years. Amag's words echo in my mind: "You must find what is comfortable for you."

Comfort—an interesting concept. Most people find comfort in having money in the bank, good health insurance, that kind of thing. Those things don't bother me. Sometimes I feel a sense of comfort when I am accepted by other people. At least I feel *uncomfortable* when I am not accepted by other people. I feel most uncomfortable when I have to try and fit in. What would I choose if I didn't care at all about what others thought of me? What would I be like if I had no concerns about the future? What if I didn't care what I might have to let go of?

I would trust that the being I met in the mirror is always taking care of me. I would allow that being-that-is-me to orchestrate the perfect day from moment to moment. I would travel the world, going wherever I wanted whenever I wanted. I would have very few possessions, knowing that everything I need will turn up.

If I did that, I would have to leave this beautiful place, my house, my friends, the animals who have shared my love. There might be a great relief in letting go of all my responsibilities and ceasing to be the very-busy-person-who-fixes-everything, but at what cost?

I gaze at the mountain, blue in the distance. I remember many other mountains—sunset in the Himalayas, turning the steep snowy slopes every shade of red; an alpine peak glistening in the moonlight; the fantastic shapes of the desert mountains around San Diego. These are only the ones I recall. There are many I have never seen. If I stay here, for fear of losing what is in front of me now, I will miss out on so much. What am I afraid of? I know that I am taken care of.

I realize that the decision, no matter how monumental, has already been made. It's been like that for me all my life. That-which-I-saw-in-the-mirror has made up its mind and won't leave me in peace until I get moving.

Joey walks up the path towards me, with that beautiful welcoming chirrup that is a cross between a purr and a miaow. "Joey, my Joey!" I laugh with delight, sitting down cross-legged on the warm earth. He stands with his two white front feet on my leg, and we touch noses. I pick him up and cradle him upside down in one arm so I can stroke his infinitely soft underbelly. He is completely relaxed.

How can I leave my gorgeous black and white boy? A sob rises in my throat, and tears fill my eyes.

I begin the long and very agonizing process of letting go of everything that is tying me down. I have a great deal to do before I can get rid of everything I own. I start taking off for a month or two at a time, then returning to work on finishing my house.

I know I can no longer be anyone's girlfriend. Although I still adore Kassie, I painfully inform her that she has to give up the concept of me as her girlfriend. Two years later we cease to be lovers, when she finds another woman who can be a real girlfriend to her. We are still deeply bonded. I ache for her touch, for the unboundaried physical ease we shared.

Joey is an independent sort, and when I'm away he spends most of his time down at Liz's. He seems pretty happy down there, although I feel anxious about leaving him for long.

One day, when I'm home, he comes into the house and sits in the middle of the floor. Immediately aware that something is wrong, I quickly discover that he's been in a fight: he has multiple puncture wounds, and can barely put any weight on three of his furry little feet. He's obviously in a lot of pain. I take him to a vet, who gives him antibiotics. He doesn't get better. He's not eating, he hardly moves around at all, and his eyes have a kind of glaze. When he lies next to me, his body is very hot and I feel regular mini-convulsions passing through him.

I'm beside myself. On the third day, I find him curled up in a corner of the back room, and I know that he is looking for a place to die. I take him to another vet who puts him on a different kind of antibiotic. The next morning he is obviously better and I breathe a long sigh of relief.

But for weeks afterwards, I find abscesses coming up along his spine. He seems to have some weakness in his front legs—sometimes they give way under him, and although he recovers quickly, I suspect he feels very uncomfortable in his body. He never quite regains his irrepressible spunk.

I spend six weeks in Hawaii, a magical place. I can barely believe the fish that I see when I go snorkeling: such an array of vivid, translucent, neon, transparent colors. And the shapes! Some are tall and narrow, some round, square, rectangular, or oblong, some with flowery fins, and some with business-like fins, some nervous and speedy, some slow and easygoing, some in shoals and some single. There are small fat black ones with white spots, very thin long transparent ones that look purple in the rays of the sun, little red ones with white stripes, white-ish grayish ones with a horizontal yellow stripe and a single black spot, tall black ones with a big vertical orange stripe. Some are red and green checkered, some are bright yellow, some yellow with black markings on their tails and heads, some with amazing feathery trailing tails, some that are pink, purple and green with vivid blue outlines, some with yellow knobs sticking out by their tails, and others with blue knobs. There are sharply black ones with bright orange spots, white ones with diagonal gold stripes, white ones with intricate web designs on them, yellow ones with two sets of diagonal stripes that meet at an angle, others outlined in iridescent blue.

The coral is also incredible: purple, blue and pink, round and smooth, stick-like, or sharp and nobbly.

And then there are sea turtles, and dolphins that I hear singing when I am snorkeling, and all the manifestations of Pele: the flowing lava, molten earth bubbling up, bright red; steam rising up out of bottomless fissures. And the tropical vegetation: waterfalls that pour over rock cliffs, trees that grow in all shapes and variations of green, producing delicious and remarkable fruits, offering homes to birds that fill the air with their beautiful sounds all day long.

I'm staying with a couple of friends on the Big Island, when Liz calls. Joey has been gone for ten days. She has looked everywhere and asked all the neighbors, but no one has seen him.

Copious, unboundaried tears flow out of my wide open heart, soaking my handkerchief. I can't do anything other than cry for the next two hours. Years later I can still burst into tears when I think how soft his fur was.

Yet I can accept he's gone. Death is always just a matter of time, after all, and why should he stay when he wasn't happy being in physical form? Years later, although I still miss his physical presence, I am very very grateful that he was in my life. He taught me more about unconditional love than any human I ever knew. What a gift.

Chapter Twenty Nine

Back in Scotland for a week, I find my parents still doing their own bizarre thing. Sometimes the way they are acting out their karma in this lifetime is quite hilarious. My father, forever the macho bully, has grown breasts. In his inimitable fashion, he seems almost proud of them. He talks about them a lot.

"Have I shown you my breasts?" he asks, standing behind one of the dining room chairs with his hands on its straight back, looking down on me as I read the newspaper.

"No, and I don't want to see them, thank you," I reply.

He's disappointed. "Oh, well…did I tell you, I actually have to wear a bra?" He laughs. "I'm producing so much milk, it soaks my shirt if I don't have these silly little pad things." He gestures at his chest.

"Do you know why it's happening? What do the doctors say?"

He waves his hand dismissively. "Oh, they don't know what they're talking about. *I* know why it happened. When your mother was ill last year, I bought a chicken at the Cash and Carry and ate it all myself. I'm sure it had some kind of hormones in it. They use all kinds of chemicals to fatten up those birds." He shrugs, running his hand over his nearly bald head. "Never should have eaten it, but it's too late now!"

My mother, once an excellent cook and the perfect hostess, has lost her sense of decorum, and has certainly lost her ability to produce a decent meal. I have to vet the food I am offered. My mother doesn't eat much. When it's lunchtime, she puts a plate of three or four different cheeses and some crackers on the table, then serves up soup that has obviously been recycled several times. Two of the cheeses are covered in mold. I simply avoid them. After we have been sitting there for ten minutes or so, my mother sees the mold and cuts it off, carefully piling the moldy pieces on her plate, and replacing the doctored hunk on the cheese plate. Five minutes later, I notice she is absentmindedly eating the moldy pieces.

My Uncle Michael is the sixth Earl of Chesterhame, although that doesn't mean much these days. The laird's family doesn't have the clout it once had. In the last forty years, things have changed in Scotland. No longer do the locals tip their hats and say 'Guid morning, m'lady,' to my mother. Many of them barely know who she is. The feudal system that was still functioning when I was a child has finally died a long overdue death.

Still, my uncle is a member of the House of Lords, which means he does have a voice amongst the rulers. And I find that a little frightening, since although he is well-meaning and good-hearted, he is not worldly wise or quick-witted. He understands almost nothing about life outside his own very narrow existence. Conversations require patience. It takes as much as a whole minute for him to gather his words to respond to a question or a comment. He married one of his father's mistresses, who is now dead—fortunately, since she suffered from severe Alzheimer's disease. Prior to being committed to a mental hospital, she became so aggressive that my uncle had to lock her out of his bedroom.

For all these reasons it is easy to make fun of him, and he wasn't on talking terms with my parents for many years. Now that they are all old and somewhat lonely, they've made peace, and since he lives just up the road, he visits often. Like my mother, he has some strange ailments. My father, with great hilarity, regales me several times with a story of how he regurgitated his food on his plate in the middle of eating a meal.

My father goes into hospital to have a benign prostate lump removed. He's very proud of how big it is, and gives everyone a blow by blow account of the whole scenario, again and again, as often as anyone will listen. I quickly get tired of hearing him describe the size of the tube that is inserted in his penis.

It so happens that I am in Scotland during the two days he is in the hospital, so I take care of my mother. My sister Elizabeth and my Uncle Michael come by for dinner. Neither of the older people have much to say. My sister, in her usual fashion, keeps the stories flowing while we sift through some overcooked fish and vegetables. In between the conversation, I hear a cough from my uncle and glance anxiously sideways. He is depositing a neat little pile of chewed food on his plate next to what has not yet been ingested. My sister barely hesitates in her story and since we were both laughing anyway, it's not obvious that we are having trouble maintaining our cool. When he is clearly finished throwing up, he mutters succinctly, "Sorry! Ruined that."

Suavely scooping up his plate, Elizabeth carries it away. I follow her into the kitchen and we both double up, gasping with laughter.

Later, in England, I stay with my old friend Nancy, who is always pleased to see me. It is a great relief to be in an atmosphere of sanity. I entertain her with stories of my crazy family. She met them some twenty-five years earlier, when she and I were lovers, so she knows I'm not exaggerating how extraordinary they are. After we have both laughed and cried a little, she says, "How did you manage to grow up so sane?"

I roll my eyes. "I wasn't always sane! I used to be really angry all the time, remember?"

She grins. "Yes, that's true. Maybe the question should be, how come you have grown up?"

"Well, my anger wasn't doing me any good. I wanted to stop feeling like that, so I did the work I had to do in order to change. And I gave up trying to change others. I recognized that everyone in the world is doing the best they can." With a mock expression of alarm, I add, "Although that is rather frightening."

"Hmm…" she frowns. "We were all pretty angry and judgmental for a while. I mean, as feminists. We were really self-righteous."

"No kidding! I was in such a fog of confusion in those days, I couldn't work out what was right and wrong. Now that I've stopped trying to play by anyone else's rules, I have some clarity in my life. I'm not trying to please anyone else. I make up my own rules."

"But very few people I know are as forgiving as you seem to be now."

"Oh! Well, I don't forgive for anyone else's sake, only for my own. It's just a matter of letting go of shit. I want to move on."

Nancy laughs. "That's very noble of you!"

I shake my head. "No, it's not. What happened to me was horrible at the time, but it's made me who I am, and I'm proud of who I am. I wouldn't be nearly so compassionate if I hadn't been through what I've been through."

Chapter Thirty

Baja California is a narrow peninsula of desert mountains. On one side the Pacific Ocean pounds steep pebble beaches, on the other the Sea of Cortez gently laps at shores of rock and sand.

I'm sitting by my fire, hugging a cup of tea. Since I can't stand to stay at crowded, expensive, dirty campsites with lots of artificial light keeping me awake at night, I've investigated other options. I've discovered, through a rather nerve-racking process of trial that turns out never to be error, that Mexicans don't have the same concept of campsites and ownership as westerners do. I can camp pretty much anywhere I want—it doesn't have to be a spot that is specifically designated for camping. So now I drive my truck along some bone-shaking dirt track till I find a remote place to spend the night, with no other humans around.

Today I'm next to the ocean, where the sound of the waves is a crashing constant. The strange grunts and yowls of a nearby sea lion colony echo eerily over the water. As I allow my fire to die, the darkness of the cloudy night takes over. Soon I'll go to bed in my truck. I've been traveling on my own for about six weeks, during which time I've spoken to very few people, and no one who isn't a stranger. In the absence of other humans, I've become very tuned into what is around me. I sit here leaning forward into the glow of the settling embers, feeling the ocean, the rocks, the whales and other living creatures.

This evening, I become aware of something greater. A sensation like a warm blanket wraps me from behind. I feel absolutely comfortable, deeply at ease, totally accepted, in the presence of very old friends who know everything there is to know about me, and will love me always, unconditionally. Tears fill my eyes. It is such a relief that, after all these years, I am aware of this vast presence within and without.

The coast of Vancouver Island is endlessly convoluted, the countless wandering inlets dotted with islands. Jo has come on an adventure with me, and we are about to take off in our kayaks to spend the night somewhere out there. As we're sorting our gear, an older man wanders towards us. Seeing him approach, I think, *he's got something to tell us.* He addresses me with a slightly bemused smile, "You going out into the bay to see the orca?"

I raise my eyebrows in surprise. "I'd love to see an orca, but I don't know where she is."

"We just got back from petting him, he's right out there." He waves at the bay. "His pod's gone back to the ocean and they left him here. He's real friendly!"

"Well, maybe we'll see her!" We smile at each other and he departs. Jo and I set off on a beautiful but uneventful trip out to an island where we find a small rocky beach to spend the night. We make a fire to roast the clams and oysters that we find on the rocks as the tide goes out.

On our way back the next day, we see a motor boat stopped in the middle of the bay, and as we get closer, there is the orca. She's rubbing her big body against the side of the boat, rolling over on her back and standing up on her tail. As we paddle closer, one of the occupants of the boat calls to us, "Bang on the side of your kayak, and he'll come right over to you!"

I slap the side of my kayak, and with graceful effortless ease, she's next to me. She is longer than my kayak. I rub her jet-black head, the skin silky and smooth. Rolling over on her back, she shows me her white belly, and opens her mouth wide. It's huge, at least two feet across, and lined with rows of perfect pyramid teeth, an inch long in the center, getting smaller to either side. "Girl, look at your teeth!" I say, impressed.

Jo calls across to me, "I saw a TV program about them, and it said they like to have their tongues rubbed!"

"I don't think I want to risk losing my hand, even though you are so friendly," I tell the huge animal, as she looks at me sideways with one large beady black eye. Then I realize my kayak is moving sideways quite fast—she's leaning on it. She swims underneath me, and I find myself lifted up.

"Hey, baby, you're gorgeous, but put me down!" I exclaim in alarm. Just as the kayak is starting to slide, she drops me back in the water, and goes to repeat her antics with Jo. For a few minutes she swims to and fro between us. She's getting a little more bumptious all the time, picking us up and rubbing against us. How are we going to get away from her?

The first motor boat has left. Soon another one stops nearby. I tell them to slap the side of their boat, and again, she responds to the call immediately. She's obviously lonely, and really enjoys the attention. As soon as she leaves us, we take off towards the nearest shore, paddling as fast as we can. She catches up with us after we have gone a few hundred yards, swimming alongside us, leaping in and out of the water with such joyful elegance that I am quite jealous. When we get closer to the shore, she departs to delight some other tourists.

Big Bend National Park is a striking series of volcanic mountains that rise out of the plains north of the Rio Grande, which separates Texas from Mexico. It is anything but a grand river—in February, normally the month of least rainfall, the river bed is twenty-five feet wide or less, and shallow enough to wade across in most places. Its original flood plain is several hundred yards wide, but so much of the water is now used for irrigation that the flood plain has become habitually dry.

There are three canyons in the Park, with walls over fifteen hundred feet high. Looking for information at one of the ranger stations, I find a woman who tells me the river is so slow moving that one can paddle upriver for long stretches, and it's quite safe to go up the canyons in a kayak. Most of the river bank is lined with bushes or very thick tall grass, like some kind of bamboo, and there aren't many spots where you can access the water. The next day I park my truck at one of the designated put-in spots, and set off upriver in my kayak. It's a cool cloudy day, and the water is slightly murky green, but I'm happy to be floating. For the first mile or so, the banks stretch flatly away from me, then I enter the canyon and the rock walls begin to rise. Soon they are towering on either side. I am held in the bosom of sheer cliffs. I have the sense they are living beings, singing to me in some alien but beautiful language, with a long slow rhythm. They are magnificent in their ancient knowingness, no one stone the same, each cliff painting its very own picture, varying from moment to moment, sometimes dramatically, as I move along the surface of the winding river. Caves, pockmarks, holes, cuts, chasms, jagged edges, boulders, promontories, rock faces, ledges, each absolutely individual, all reveal themselves and then disappear again as I paddle by.

Once I'm in the canyon, the wind is behind me and helps me along, sometimes even blowing me upstream where the current is very slow. When I come to rapids, I'm always able to get out and walk along a gravelly beach beside the water, pulling my kayak, until I reach a place where I can get back in. I see a few turtles, and paddle past a group of people having lunch at a table on a beach, their canoes pulled up out of the water. The table is even decorated with a cloth. I say hallo, though I shake my head in puzzlement. How much is the guide being paid to carry that table? Are people afraid to sit on the ground? Is there some kind of dangerous insect that I don't know about? Snakes, perhaps?

Overhead, in the narrow space between the cliff tops, the clouds gather thick and black. Around a corner from the party, I hear a few rolls of thunder, then drops of rain and a flash of lightning. I take shelter under an overhanging cliff, watching as the raindrops thud into the water. The storm is fierce but short, and soon I carry on. I have to paddle hard to stay warm though, and when the day is half gone, I'm happy to turn back. Floating downriver is gloriously easy, and it's fun to go through places where the water runs swift and narrow, sometimes striking off a rock face or a jutting boulder, so that I have to paddle fast and furious. The river is low enough that I never feel endangered.

That night it rains, and the following day is cloudy and a little drizzly. After a long hike into the mountains, I drive to a camping spot below one of the other canyons, hoping that the weather will improve and the river will not flood. The next morning dawns clear and blue, the river still calm and slow. I am in luck. I set off up the canyon, enjoying the warmth of the sunshine. Once again, as the rock faces envelope me, I bask in their ageless wisdom. Turtles galore are sunning themselves on rocks, watching me balefully as I pass, their long necks twisting to track my progress, ready to vanish with a splash if I get too close. Most of them are no bigger than my hand, but I find one slow soft-shelled turtle that is as big as my head. Swallows and other birds I don't recognize flit over the surface of the water, one repeatedly singing a scale from high to low, sometimes far up near the tops of the cliffs, sometimes perched on one of the stunted trees that occasionally decorate the river bank.

I paddle about five miles, until I can see the entrance to the canyon ahead of me, the cliffs scaling down on either side. Taking my time going back, I let my kayak be carried slowly on the current, and admire the way the rocks are shaped by the water, running my hands over them, feeling their hard rough solidity, warm in the sun or cold in the shade. One huge black rock I find, at a deep spot, is worn into a smooth spiral on the downriver side, where the water must have swirled. The spiral is so narrow and deep that I cannot reach my hand all the way to its far wall.

By the time I return to the place where I have camped, I'm tired. I very rarely leave my kayak on the edge of a river in case of a flash flood, but I figure this time it's safe, since we've had no rain for thirty-six hours. So I leave the boat there, about two feet above the water level, for maybe twenty minutes, while I walk back to the truck, and change my clothes. I have a quick handful of trail mix before I return to the river's edge. I stand aghast between the thickets of bamboo—the water that was previously clear is now thick brown, flowing steadily and unrelentingly in a swathe more than fifty feet wide. It has risen at least three feet! Gone are the gently sloping beaches. My beloved pink kayak has been lifted from where I'd beached it, and a glance to my left reveals it floating downriver, not yet out in midstream.

Cursing once, loudly, I make a very quick decision. Ripping off my jeans and my boots, I leave them in a pile on what remains of the river bank. Wearing only my underpants, a T-shirt and a baseball cap, I leap into the muddy water, swimming as fast as I can, occasionally kicking off the river bottom in places where small beaches were so recently above the water surface. About a hundred yards down I realize that the water is still rising, and I have left my jeans—with my wallet in the pocket—where they will be carried away if the water rises far enough. *Too late to turn back now*, I think, cursing my stupidity. Perhaps it will be a fair exchange, my kayak for my wallet.

In midstream, I am carried swiftly, but the kayak is light and moves easily on the water, so I'm about a quarter of a mile from where I started before it is in my reach. I'm in the nick of time, for now it has been caught in the main current. The first time I grasp for the loop of rope that hangs off the end, I miss, and realize that the kayak is beginning to move faster than me. Launching myself out of the water with all the force I can muster, I grab wildly at the rope and successfully get hold of it. Now I have to get to the bank, without wasting any further time, for the river is narrowing and the water here is flowing more fiercely. I'm closer at this point to the Mexican side, so that's where I go, resisting the strong pull of the kayak wanting to follow the water to the ocean.

Once at the edge of the bank, I think I'll be able to make my way upstream, since it's shallower here. But it is still at least four feet deep, the current is still surprisingly strong, and branches of trees and long stalks of the thick grass hang in my way. I struggle for a while before I decide that I should beach the kayak and somehow return upstream alone, in the hope of rescuing my jeans and wallet. I drag the kayak up onto the bank, which is steep at this point, and secure it as best I can on some tree branches. Without further ado, I leap into the implacable torrent of brown water, swimming upstream and sideways as hard as I can. Although I make no headway upstream, I do manage to get across without being carried downstream too far. Once again I try to make my way through the water along the bank's edge, finding it no easier without the kayak. I'll have to get out of the river, which means fighting my way through the thick bamboo grass that lines the bank.

My legs and feet are bare and, because of the thick growth, I can't reach the ground, though I can see it two or three feet below. I have to force the thick stalks of the bamboo sideways so that I can walk on them. It's slow going. About ten feet in, I stop to rest, and make the mistake of thinking about what I'm doing. *I can't get through this stuff! I can't even see where it ends! Well*, I tell myself grimly, *you don't have any choice.* I clamber on again and in another ten feet I am delighted to see that it's thinning out. My pleasure deflates when I reach the edge of the thicket and realize it's lined with very thorny bushes. I carry on regardless, and then I'm standing on the sandy desert floor. In spite of the fact that my legs are covered in blood from thigh to ankle, I set off running at full speed. Somehow the bottoms of my naked feet don't suffer at all, which just goes to show that anything is possible. I reach the point where I started. My jeans and boots are sitting right there, with the water lapping an inch below them.

Taking my jeans and boots back to the truck, I don a pair of sneakers and a life-vest, pick up the paddle and set off again. This time I let the water carry me. As I float down midstream, I see a Mexican at the edge of the water thirty or forty feet away. He looks at me and I look at him. *Shit, I'm going to have to tell him what the hell I'm doing.* I start to explain, speaking very broken Spanish.

"Hola! Mi kayak es para la…"

"Hola! What are you doing?"

Well, that's a boon, he speaks good English. "My kayak was carried away by the flood and I'm going to get it. It's on the bank down there."

"Your kayak?"

"Yes, my kayak!"

"Oh…where are the others?"

Damn, I should have expected this question. I don't want to admit I'm on my own. That would be hard to explain.

"They're back there!" I take one hand off the paddle to wave behind me.

"Oh…and your kayak was carried by the water?"

"Yes, it's down there." I nod forwards. By this time I'm nearly too far away to talk any more, but he has one more question.

"Where are the others?"

"They're back there!"

"Well, don't get drowned!"

As the water carries me onwards, I maneuver further towards the Mexican bank. To my relief, I see my pink kayak just where I left it. Evidently the water has stopped rising. I pull it back into the river, and with some difficulty, because the water is still trying to carry me downstream, I get into it and start to paddle upstream. Of course I get nowhere—I don't know why I ever thought I would. My adrenalin rush is fading but I summon all of my remaining strength to drag the kayak to the top of the very steep bank. I glance down at my legs— the water has done a good job of cleaning off the blood, though there are some fairly spectacular scratches. I set off along the bank, thankful that I am wearing shoes. After a hundred yards, I meet the Mexican outside his little shack with a large herd of goats.

"You found your kayak!" He smiles.

"Yes!" I smile back, walking onward.

"Where are the others?"

"Up there!" I nod forwards.

He looks puzzled. As I pass, I turn back to say, "Thank you!"

He looks more puzzled. "What for?"

Now *I'm* puzzled. *What* am *I thanking him for?* It isn't until much later that I realize I'm thanking him for leaving me alone.

I arrive at a small ravine, which stops me going any further. Shrugging, I drag the kayak down to the water—it's rocky here, and there are some stunted trees, but none of the horrible bamboo grass. At the edge of the muddy torrent, I find I'm directly opposite the place where I need to be on the American side. Getting into my kayak, I paddle like hell. Again the water is kind to me, and I'm soon wearily dragging my boat across the ground towards my truck. The sun is just setting. I'll have light enough to make myself a cup of tea before I collapse.

Back in California a few weeks later, I tell Jo about my narrow escape. It makes a great story, much more fun to talk about than it was to go through. She exclaims in horror at all the right moments, and at the finale, she says, "You were so lucky!"

"Well, no," I reply, shaking my head. "If I'd been one minute earlier, I'd have caught my kayak before it was carried away. If I'd been one minute later, it would have been out of sight. If I'd been in the canyon, I'd probably have drowned. The whole thing was perfectly timed."

She purses her lips. "Well, the obvious question is, by whom?"

"I can only answer that by saying that my whole life is orchestrated by That-which-I-met-in-the-mirror."

Jo nods—she's heard about my epiphany with the mirror. "But why?"

"Well, I spent most of the night after it happened mulling over that question." I sigh. "I think that the reasons why things happen to us are often very hard to divine from this limited human perspective. From the perspective of All-that-is, things aren't so serious. Often they are simply experiences. My most vivid memory about that river is the delightful sensation of being carried by the water. I learned a great deal, firsthand, about the power of water."

"Hmmm…and I guess you didn't lose anything in the end."

"No, even my scratches were far more spectacular than they were painful. I had a deep throaty cough from all that intense exercise, but that was probably a good thing. I got rid of a lot of phlegm, stuff from the bottom of my lungs that needed to be dredged up."

"Well, no one can deny you are taken care of!"

I smile. "Right. And I just have to trust that. It has nothing to do with being adventurous or lucky."

Chapter Thirty One

I tend to be afraid of the wind. Its raw power and destructive ability make me nervous. I decide to take up windsurfing, thinking that it will be an outlet for my physical energy, and it will enable me to make friends with the wind. Windsurfing proves to be tricky to learn, and involves some bulky equipment. The first time I see someone zipping over the water on a small board with a huge kite high up in the air, I think, *I'm going to do **that**!*

Receiving some unexpected money from my family, I blow it all on kitesurfing gear.

At the time, I'm in Adelaide, Australia. The dealer who sells me my Boxer kite—which is what he recommends for a beginner—gives me one lesson, and then I'm on my own. I go to a beach where I find two other kitesurfers, and a very strong wind.

I introduce myself. "I'm not sure I should try to put the kite up in this wind," I say. "I've only had it up once before. I'm not even sure how to rig it."

One of the blond, muscular young men says, "Oh, give it a try, you've got nothing to lose. I'll help you rig it."

Later, I learn you always have something to lose. It's called your life, and it's quite easy to lose it kitesurfing. But I naively trust the young man. We rig the kite.

It is a twelve square meter C-kite—about as big as a small to average sized room, although it packs up very small. One edge has to be inflated with a pump. Four lines, around seventy-five feet long, attach it to a bar which controls the kite. The bar is attached to my waist by a harness. I also have a board, but the primary, all-important aspect of kitesurfing is learning to control the kite. I am practicing body dragging—that is, getting in the water and allowing the kite to drag me. The problem is a C-kite only operates well in a fairly small wind range. By the time my new-found friend and I have the kite up, the wind has risen in strength. I manage to get myself to the water, before the kite takes over, smashing into the water with a resounding bang. Somehow or other, it picks itself up again, and me with it. I fly over the surface of the water at alarming speed. The kite hits the water again. Even when it's just sitting on the water, it drags me downwind at a startling rate. I am out of my depth (in a couple of senses) and I struggle gradually towards shore, hoping the kite doesn't pick me up and throw me down on hard land. I notice that my blond friend is running along the beach parallel to me, shouting something which I can't possibly hear over the crashing of the waves and the roaring of the wind.

I'm completely exhausted by the time I feel solid ground under my feet again. The young man agrees that the wind is too high, and wades out to grab the kite which is bouncing merrily on the water. He helps me take it back to where we started—the first of many long walks up the beach, one arm tucked around this great flapping thing behind me, that very badly wants to fly, with or without me.

He goes out with his kite while I pack mine up. When I'm done, I walk along the beach to see how he's doing. I meet him trying to walk back, his kite way up in the air above him, pulling him up on his toes. When I ask if I can help, he says, "Yes, you can hold me down!" So I haul him back up the beach, holding onto the handle at the back of his harness (all kiting harnesses have a handle for exactly this purpose). His feet only occasionally touch the ground.

I decide I should have a lesson, which costs a lot of money, and only confirms my growing sense that this is a dangerous sport. The kite has a mind of its own. It is an extremely powerful, capricious toy, and it scares me. Still, if all these other people can learn to control it, so can I. I need practice.

One day it picks me up and flings me down on the ground like a rag doll. I can barely walk for the next week. I'm not sure this is fun.

In Melbourne, I find a beach crowded with kiters. A very sweet Spanish man, who is teaching there, quickly recognizes me as someone who doesn't know what she's doing, and takes me under his wing. "This is a dangerous kite," he says, with kind laughing eyes, pointing to my gray and black monstrosity. "Boxers are not good kites for beginners unless the wind is very regular and steady. Try this foil, you'll like it."

He's right. A third of the size of my Boxer, it feels much safer and yet still powerful enough to pull me along. It is a different design, with no inflatable edge. I buy the kite and have lots of fun with it over the next few weeks. Back in the U.S., I go to the Columbia River Gorge in Oregon, which is a beautiful spot on a wide river, well-known for its excellent winds. It is ridiculously crowded with kiters, and I quickly discover two things: that crowded beaches are not safe, and there is a great deal of snobbery in wind-sports. Almost everyone has the inflatable type of kite, like my Boxer, and they all turn their noses up at my foil, which is a different kind of kite altogether. None of them have ever tried it. The only people who think my little foil is any good are those who have one of their own, and there are very few of them.

But one of the real problems with learning to kite is that if you don't have adequate power and speed, you will not be able to stand on the board. You have to be moving fast to get the board to skim over the surface of the water. Although my little foil is a safe toy to learn about kite control, it doesn't really have the power I need. So I return to using my Boxer. I usually take it out on the water in the mornings when the wind is lower. One day, I'm lying back in the water with the board on my feet, thinking it's time to go back to shore, when all of a sudden a gust catches me. Without any warning, I am standing on the board as it shoots towards the beach, where two people are sitting watching. I just have time to register the alarm on their faces, when I manage to miss them by a foot or so. As the board hits the sand, I'm somehow able to remove my feet from the straps, leaving the board lying there by the water. The kite doesn't stop. I continue on my trajectory, leaning backward so that my feet lead the way, digging grooves in the sand in front of me. Two kitesurfers are rigging a kite nearby. As I pass them, one says, "Need some help?"

"Yes!" I reply, and he grabs that oh-so-convenient handle on the back of my harness. Between the two of us we bring it to a stop, and he holds on to me while I ease the kite down to the ground so that his friend can get hold of it.

After packing my kite up early one afternoon, I'm walking along the beach when a smiling young man accosts me. He points to the kite laid out beside him. "Do you know how to put these things up?"

I nod. "Yes, I know how to rig them."

"Well, I just bought this. Would you help me get it up?"

I'm a little nonplussed. "Um…you've never flown a kite before?"

"No, but I've been watching these guys out here, I think I know what they're doing." He's still smiling, with a slightly pleading look on his face.

I hesitate. *I can sympathize with your desire to be flying over the water, and your frustration at not being able to figure out how to rig the kite, but no one can possibly learn this sport by watching others— the movements that the rider is constantly making are far too minute and subtle. You're probably going to kill yourself, or someone else.* "You need to take a lesson."

"They're so expensive. I can see what these guys are doing, I've watched them for hours."

I know they're expensive, but how much do you value your life? You're deluded. What the hell, it would be a good experience for me to play around with a different kite.

"OK, I'll help you get it up." I put down my own kite and within fifteen minutes I have his kite ready to go. I instruct him how to hold it while I launch it. Once it's in the air, I play around for a minute or two, before handing it to him.

"What do I do now? What do I do now?" He shouts excitedly, with a death grip on the bar. Then he does what beginners usually do—pulls the bar down towards his body, which powers up the kite. It loops around in the air before crashing to the ground. Only the fact that I'm holding onto his harness stops him from being dragged. Taking the bar, I re-launch it. That is my mistake—I should have checked the lines weren't twisted. As soon as the kite is in the air above me, I see that they are, but before I can do anything, the kite takes off. He's holding onto my harness. It drags us, on our bellies, about twenty feet over the sand before it hits the ground and stops. I jump up, handing him the bar, and run to catch it. As soon as I have secured it safely, I walk back to the would-be kiter. To my surprise, he's shaking. "It just dragged both of us, it just dragged both of us," he keeps repeating, in an agitated tone.

I shrug. "You'll have to get used to being dragged if you want to learn to kite. That's one reason to wear a wetsuit. Maybe you'll have a lesson now?"

He nods vociferously. "Yes, yes, I'll have a lesson!"

I walk off, looking back once to see him hurriedly deflating the kite and folding it up. I wonder if it will ever see the light of day again.

One of my friends, hearing about my adventures, tells me I am her model of fearlessness.

"I'm not fearless at all," I say, shaking my head. "I'm very intimate with fear. I just decide to do things anyway, even though I'm scared. Some of these guys kiting out there, they *are* fearless, and in one day they can learn to do things that I take a week or a month to learn." I'm frustrated with my slow rate of progress.

My next stop is Hawaii, where I have heard there are very reliable winds, and several kite schools. I discover some problems as soon as I get to Kite Beach on Maui. The beach is the size of a postage stamp, so there is no room for mistakes when launching the kite, or bringing it down. The wind inshore is quite low, whereas further out, it's very high. There are lots of rocks around. None of that spells well for beginners.

I have planned to be here for a week. I get my lines tangled in a tree and bust them on a fence; my board disappears forever in the swells while I struggle with the kite; worst of all, I am dragged over some big rocks when my kite takes off unexpectedly. I already have some scars down my right side from similar, less spectacular episodes. This time I am bloody for several days. By now I am seriously addicted to this exciting sport, so these misadventures don't stop me going out. I find a man who gives lessons, and on his advice, buy another smaller C-kite and a new board to replace the one I just lost. He agrees that I probably need practice more than I need lessons.

A couple of months later, I'm on the west coast of Australia, near a town called Geraldton, famous for its winds. I am easily the most inexperienced person on this beach, and a lot of the macho young kiters are looking at me askance. Like every beginner, I make a fool of myself through my lack of experience, and perhaps more so because I am nervous of kiting in crowds. Being that kind of person, I am often asking questions, and I have been in the habit of pumping other kiters for information. I am learning that many of them simply want to sound like they are knowledgeable. Kitesurfing is a new sport: there are plenty of things a kite can do that these young men have no idea about, and there are many different kinds of equipment that they have never heard of. After following the advice of one man about which of several different line connections to use on my kite, I discover, to my cost, that he's told me to use the ones that give me maximum power. The women in the sport are not a lot better: one tells me authoritatively that I have my safety leash attached the wrong way round, and I only find out that's rubbish when it releases abruptly, so that I almost lose my kite altogether. Both these people are well paid teachers.

In Geraldton, I take out my new smaller kite, an eight meter. Smaller kites, for use in higher winds, typically move very fast, which makes them more dangerous. This innocent-looking little kite *tea-bags* me several times. Tea bagging is a phenomenon where the kite swings from side to side in the air, picking you up and dunking you in the water, often three times in quick succession. It doesn't occur gently. After that, I seldom use that kite. Rarely forgiving enough for a beginner, it is downright evil in a gusty wind.

As the months and then the years pass, kite designers come out with much safer kites, and I find myself with money to spare from the sale of my land. I start buying myself some really good kites. Improved skills and improved equipment make for more fun. Once you have good kite control you can jump off the water, sometimes up to twenty or thirty feet, hanging in the air for several seconds. I'd seen a video of people kiting on snow, where you can get up very high speeds because there is no friction. They were jumping over houses. I want to do that. I've spent months learning how to *stop* the kite from picking me up. Now I am learning how to *make* it pick me up. The tricky part is landing. Whenever I find myself up in the air I get so excited that I forget to control the kite, and end up crashing into the water.

I spend a month in Thailand, at a place called Hua Hin, where there's a beach used by kiters, mostly westerners. The water is flat, so you don't have to contend with waves knocking you off your board. I hang out with two other kiters less experienced than me, which is new and different. I'm delighted to pass on a few of the pearls I've picked up on my educational journey. After watching John trying to get up on the board, I say to him, "Don't *try* to get up on the board. Just put it on your feet, lie back in the water, and work the kite to get some power. When there's enough power, the wind will pick you up and you'll just find yourself standing. No matter how much you try, you'll never get up until there is enough wind."

He goes off, and comes back a half hour later looking pleased with himself. "That was good advice. Thank you!" he says.

I nod, smiling. "Yes, I wish someone had said that to me when I was learning!"

I go to Fortaleza on the Brazilian coast, one of the best places in the world for wind. Again, the delightfully wide and empty beaches are primarily frequented by westerners. Like Hawaii and northern Australia, the water is warm enough to go out without a wetsuit. I spend three weeks improving my skills in winds that once would have terrified me. I'm getting bolder, although I spend too much time picking weed off the strings of my kite after it drops in the water as I am trying to get away from the beach. You have to be very confident and aggressive to get beyond the breakers fast enough that they don't bowl you over. If the kite strings dip into the water, they rapidly pick up lots of weed, and they don't let go of it easily.

Nevertheless, I am beginning to look and feel good with the kite. I am going fast enough that I find myself a long way from the beach in no time at all. A few times I drop the kite when I am all the way out there, can't re-launch it, and have an agonizing swim back. But on the whole I am actually having fun.

One day, coming back in to shore, I slide through the last few feet of shallow surf on my butt, a fairly normal procedure to slow myself down. Suddenly I feel a very sharp jab in my left buttock. I leap up, the kite goes out of control, smashing down onto the ground, and I'm jerked off my feet. Finding myself lying on the sand, I twist myself round to see what's going on. A small catfish is attached to me. One of its sharp spikes has impaled itself in my butt, through the thick material of my harness. I pull it off. "Damn, that hurt!" I say. It looks at me with a very sorrowful, frightened eye, and I throw it back in the water. *Another thing to add to my list of potential kitesurfing hazards.*

In northern California, the average man is less macho than in other parts of the world, and beach goers are usually friendly. That makes it one of my favorite places to be, in spite of the cold water. Kitesurfing is a spectacular sport. People recognize you by the color of your kite, and often make comments to you when you come in. One old lady, walking along the beach, says to me, "You were having fun out there! *You* know what you're doing with that kite. Now him over there—" she points with her walking stick "—he doesn't know how to control that thing."

One older man, who's learning to kite, introduces himself as Mad Max. "I live in an apartment right here on the beach, and I watch you a lot. You're always the first one out and you can stay upwind when no one else can even keep their kite in the air," he says.

I grin. "That's because I have a better kite than everyone else." I'm talking about my latest foil kite. I've replaced my Pulse with a Psycho. Who makes up these names? When I first heard of a Psycho, I thought, *I'll never buy a kite with a name like that.* Then it turned out to be one of the best foils on the market. Later I have a choice between a Havoc and a Flow. I decide I would rather go with the flow than wreak havoc, at least when it comes to kiting. Now I'm choosy about the colors of my kite too. My Flow is aquamarine and I have a Bullaroo that's purple.

Even though I am pretty good with the kite by this time, I still drop it on the water now and again, or lose my board and can't retrieve it, so that I have to swim in. One evening as I am packing up, Mad Max comes up to me saying, "I heard you had a bit of trouble out there today."

I shrug. "Not really, I had to swim in because I lost my board, but I got it back. It was washed up along the beach." I'm much more concerned about losing my board than I am about having to swim in.

"Well, I was having a nap and my wife woke me up. She said I should get out there and help you, because you were in trouble."

I laugh. "Well, it's a good job you didn't, because you'd have been wasting your time!"

He nods, laughing. "That's what I told her. I said, Chris knows what she's doing!"

Although I've never met his wife, she evidently knows which kites are mine. A few days later there is a fierce wind, and although I have a small kite, I am overpowered. Before I launch it, I ask another kiter to hold onto my harness. Between the two of us, we probably weigh 350 pounds. I bring the kite up carefully and slowly. When it is directly above my head, I feel my feet leave the ground. I assume the other kiter has let go of me. When I come back down to the ground—on my feet—I discover he is still holding on. It lifted us both.

The next day Mad Max tells me his wife woke him from his nap again, telling him to go and help me.

Now that I am more confident, I enjoy the idea of entertaining people on the shore. This really comes home when one of the local kiters tells me, "The guys on the beach were asking who was that guy catching all that air today." He's using kiter slang for jumping. "I told them, that's no guy, that's a woman." He grins.

Now I just have to get really good.

I am becoming the woman who follows the wind. Kitesurfing is all I want to do. I even go kiting when I am in Scotland, where the temperature doesn't encourage anyone to go in the water. I always visit Nancy when I'm in the UK, and tell her about my latest adventures. She asks what it is that I enjoy so much about this sport.

"Well, now that I'm no longer constantly trying to fix everyone and everything, I have to have something to fill my time!" I quip, laughing. "No, seriously, when I'm out on the water, dancing with the wind, nothing else matters. There's just me and water and the wind, and I have to be absolutely focused on this present moment, listening to the bidding of the wind. Everything else falls away."

"Don't your arms get exhausted holding the kite?" she asks.

"No, you're using your whole body to balance the power of the wind, leaning back against the kite. Your arms are quite relaxed. In fact, you don't have to be holding onto the bar at all. The kite's attached to your harness and you are constantly feeling what's going on through your belly. It's very subtle and very immediate, and it's a body thing. Every split second you're responding to the messages you get through your belly, making very slight changes of weight and position."

"It sounds difficult."

"Well, you have to bypass your brain, because its responses are not quick enough. You have to be absolutely present. I think that's what I find so delightful about it. You are required to be one hundred per cent focused on being alive. I see it in people's faces when they come in from a ride. They're renewed, refreshed. They remember that life is worth living. Really, it's a spiritual thing."

Nancy smiles. "I can see what you mean when you say that, although I don't suppose there are many Buddhists or Christians who would agree with you. I can't quite see Mother Teresa on a kiteboard!" We both laugh at this image.

"Well, people think that being in service is the only way to be spiritual, but that's nonsense. First of all, if you aren't enjoying what you're doing, then you aren't doing the world any good, no matter how *good* you are. And secondly, we're all spirit experimenting with being human, not humans trying to be spirit. So we're all leading spiritual lives whether we like it or not!"

"Do any of the other kitesurfers you've met think it's a spiritual pastime?"

"I don't think so!" I laugh, thinking of the beer-drinking guys I've made friends with. "I did hear one guy say that it's better than sex. He was pretty young so he may not have had very good sex, but still, he was saying that it's the same kind of energy, and I would agree with that. As you know, I think sex is a very spiritual pastime."

One morning, in the midst of all my adventures, I'm in a store getting a cup of chai. A stranger steps backwards into me, immediately turning round to apologize in wide-eyed anxiety. "Oh, I'm sorry, I'm so sorry!" she exclaims.

I smile into her alarmed face. "That's quite all right, don't worry about it!" As I speak, I am aware of my heart bursting open with love. It's a physical sensation: a huge, delightful warmth pouring out of my chest in an endless wave. I leave the store hugging my chai, and walk down the street, vitally conscious of the love still flowing through me.

Those of us who claim the treasure that I found first in the aviary are the wealthiest people in the world.

Other books by **Mikaya Heart**:

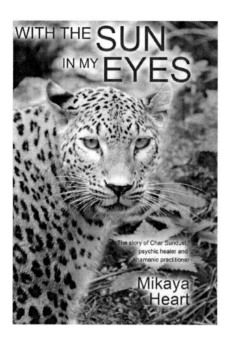

With the Sun in My Eyes: the story of Char Sundust,
psychic healer and shamanic practitioner.
ISBN: 978-0-595-51203-4

This unusual book is an excellent introduction to practical applications of the shamanic arts. Mikaya Heart spent two years with the Northwest healer, **Char Sundust**, delving into her healing work. A skilled interviewer, she spent many hours with Char's family, friends, students and clients, gleaning in-depth information, then spinning that into a gripping narrative. The result is a very read-able book that describes Char's childhood, her training as a shamanistic practitioner, and the extraordinary healing work she does now, with vivid concrete details of the different realms, entities, power animals, energies, archetypes and spirits she relates to on a daily basis.

This not only a delightful adventure story, it is also educational, chronicling in detail how healing of all kinds can be addressed on levels other than the physical.

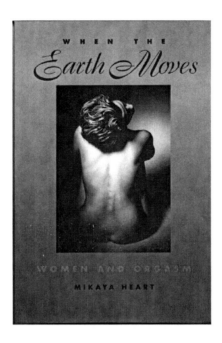

When the Earth Moves: Women and Orgasm
ISBN: 978-0-890-87875-0

The result of numerous interviews as well as personal experience, this book is a thorough examination of women's sexuality, and an invaluable guide for couples who want to take their sexual relationship further. Here's what others have to say about it:

"The most honest approach I have ever read! I now know what my wife really needs to feel sexually satisfied."

"A life-changing book! MikayaHeart examines so many different angles of orgasm, from emotional, to technical, to spiritual. She also includes the words and experiences of many women. I could finally see there are other women out there like me. It was so empowering!"

"This book has been a life saver for my husband and myself."

The Straight Woman's Guide to Lesbianism
ISBN: 0-9615129-4-6

How do women know they are lesbians? How do they get to the place of deciding they're gay? And how does it change their lives? This short book is a down-to-earth explanation of the many different ways that women come out, including quotes from a variety of lesbians with wide-ranging points of view. Cartoons by Jesse Cougar make the book a fun-read. Here's what others have to say about it:

"I never realized that lesbianism could be such a hugely life-altering choice! This book was a real eye-opener for me, as a straight woman. I now have a much greater understanding of what it's like to be gay."

"I didn't know how much I didn't know! Reading this book was really educational—and fun. Good work, Mikaya Heart!"

"I was in the process of coming out as a lesbian when I read this book, and it made everything so much easier."

LaVergne, TN USA
24 September 2009
158791LV00004B/21/P